THE POLITICS OF DISSENT

A BIOGRAPHY OF E D MOREL

THE POLITICS OF
DISSENT

★ ★ ★ *A Biography of E D Morel* ★ ★ ★

DONALD MITCHELL

SilverWood

Published in 2014 by the author
using SilverWood Books Empowered Publishing®

SilverWood Books
30 Queen Charlotte Street, Bristol, BS1 4HJ
www.silverwoodbooks.co.uk

ISBN 978-1-78132-178-2 (paperback)
ISBN 978-1-78132-179-9 (ebook)

British Library Cataloguing in Publication Data
A CIP catalogue record for this book is available from the British Library

Set in Sabon by SilverWood Books
Printed on responsibly sourced paper

Contents

The Early Years

Why? Why this enslavement and destruction of a people? The same old motives which from the beginning have been responsible for all the great world tragedies: human ambition, greed, and selfishness.

E D Morel
Red Rubber, 1970

To say that your intention is to 'free' the subjects of another of your enemies from the "domination" of their government, or, in other words, to insist upon the disruption of the empire of another of your enemies, is not a peace proposition; it is a proclamation of conquest...If conquest, and not peace, be your intention, well and good. Have the courage to acknowledge it.

E D Morel
Thoughts on the War: the Peace – and Prison, 1920

Powerful establishments have many ways of silencing embarrassing critics. At worst, they simply assassinate them. Alternatively, they exile or imprison them. Almost always they vilify and discredit them. And finally, if the elite survives to supervise the writing of history, and particularly if a critic's comments remain pertinent, they do their utmost to airbrush him or her from the narrative, and ensure that the destabilising influence is cloaked in obscurity.

All these measures, excepting unmediated murder, have been directed against the person and the memory of E D Morel.

During the last two decades of his life, Morel became both a famous and a highly controversial figure. His concerns are highly relevant to today's global dilemmas, for his work has a direct bearing on many of the critical issues of our times. In particular, his campaign regarding what was then the Congo Free State illuminates many of the problems that continue to beset the Democratic Republic of Congo (DRC), while his views on democratic participation and control are highly pertinent to the present-day debate on political accountability. This latter perspective has direct relevance to the recent decision to engage in a pre-emptive war on Iraq – a conflict based on mendacious intelligence and gross misinformation, which has brought death and destruction to hundreds of thousands of innocent people.

Morel was an author, journalist, radical campaigner and Member of Parliament. His pursuit of social justice and human rights, his trenchant critique of the establishment, and his extraordinarily prolific output made him both loved and hated by his contemporaries. In January 1924, he was nominated for the Nobel Peace Prize, with the Prime Minister, Ramsay MacDonald, and 120 members of the Labour Party as signatories to the nomination. At the same time, *The Times* of 31st January ended a pejorative article by saying that, '...members of the British government will not make their task easier, nor will they increase British prestige by giving him a memorial.' For reasons that are not clear, no one was awarded the prize.

By the end of the year Morel was dead, at the early age of 51. He had been responsible for the first great human rights movement of the 20th century, and although there were dissenting voices, he was mourned as a national hero. According to his obituary in the *Frankfurter Zeitung*, 'The knightliness and uncommon personal charm of this handsome, noble and proud man brought him the regard even of his enemies, (who, truth to say, were not few) and often their surreptitious admiration, and there is no question that the whole of the British people would without exception have honoured him if the British mentality had not been prey during the years of war to bitter internal conflicts and perplexity.'

Much later, in his autobiography published in 1937, Viscount Snowden, Chancellor of the Exchequer from 1929 to 1931, wrote that:

> Mr E D Morel...was of a very different type from the majority of Labour members. He had come into prominence by his critical attitude to the War and had served a term of six months imprisonment for a minimal offence against the Defence of the Realm Act. I well remember the effect his first speech in the House of Commons made upon the Tory Party. They had heard of him through his wartime activities and imagined him to be a wild and ignorant person. On the contrary he was a man of impressive appearance, a cultured speaker

and an attractive debater. I remember Lord Robert Cecil, after Mr Morel's first speech, expressing to me his great surprise to find Mr Morel so different from what he expected.[1]

It is now almost 100 years since the winding up of the Congo Reform Association (CRA), Morel's vehicle for reform of the Congo, which after a decade of remarkable campaigning saw control of the country pass from King Leopold to the Belgian government, and subsequently to the implementation of reforms. The impact of the red rubber trade in the Congo during Leopold's rule had been totally devastating. It had unleashed a reign of terror across the entire colony and ravaged the population in large parts of the region. The amputation of hands and other limbs, vicious and frequently fatal flogging, casual killing and widespread rape were commonplace, and had become institutionalised on a routine basis wherever rubber was collected. It is estimated that some 8-10 million Africans, out of an initial population of around 20 million at the time of colonisation, died from displacement, starvation and murder over the twenty-four years that Leopold exercised total control over his domain, a level of mortality almost as great as the death rate of all the combatant countries combined during the First World War.

At the outbreak of the conflict in 1914, Morel embarked on a further campaign as secretary and prime mover of the recently formed Union for Democratic Control (UDC), which called for parliamentary oversight of foreign policy and a moderate peace settlement. This time, his campaign was directed against the secret diplomacy conducted between the major European powers: France, Russia, Germany and Britain, which preceded the conflict. After the War he devoted his remaining years to attacking the Treaty of Versailles, warning that 'if we do not build upon a foundation of truth, the Europe which emerges from this war will be even more unstable than the Europe produced by the Treaty of Vienna a century ago.'[2]

It is unlikely that any campaigner for truth and justice has had such a prodigious output of books, articles, pamphlets and letters as E D Morel. At the London School of Economics, the index to the Morel archives alone exceeds 340 pages. But although the political implications of his campaigns have been studied, and he is mentioned in literature on the role of the European powers in Africa in the early part of the 20th century, remarkably little attention has been accorded to his work, or to the extremely high profile he achieved during his lifetime. Much has been written about his close friend, Roger Casement, whose career and commitment to native peoples was equally great, but by contrast Morel's life and achievements remain largely unrecognised. In a recent book on the Edwardian era, neither Morel nor the Congo merit a single mention.[3] An unpublished PhD, *The Idea of Economic Imperialism, with Special Reference to the Life and Work of E D Morel* was completed by Wuliger in 1953, and Morel's campaigning was given recognition both by Catherine Cline in *E D Morel: Strategies of Protest* published in 1980, and by Adam Hochschild in *King Leopold's Ghost,* published in 1997, but the only book with a claim to being a biography is *E D Morel: The Man and His Work*, published by Morel's devoted friend, Seymour Cocks, in 1920.

At the time Morel's campaign against King Leopold came to a successful conclusion and he was at the peak of his power and popularity, it was said that there was no position in diplomacy that he could not fill with distinction. It is clear that he was passionate about his work, as 'convinced of his cause as any 17th Century religious zealot,'[4] as Cline puts it, but the man himself, beloved by so many, yet reviled by others, remains a shadowy figure. Only Seymour Cocks's book, written before his death, gives some idea of his profound faith in human nature, and of his stature as a social activist. As W S Adams remarked forty years ago in his book *Edwardian Portraits*, Morel's biography remains to be written.

The reason for this silence must surely lie in the last years of his life, which were devoted to the exposure of the secret diplomacy, falsehoods and treaties that led up to the First World War, and to the search for a peace based on justice (rather than on revenge) that might prevent a further conflict. This quest set him on a directly confrontational course with the government, and most particularly with the Foreign Office, and he became increasingly isolated during the war years as patriotic fervour rose around him. He was often abused in the national press, and his popular standing never wholly recovered. In 1917 he was found guilty of a trivial offence under the Defence of the Realm Act, and imprisoned for six months in Pentonville. On his release, he continued to campaign, directing a great part of his energies towards his powerful critique of the Versailles Treaty, and in 1922 was elected as a Labour MP for Dundee, defeating Winston Churchill, who was the sitting member.

In later years, as another war became imminent, even those who had been his supporters began to question his legacy. The fact that he had brought professional diplomacy into such disrepute, and had condemned the Treaty of Versailles, was seen as contributing to the formulation and acceptance of the appeasement policy of the late 1930s, which was deplored by many of his former followers. Yet it was plainly irrational to hold that the policies he had promoted for dealing with the Weimar Republic were in some way responsible for the concessions made to Hitler's Germany. Rather, in view of the principles for which he had struggled so persistently, there is every reason to believe that he would have resisted any compromise with such a barbarous regime. Nonetheless the decline of his reputation in the years following his death seems to have left him marginalised; at best perceived as oblivious to the importance of power politics, at worst regarded as a virtual traitor to his country.

At the end of the Second World War, however, there was a fleeting revival of interest in Morel. There were calls for his life and work to be recorded, from amongst others, Bertrand Russell, the philosopher and pacifist, who wrote to Morel's wife, Mary, from Trinity College, Cambridge in 1946 asking if someone could be found to write a biography of her husband.[5] Douglas Goldring, the radical British journalist and writer, also wrote in the same year of his 'exasperation that none of his [Morel's] close political associates, with the necessary qualifications had done anything to keep alive the memory of both the man and his message.'[6]

Tragically, nothing can now be done to alter the vilification Morel endured during his lifetime or to redress the injustice of his imprisonment, which arguably led to his early death. The fact that virtually all of his domestic papers, including his personal letters, were destroyed by his descendants after his death, makes it particularly difficult to present a fully rounded picture of a man who was clearly held in great affection by those who were dear to him, including his exceptionally supportive wife. But although such details as remain of his family life must be allowed to speak for themselves, this book at least seeks to re-establish his name as a far-sighted and fearless humanitarian activist; a man who fought for justice against enormous odds, and never flinched from questioning the zeitgeist of his age.

Georges Edouard Pierre Achille Morel de Ville, to give him his full name, was born in Paris in 1873. His French father, Edmond Morel de Ville, was described as a man of considerable ability but little ambition; apparently he was not only a considerable linguist and brilliant chess player, but possessed such a fine tenor voice that he received several tempting invitations to sing at the famous Paris Opera – offers which he did not pursue. Morel's mother, Emmeline de Horne, was English, and came from a long line of de Hornes who had fled from Flanders to escape persecution in the 16th century and settled in Essex. The couple had first met in Paris in the 1860s, and married in 1870 following the restoration of peace after the Franco-Prussian war. Morel de Ville was then 48, and Emmeline twelve years his junior.

After their marriage, Morel's parents lived with his paternal grandmother, to whom his father was apparently devoted, and with assorted other members of the family in the Avenue d'Eylau in Paris. It was there that Morel was born. Before he was four years old his father died, and in due course his mother left the family house, largely, it would seem, to escape the overbearing presence of her mother-in-law. She subsequently eked out a living as a music teacher in Paris, and being determined that her son should have an English education, sent him to Madras House, a private school in Eastbourne, at the age of eight.

During these early years, there was little indication that Morel would shortly develop into a campaigner and writer of remarkable talent. He appears to have been happy at Madras House, delighting in going out into the countryside to pick violets to send to his mother, and enjoying swimming from the beach at Birling Gap. Later, he described himself as a 'delicate, weedy, passionate, and abnormally sensitive boy, with an instinctive love of the beautiful.' This awareness extended to a particular interest in moths and butterflies, and indeed Morel became something of an expert lepidopterist later in life. Although he appears to have been mildly reproved for this hobby when he moved on to Bedford Modern School, his housemaster was indulgent, even allowing him to keep caterpillars and pupae in his school box. His academic record shows no exceptional ability in any field and surprisingly, given his early years in France, his French was considered rather poor.

After only two and a half years, just before he was 16, he left Bedford Modern and went back to Paris, mainly on account of his mother's ill health. She had found a place for him in the American banking house Drexel, Morgan and Company, and he worked there for two years until it became apparent that Emmeline's longing to go home to England was becoming overwhelming. It was clear that they could only return if Morel could find work to support them, and eventually an offer was received from Elder Dempster and Company, a Liverpool shipping firm. Their first offer had been the post of purser in one of their ships employed in the Congo trade, but as Morel did not wish to be separated from his mother, a place had been found for him in their office.

In 1891 mother and son returned to England, ending what Morel later described as their 'exile', and he began work as a clerk at Dempster, where his now fluent French proved a great asset in deciphering business documents from the company's trading partners overseas. His salary was £70 a year, and since family finances were extremely straitened at this time, he supplemented his income by giving French lessons at 2s 6d an hour, although this was considered rather a demeaning occupation.

The office in which he now found himself was the centre for West African interests in Liverpool, and the continent at once began to exert an influence upon him.

> There was something very huge and mysterious about the whole subject which exercised an increasing fascination over my mind... I plunged into the old West African literature: learned the geography of the coast, section by section, with the help of maps and steamer charts; studied its history, its trade and its people and customs, its fauna and flora, laid myself out to read up everything I could find about the current problems in the newspapers...The more I read the more interested I grew; the more clearly it seemed to me...that the newspapers seemed extraordinarily ignorant of the whole subject.[7]

When his mother remarked that he had a gift for writing that might be put to good use, he took up the suggestion with enthusiasm, and in December 1893 his first article dealing with the subject of French colonial policy in West Africa appeared in the *Pall Mall Gazette*. In 1895, when he was only 22 years old, he was appointed head of the Congo department where he apparently earned the reputation of being a 'devil for work'. A colleague later wrote that Morel was the first to find a market for articles about the West African Coast and that he became the recognised expert on the subject, driving himself hard and 'proving difficult to work with if you did not share his keenness'.[8]

Morel's development was not unlike the sudden hatching of the pupae that he cultivated; almost overnight, an unremarkable boy had metamorphosed into a formidable crusader. As he passed into adulthood he was clearly filled with a driving idealism, and an urge to pursue justice in the face of unprincipled evil and the devious political processes which allowed it to flourish. The de Horne family had been associated with the Quakers, who had been in the forefront of the opposition to slavery in the 18th century, and many years later, as Morel exposed the horrors of the trade with which he had unwittingly involved himself, he remarked in a letter to a friend that he wondered whether his reformist zeal was 'more than an unconscious following of hereditary and constitutional instincts? If one had not this in one's blood...would one have done it?'[9] Certainly, it is more than likely that his upbringing by his mother, herself a product of a long Quaker tradition, was very influential, and that a secularized form of her beliefs formed a foundation for his altruism.

However, although his desire to challenge the ills of the world was fundamentally humanitarian, he undoubtedly harboured ambitions for himself, albeit fairly modest ones compared to those of the many aggressively competitive men of his day. Indeed, he confided to a friend in a rare moment of self-criticism that he was 'not the high moral kind that can rise above egoism'. But it is hard to hold that against him; the desire for public recognition of one's endeavours is the most common of human vanities, and there are few in any walk of life who do not seek it. Moreover, no one who lacked Morel's astonishing work ethic could have hoped to match his output and achievements, and he could hardly have been unaware of his own ability. Modesty is not a characteristic that sits easily with commitment to a contentious cause, and no doubt it was partly the conviction of his own rectitude that enabled Morel to take on the establishment with 'the gloves off', regardless of the risk to his personal reputation. Although his campaign on behalf of the people of the Congo ultimately earned him great public adulation, his opposition to the First World War led to his imprisonment, and he pursued both with the same single-minded determination. In the sense of the aphorism attributed to Edmund Burke, that 'all that is required for evil to prevail is for good men to do nothing', Morel was indeed a good man, and one with exceptional endowments who did more with his particular virtues than most men would have done.

The Congo Campaign

For nearly twelve years an invisible war has ravaged this beloved, beleaguered country. Over five million dead, hundreds of thousands of women and girls raped and sexually tortured in unimaginable ways, 800,000 internally displaced since January 2009 and close to 350,000 forced to flee to neighbouring countries. The violence is fuelled by the world's need for minerals, most recently due to the economic crisis. Congo, the sixth most mineral rich country in Africa has become the stage for a regional war fuelled by economic interests.

The Guardian
19 June 2009

The country that we now call the Democratic Republic of Congo (formerly known as Zaire) was established at the time of the scramble for Africa, when the European nations agreed on the rules for dividing up the greater part of the continent between them at the Berlin Conference of the Powers in 1884–1885. Its borders enclose a vast area, some eighty times the size of Belgium, and include the whole of the Congo River Basin. Among the land's early inhabitants were the Bantu, who migrated from what is now Nigeria in around 2000BC. Thereafter other peoples, amongst them the Kuba and the Luba, settled in and around the Congo Basin, and the Kongo Kingdom emerged in the 13th century. Although these cultures were often regarded as 'primitive' by Europeans, there is nonetheless widespread evidence of very early copper and iron smelting techniques in the region which, together with the excavation of wooden artefacts, has led archaeologists to conclude that at least some groups in ancient Congo had developed centralised political units around the end of the first millennium.

When the Portuguese reached the mouth of the Congo River towards the end of the 15th century, they established long-lasting relationships with the Kongo. Catholic missionaries followed the Portuguese, in time transforming their territory into a Christian kingdom. Over the next three centuries, other Nilotic peoples from the upper regions of the river migrated into northern and central Congo, and a number of chiefdoms and kingdoms emerged (including the Kuba and the Luba), exercising control and influence over much of the area.

Contact with Europe brought new crops and farming methods, as well as new cultural and manufacturing techniques, but early in the 18th century penetration from the east (particularly from Tanzania) by traders searching for slaves and ivory had a profound impact, and by the time Leopold claimed the Congo as his own there was no overall political unity.

In the 15th century the Portuguese had been the first Europeans to trade extensively along the west coast of Africa, setting up numerous trading posts and establishing a colony, Angola, in addition to Mozambique on the east coast. However, their success in Africa was soon overshadowed by the discovery of the New World and its riches. As Thomas Pakenham puts it, 'the trickle of African gold and the tusks of ivory and ostrich feathers could not compare with the flood of treasures from the East and West...Africa slipped back into the shadows'.[10] But another African export was soon to come onto the market, a commodity that was more important for world trade during the next 300 years than anything that had previously emerged from the continent: human beings themselves.

The establishment of cotton and sugar plantations all over the New World created a demand for labour, and the African continent afforded a limitless supply. The slave trade required no penetration into the interior, and there were African tribes to be found who conspired with the colonial powers in the enslavement of their fellow countrymen. This led to what has been described as the most terrible of all migrations: some 10 million black Africans were exported like cattle during the three centuries after the Portuguese invasion, and up to a third died in transit.

By the middle of the 19th century, however, slavery had largely ended, and thanks to the steamboat, merchants on the west coast had found more acceptable alternatives to the now prohibited market in human beings. Great ports such as Liverpool, whose wealth had stemmed from the barter of manufactured goods for slaves, could now become even wealthier by exchanging those same goods for tropical products such as groundnuts, peanuts, and palm oil. This new profitable trade was pursued with vigour. 'Here was the antidote for slavery, "legitimate trade", a cure for the open sore of Africa, applied miraculously by steam.'[11]

Until the 1890s there had been little need or advantage to British merchants in acquiring African territory, and they had confined most of their activity to the coastal areas. Their position was backed up by naval forces and secured through treaties with native chiefs, and competition from traders of other European nations was minimal. But these easy-going relationships, which avoided the costs and difficulties of direct administration, were threatened by this scramble for Africa following the Berlin Conference. By the time Morel started work in Liverpool, French traders had begun moving into the hinterland of the Gold Coast, Gambia and Sierra Leone, thus reducing the flow of goods to the British merchants on the coast.

In his first article, dealing with French colonial policy, Morel also urged the need for more extensive railway construction in the British Protectorates and Crown Colonies, a development in which Britain lagged far behind both the French and the Portuguese. From this time on, a steady stream of his articles concerning African affairs appeared in the press: in the *Manchester Guardian*, the *Liverpool Daily Post*, and the *Liverpool Journal of Commerce*, amongst other publications. Besides laying the foundation for the campaigns to come, his financial position was considerably improved by this foray into part-time journalism, as well as by two legacies from one of the Morel de Ville uncles: £800 to his mother and £1500 to himself. This increase in his income allowed him to marry Mary Florence Richardson in 1896.

Mary was the daughter of a Liverpool printer, John Richardson, and of Anna Carwithen, a member of a well-known Devonshire family, who for many generations had been vicars of the parish church at Manaton, a small village on the eastern edge of Dartmoor. Morel had met her through her parents, who had asked him to tutor their two younger sons in French, in order to help with their applications for Naval College. She believed implicitly in Morel's work, and their union proved an enormous source of strength for the rest of his life. The secure and loving family base that she provided was to sustain him through the many vicissitudes that lay ahead. She eventually bore him five children, and their daughter, Stella Emmeline, was born a year after their marriage. Around this time Morel had become a British citizen, and he decided to drop the second half of his full surname 'Morel de Ville', and to use the first half only. In future he used the initials EDM and the signature E D Morel.

In these initial years, the views that Morel expressed through his journalism on imperialism and the expansion of trade were entirely conventional; he had not yet begun to question the prevailing dogmas of his day. Later, when the Congo reform movement was underway, he was accused of having been the spokesman for the Liverpool shipping interests, and it is true his early work pleased both his newspaper clients and his employer, Alfred Jones, Chairman of Elder Dempster.

Alfred Jones was a significant figure in the business world. In addition to Elder Dempster he controlled a number of other shipping lines, founded the British Bank of West Africa, established both the African oil-mills in Liverpool and the Liverpool School of Tropical Medicine, and owned hotels in Jamaica, the Canaries and West Africa. His success can be best measured by the scale of his philanthropy. Amongst other donations he gave £10,000 towards the building of a cathedral in Liverpool, a remarkable sum by any standard, and worth approximately £1m in today's terms. However, there was little evidence of this philanthropy being extended towards the creators of his fortune. He never expressed concern about the circumstances under which the African population laboured to produce the materials in which he traded, and he appears to have been deaf to the descriptions of exploitation and ill treatment of native peoples that had been received from missionaries and travellers and others. In fact, these had been circulating in Europe for a number of years, and the Aborigines' Protection Society (APS) had appealed unsuccessfully to the British government on behalf of the natives of the Congo in 1896. The following year Sir Charles Dilke, the Liberal and reformist MP, had also brought the question before the House of Commons, suggesting that the government should takes steps to convene an international conference on the subject.

The suggestion was declined, but a public meeting was convened by the APS at which Dilke and others spoke, as did a Swedish missionary called Sjöblom, who made damning accusations against Congolese officials, charging them with committing appalling atrocities upon the natives who were forced to collect rubber. Morel's eyes were not yet open to the horrors of the exploitation of the Congo, and in response he told readers of the *Pall Mall Gazette* that he would give them the facts as they were, '...not as disappointed adventurers, needy place-hunters and misinformed philanthropists would have us believe'. As for stories alleging the ill-treatment of natives, even if they were true 'what European nation which has undertaken the heavy responsibility of introducing the blessings and vices of civilization into the Dark Continent can claim immunity for its representatives in this respect?'[12]

In taking this supremacist attitude, so totally opposed to his later views and writings, Morel was simply reflecting the ubiquitous beliefs of his day. That even enlightened colonial explorers and administrators held these opinions is illustrated by Sir Harry Johnston's introduction to Morel's *Red Rubber*, published in 1906, long after Morel's own attitude to the exploitation of Africa had changed. Although the book is a passionate indictment of Leopold's regime in the Congo, and is itself in no way racist in tone, Sir Harry's preface condescendingly remarks that 'negroes' were 'leading lives not much superior to those of brutes, although there were none not emphatically human and capable of improvement'.[13]

A decade before the publication of *Red Rubber*, however, Morel was still voicing the conventional presumptions of his day. On one occasion, he even wrote that he saw a great future in store for the Congo and those vast territories secured to their country by King Leopold II. His first experience in creating an organised public protest on a question of public policy, an activity in which he was to spend the better part of his career, was on the issue that most concerned the Liverpool merchants: French expansion in the hinterlands of British territory. He campaigned to persuade the Foreign Office that they should demand the equality of British merchants with the French in their trade with the French colonies.

Morel's commitment to the interests of Liverpool shippers remained throughout his period of employment with Elder Dempster, but he gradually became more and more concerned with issues other than the rights of competing commercial interests. He travelled back and forth across the English Channel, visiting Brussels and Antwerp as his company's liaison officer, dealing with the handling of cargo, and meeting Leopold's Congo executives.

By the time Morel stumbled upon what he called 'a secret society of murderers with a King for a croniman', the million square miles of the Congo, with its millions of inhabitants, had already been under the absolute rule of Leopold II, King of the Belgians, for fifteen years. The Berlin Conference had been set up in 1884 to establish a series of principles for regulating European policy in tropical Africa, and the fate of the continent had been determined by fourteen European representatives who had never set foot on African soil, and without the presence of a single African at the negotiating table. The recognition by the powers of the International Association of the Congo (later to be known as the Congo Free State) successfully climaxed nine years of intrigue and plotting, during which Leopold had transformed a private international association, originally established to support scientific expeditions into Central Africa, into a state over which he had total control. Such power enabled him to issue decrees giving the State rights of proprietorship over all vacant lands throughout the Congo territory, and reducing the rights of the Congolese over their land to the narrowest limits of native villages and farms.

It is difficult to grasp the size of the country over which King Leopold now held sway, and which he regarded as his own property. Morel's book, *Red Rubber*, shows a map of the Congo River and its tributaries superimposed on a map of Europe, with the Congo covering an area in the north reaching from John O'Groats in Scotland, east to Bergen in Norway and Stockholm, while in the south it extends from Istanbul west to Athens, the south of Italy, Corsica and the Franco-Spanish border. All this was Leopold's fiefdom, and his alone.

Although he was deeply involved in African affairs and had become well informed about developments in the centre of the continent, Morel acknowledged he had been 'slow in finding out the facts.' In a rather inadequate apologia for his past unreconstructed views on the native people of West Africa, he attributed them to 'my youth and inexperience; the elaborate secrecy with which the high officials of the Congo Free State in Brussels conducted their masters' business; the natural obstacles to a young man in a shipping office going outside his province to investigate the conduct of a foreign government in purely business relations with his employer.'[14] This description of himself as an ingénu seems inadequate to account for the radical change he had undergone from apologist for the regime in the Congo into a champion of native rights, but one additional influence seems to have been crucial to informing his new perspective. At the time he was becoming aware of the gross imbalance of trade between the Congo and Europe, and awakening to the reality of violence in the interior, he had become a friend of the writer and explorer, Mary Kingsley.

While studying anthropology, and following the death of her parents in the mid 1890s, Mary Kingsley had travelled in Africa for three years to finish a book by her father. She was sympathetic to African culture, and she saw and understood the profound impact that European colonialists and missionaries were having on the continent. Her own publication, *Travels in West Africa*, was amongst the first to present Africans as human beings. Morel was profoundly affected by her attitude, and the forward to his first book, *Affairs of West Africa*, carries a glowing tribute to her. 'The nature of the work she had undertaken, the intense fervour with which she devoted herself, body and soul to preaching the morals it was given her to inculcate...no mortal being could have endured for so very long so perpetual a mental and physical strain...The truest, kindest, staunchest friend that ever breathed – such was Mary Kingsley.'[15] It is clear from his subsequent writings that her opinions continued to influence him deeply; her views on land tenure, for example, soon became his own. 'Speaking generally,' he later declared, '...throughout tropical Africa there is no such thing as unowned land where there is population...With few exceptions, native tenure takes the form of communal ownership of the land and its fruits; a form proper to the condition of native society and immemorial custom.'[16]

Mary Kingsley was also a staunch advocate of free trade, believing it would be the most principled and humane mechanism for bringing Africa into the modern age, and again Morel enthusiastically adopted her view. 'Native ownership in land,' he wrote, 'must needs be the foundation-stone of all normal European rule in the African tropics, because the economic object of normal European rule is the development of commercial relations, and because any commercial relationship between the European and the native is impossible, unless the native has articles to sell with which to purchase the manufactured goods.'

King Leopold's decrees, asserting rights of possession over so-called 'vacant land', completely destroyed such traditional systems, leaving the African population with nothing to trade, and to Morel this was the greatest outrage inflicted upon the people of the Congo Free State. In a trenchant criticism of the prevailing colonial practice of land seizure that has had such disastrous repercussions for Africa, he declared that the situation could be summed up in three sentences:

> The rights of the natives to the produce of their own soil are taken from them and vested in aliens living thousands of miles away. The natives ceased to be owners of property and consequently cease to be economic units; the alien claiming the right to extract from the native, as representatives of a superior civilization, the labour which is required for the collection of this produce and its shipment to Europe, where it is sold for the exclusive benefit of the alien in question. The proceeds of this sale form the principal asset of the alien administration and its affiliated corporations; the natives are thus systematically robbed of their natural wealth and the power to enrich themselves by trade and labour.[17]

Land appropriation of this kind had an added benefit for Leopold. At the time he took over possession of the Congo Free State, it contained an estimated population of some 20 million people, and it was not necessary to transport labour across 3,000 miles of ocean to a destination in the New World, as it had been before. Instead, thousands of tons of tropical products, principally rubber, could be shipped direct to Europe from Africa, and this vast transfer of commodities came at a minimum cost to his own regime. The details of this trade were not normally scrutinised, but Morel's work at Elder Dempster drew them to his attention, and what finally convinced him of the accuracy of the reports of abuses in the Congo was his unexpected discovery that the records he kept so carefully for the company did not conform with the trade figures that the Free State of Congo announced to the public.

On examining the ships' manifestos, he found that much of the rubber and ivory shipped from the Congo in the company's steamers were not included in the statistics issued by the Congo government. A great deal more was being exported than was included in the returns. He also discovered that some of the companies which controlled vast areas of Congo territory, and were intimately connected to King Leopold and his minions, were making immense profits so immense, in fact, that shares which were nominally worth about £20 apiece were changing hands at anything from £800 to £1000 per share (enormous sums in today's terms), whilst shareholders were receiving dividends bringing in from 300 to 800 percent on their investments.[18] But none of this wealth was returning to the Congo. In other words, although exports were generating vast fortunes for Leopold and his business cronies, the people of the country were receiving nothing, or next to nothing, for their commodities or their labour.

It is virtually impossible to persuade anybody to work for no return without employing coercion, and Morel's examination of the nature of the country's imports bore out this appalling fact. Although there were few imports into the Congo that could be construed as normal articles of trade, he discovered that the steamers returning to the country had been shipping vast numbers of ball cartridge and thousands of rifles and other weapons to the State itself, or to sundry Belgian 'trading companies'. It was plain that the guns and ammunition were being used for the subjugation and exploitation of the native population, and it became abundantly clear to Morel that what he had unearthed was, to all intents and purposes, a system of slavery. 'I have stood on that quay of Antwerp,' he wrote, 'and seen that rubber disgorged from the bowels of the incoming steamer, and to my fancy there has mingled with the musical chimes ringing in the old cathedral tower, another sound – the faintest echo of a sigh from the depths of the dark and stifling hold. A sigh breathed in the gloomy equatorial forest, by those from whose anguish this wealth was wrung. *They* knew not their merciful Emperor. Yet that echo took form of words in my mind, "Imperator" – it has seemed to whisper – "Imperator! *Morituri te salutant!*" (We who are about to die, salute thee, Emperor!)'[19] Appalled by his discovery, he immediately went to confront Alfred Jones.

At the time, and in spite of the concerns expressed by the APS and foreign missionaries, very few people in Europe were remotely aware of the extent of the violence being inflicted upon the people of the Congo Free State. Morel's original response in 1897 had been typical of most of his contemporaries: the Congo was a faraway place of which they knew nothing, and besides it was inhabited by a backward and uncivilized people. As a result, the land question alone might not have been sufficient to fuel Morel's campaign against the King. There seems to have been little opposition to foreign corporations obtaining immense 'concessions' – a polite description that legitimised theft – from Leopold for the production of palm oil or the extraction of minerals. The dispossession of native peoples from their land was common practice in modern history, and had been so since the discovery of the Americas. Indeed, it is often practised today as both developed and developing nations pursue their needs for minerals, fossil fuels and agricultural land, with little regard to the rights of indigenous populations. But until Morel's campaign, the appalling orgy of brutality inflicted upon the Congolese people was unknown to the general public, and horrific reports such as that of the Swedish missionary Sjöblom went largely unnoticed.

Many of these writings were harrowing in the extreme; for example, on the collection of rubber Sjöblom wrote:

> If the rubber does not reach the full amount required the sentinels attack the natives; they kill some and bring the hands to the commissary…Two or three days after a fight a dead mother was found with two of her children. The mother was shot and the right hand taken off. On one side was the elder child also shot, and the right hand also taken off. On the other side was the younger child, with the right hand cut off, but the child, still living, was resting against the dead mother's breast…A sentinel passed our mission station, and a woman accompanied him, carrying a basket of hands. We counted eighteen right hands smoked…they belonged to men, women, and even children…one of the soldiers told me…'The commissary has promised us if we bring plenty of hands we will shorten our service. I have brought in plenty of hands already and I expect my time of service will soon be finished'. [20]

However, when Morel presented his chairman, Sir Alfred Jones, with evidence of what was taking place in the Congo he received little interest or support. Sir Alfred simply assured him that Leopold would not tolerate such abuses and advised him to keep quiet about it. This bland response was scarcely surprising given Sir Alfred's wide ranging business interests.

He was described as the 'uncrowned King of West Africa',[21] and being one of Leopold's best customers, had been appointed as the Congo's Honorary Consul in Liverpool. His services were further recognised by Leopold's donation of £2,600 to the School of Tropical Medicine.

Morel, however, ignored Sir Alfred's opinion, and disregarding the effect that his actions would inevitably have on his own career, wrote a series of articles in *The Speaker* exposing the Congo scandal. Thus began what has been described as 'a great moral crusade and a remarkable and unequalled period of investigative journalism.'[22] Over the next few years, three full books and hundreds of articles for all the major British newspapers, as well as others in French for papers in France and Belgium, flowed from Morel's pen. As Hochschild puts it, 'He was renowned for his meticulous accuracy, amassing evidence as painstakingly as a lawyer's brief, and both admirers and enemies searched his work for factual errors with scant success.'[23] It was asserted that no one ever ridiculed Morel; when he touched a subject he mastered it until there was nothing more to be said. This amazing output continued unabated in the face of considerable financial problems and withering attacks from Leopold's supporters.

Under the circumstances, Morel felt that he could not remain at Elder Dempster much longer. In 1901, the year of Queen Victoria's death, he resigned, in spite of Jones offering him a post abroad with a substantial salary. This must have been an extremely difficult decision; Morel had very limited private resources, and by this time he and Mary had three children: Stella, Roger and John, born in 1897, 1899 and 1901. Moreover, the house in West Kirby where they had lived since their marriage, and which commanded a spectacular view over the River Dee estuary, was becoming inadequate for their needs. Unable to support his family by freelance journalism alone, he managed to secure a post at £300 a year on a weekly paper, *West Africa,* run by Haigh Chalmers.

Morel's first article in the paper was a vigorous condemnation of the Hut Tax in Sierra Leone, which had been instituted to provide revenue for the Protectorate to meet its administrative costs, and he continued to address this subject for some time. The Tax was 'a ghastly political mistake…The immediate result was a local insurrection developing into a general rising, which led to the massacre of hundreds of the educated native element established in the interior.'[24] As he would continue to do over the coming decade, he emphasised 'the point we have urged again and again, viz. the rights of the native owners of the soil.' He followed this up with another lengthy article in June, addressing the Administration of British West Africa and the importance of native cooperation.[25]

Neither article questions the imperial project, but they demonstrate his increasing awareness and concern about the manner in which the colonising powers were exploiting their new territories. Today, his words, written in 1901, sound immensely patronising. He asserts, for example, that 'if Englishmen mean to make a success of their West African Empire, they must take the trouble to understand what is passing in the mind of the best type of educated West African on the problem of native representation in administration', but at the time, very few people held such comparatively enlightened views. His scope was also unusually wide. He wrote about Northern Nigeria, its people, social systems and conditions; Great Britain's relations with Bornu and French political activity around Lake Chad; Germany and free trade in Western Africa; the Lagos 'Native Councils Bill'. Indeed, there seemed to be little which escaped his thoughtful and detailed comments, and at this early stage in his career his post at the paper confirmed his reputation for having a remarkable command of a wide range of issues.

In addition to his journalistic work, he published his first book, *Affairs of West Africa*, towards the end of 1902. It included many illustrations of people, places and activities, and is another impressive example of an authoritative work on further issues in West Africa. Much of the book was again devoted to Nigeria, but it also addressed matters such as land tenure and labour, and included chapters on the cotton industry, the concessions regime in French Congo, the mahogany trade, and an article on sanitary affairs by a Major Ross. The final three chapters were built on Morel's earlier articles in *West Africa*, and are a swingeing attack on international monopolists and the Congo – the 'Domaine Privé' of Leopold, as he called it – and the trade in rubber. He ends the book as he began it, with a quote from Mary Kingsley.

> The moulding of that history (of the African race) is in the hands of the Europeans, whose superior activity and superior power in arts and crafts give the mastery; but all this mastery gives is the power to make the future of the African and the European prosperous, or to make it one of disaster to both alike. Whatever we do in Africa today, a thousand years hence there will be Africans to thrive or suffer for it.[26]

What is astonishing is not just the quantity of writing, but its comprehensive command of facts and figures, particularly in view of the fact that at this stage Morel had never visited any of the countries concerned, other than Belgium. *The Times*, though generally approving of the book, was critical of the author for '…having fallen into error based on an insufficient knowledge of the operations of both countries in the interior,'[27] a criticism that was difficult to refute. On the other hand, *The Speaker* (though hardly an impartial source, since it had published Morel's earlier articles) reported the book as being '…so full of good suggestions for the greater prosperity of West Africa that it cannot be too widely or too carefully studied.'[28]

In March and April 1902, *West Africa* reproduced two articles by Morel previously published in the *Contemporary Review*, both entitled *The Belgian Curse in Africa. A startling attack on the Congo State.*[29] These followed his articles in *The Speaker* and represented his first attack on King Leopold's regime. Complementing these publications, the April edition also carried a copy of a further statement, *The Treatment of Natives in the Congo*, submitted to the British government again on behalf of the APS, and signed by their secretary, Richard Fox Bourne.

During the same year, Morel's family moved to Stafford House in Hawarden, then a village on the Welsh borders, about seven miles west of Chester, and their fourth child, Geoff, was born there in 1904. They remained at Hawarden for five years, and over this period Morel conducted his campaign almost entirely by correspondence, only travelling to London on important occasions. His friend, Seymour Cocks, writes of his retiring disposition and strong affection for country life,[30] which perhaps allowed him to find time for his lifelong hobby of collecting moths! This habit of seclusion, and reluctance to mix with the well known figures of contemporary life, apparently led to some of his opponents picturing him as a sinister Machiavellian figure lurking in the background.

At the time Morel went to work for Chalmers, the Congo had made little impression upon the public conscience, despite five years of intermittent press attention. The Boer War had monopolised public opinion, and official circles had small appetite for rocking the boat of traditional Anglo-Belgian policy. Reports received by the Foreign Office from its consuls in the Congo had largely been suppressed. It was said that Queen Victoria opposed a strong line of action being taken against the son of the man for whom she had entertained such strong affection, while the three Chambers of Commerce most closely associated with West African trade, Liverpool, Manchester and London, had sent delegates to the Berlin Conference and agitated in favour of Leopold. In addition to Alfred Jones's honorary consulship, the chairman of Manchester's Chamber of Commerce African Section ran a firm selling cotton goods to the Congo Free State; his partner was Belgian Consul in Manchester. In London the President of the Chamber of Commerce was a Knight – Commander of the

Order of Leopold.[31] It was obvious that the merchants, with their major business interests in Belgium, had no incentive to go elsewhere.

Nonetheless, not all traders were in the pocket of the King, or unsympathetic to Morel's views of how business should be conducted. In 1899, through Mary Kingsley, Morel first met John Holt of the Liverpool shipping firm that bore his name. Holt was nearly sixty when Morel first encountered him, and he grew to hold a strong personal influence over the younger man. Over the years he was to provide Morel with encouragement, contacts, business advice and subscriptions for his publications. It was said of Holt, who was then Vice President of the African Trade Section of the Liverpool Chamber of Commerce, that he had 'no contempt for the African'[32] and indeed his concern for Africans was deep and genuine. He had spent many years in West Africa building a thriving business through direct transactions with the native peoples, and had a reputation for fair dealing, a practice now threatened by a growing system of concessions and monopolies.

It was Holt, with the help of Alice Stopford Green, who arranged Morel's first public address to the Women's National Liberal Association in London in 1901. The talk was principally on the need for imperialists to govern through established native land rights, institutions, customs and law. Alice Green, widow of the historian John Richard Green and herself an historian, was Vice President of the African Society and an outspoken critic of British colonial policy in South Africa. She lived in Kensington, was well acquainted with many influential people, and was to prove one of Morel's great allies, editing his views and helping him to place his articles.

The Campaign Gathers Pace

At the start of the 21st century, when communication is provided by satellite at the touch of a button and through a variety of sources, it is difficult to appreciate the scale of the task that Morel had set himself in attempting to raise the conscience of a nation. To begin with, he had never travelled to Africa, and had no first-hand knowledge of the Congo, and Leopold had now banned all unsympathetic journalists from visiting the country. At home, communications were by today's standards time-consuming and cumbersome, although it must be said that they were also swift and efficient, with the mail service reaching its peak performance in the decades before the war. Some parts of London had up to twelve deliveries a day, with other major cities, Birmingham, Manchester and Liverpool, having six to eight deliveries. Intercity letters could even arrive on the same day, thanks to sorting rooms on mail trains and the special underground network in London.[33] Nonetheless, in 1900 the telephone and telegraph were in their infancy, and leaving aside the horse, the only swift method of transport within the country was by train. Newspapers were widely available, but whilst use of a typewriter was becoming increasingly common, many contributions would still have been handwritten in either pen or pencil. Fortunately Morel himself mastered the typewriter and the use of the carbon copy early on in his career, making it infinitely easier to read his voluminous output.

In addition to these technical problems, the strength of the opposition was formidable. Leopold was one of the ablest monarchs in Europe and was related to many of its royal families. He was clever and shrewd, skilled in diplomacy, crafty and unscrupulous, and he could exercise his influence through a multitude of social, economic and political channels. He was essentially the embodiment of a vast capitalistic conspiracy, with tentacles reaching into every financial centre on the Continent; he influenced the press of a dozen countries, and in some cases even their religious organisations. A compliant press bureau was equipped to release all manner of misrepresentations in every form, whether through books, pamphlets or special articles. As Morel put it, such a body was capable of 'rallying the latent forces of moral reaction to its side and infusing them with renewed energy and power'.[34]

Confronting this hegemony was a small group of committed men and women, devoted to their cause but possessed of little wealth and with practically no financial backing, and initially commanding very limited public support. Their task was to awaken Parliament to an urgent and shocking issue at a time when much else was happening on the international scene, and when the government would have greatly preferred to take the least difficult and inconvenient course (as governments so often do) and 'let sleeping dogs lie'.

The three articles in *The Speaker*, exposing the Congo Scandal, had been published unsigned, but they came to the notice of Sir Charles Dilke, the MP whose views Morel had criticised earlier, and Henry Richard Fox Bourne, both of whom had been denouncing the ill treatment of the natives in the Congo. Enquiries to the editor of the paper revealed Morel to be the author, and he was soon advising them on their campaign. In effect, he had launched his offensive, but not, it seems, without some reservations. In writing to Holt he asked, 'Am I a David to face this Goliath? God knows I would like to see the horror of the Congo put a stop to, but are you and I sufficient for attaining such a thing? Have I the power to secure the freedom of millions of the Congo region from the scourge of European brutality being inflicted upon them?'[35] But in the event he put such worries aside, and the campaign to come revealed his extraordinary ability to concentrate all his energy on the objective of reform.

It was unfortunate that shortly after the start of the campaign Morel became involved in an unseemly dispute with his employer, Haigh Chalmers, and carried out a vituperative campaign against him which brought his time at the newspaper, *West Africa,* to an unsatisfactory conclusion. Chalmers had revealed plans to incorporate the newspaper and Morel was incensed that he had been given no role in the new organisation. To make matters worse, the financial disclosures entailed in the change did not correspond to Morel's expectations. He had been under the impression that the paper was losing money, whereas the figures showed that it had been making money all along, and Morel now claimed that its success and prosperity was largely due to his efforts.

Understandably, he resigned a few months later when his contract expired. But not content with resigning, he went on the offensive against Chalmers with the aim of destroying his influence and reputation in Liverpool. Morel was determined to start his own newspaper, but there seemed little chance that two newspapers principally interested in West African affairs could co-exist when their success depended upon support from firms engaged in the West African trade. Vilifying Chalmers and his character, whilst at the same time currying the favour of the commercial and business community in Liverpool, was an unedifying use of Morel's journalistic and writing skills. He proposed to one of his allies in the London office that Chalmers be told he must make an offer to sell the paper within a week, or members of the staff familiar with his dubious affairs would desert to join the opposition paper. He also approached a firm which had declined an invitation to advertise in his own publication, recalling that in his book he had gone out of his way to refer to its role in opening up the West African rivers, and that he had fought for the 'merchant's interests' for years. In the end Chalmers refused to be intimidated, but in spring 1903 Morel nonetheless went ahead and launched his new paper, the *West African Mail.* The major stockholders, in addition to a number of other smaller investors, were Morel himself, and somewhat surprisingly, Alfred Jones and his rival, John Holt, each of whom invested £500.

It is interesting to reflect on the motives that drove Morel to act in such an unscrupulous manner. It was not long after the publication of 'The Congo Scandal' series, yet here was its author behaving in a way quite contradictory to his own concerns. How principled was the journalist, who in order to advance his career, attempted to gain the financial support of the commercial community by the promise of a favourable press? Morel himself appears to have been unaware of his anomalous behaviour, believing that in becoming the most influential voice in West African journalism he would be a power for good, and advance the cause of the Congo people. Furthermore he believed strongly in free trade, assuming that what was good for the Liverpool merchants was good for West Africa. These views typically lacked any nuance or self-doubt; later in his career he would be accused of not taking other important issues into account during his campaigns, and of lacking the ability to examine his own motives in trying to achieve his objectives.

The Chalmers affair is perhaps the first occasion when Morel's single-mindedness became glaringly obvious. In the light of what was to follow, it seems most unlikely that he wrote his early articles on the Congo simply to advance his journalistic career, but his actions at the time are certainly an example of his occasional tendency to employ ruthless means to achieve his objectives. However, although it has been said that the circumstances surrounding his founding of the West African Mail reveal an ambitious and self-righteous disposition, Morel could never have achieved his aims without steely determination to succeed and a conviction in the rightness of his cause. He may have possessed what has been described as 'tunnel vision', but with an opponent as powerful as Leopold there was plainly little room for scruple. Arguably, no true reformer, when faced with a major injustice, can be anything other than pitilessly focused on the task in hand. Morel's own feelings were well expressed in his critique of Fox Bourne, whom he described as 'an honest, sincere and genuine philanthropist, whose efforts were beyond praise, working for pure zeal on behalf of oppressed peoples all over the world.' However, he considered 'the very catholicity of his sympathies to be a popular weakness in a case of superlative wrongdoing.' Although Fox Bourne aroused a certain amount of interest in the Congo it was very restricted and had 'no driving force'. [36]

Morel was convinced of the impracticality of leading a crusade against the Congo by invoking humanitarian sentiment alone. He was certain that it would be impossible to arouse anything more than the most ephemeral public concern by concentrating solely upon the scattered reports of savage brutality perpetrated upon the native population. He was determined to emphasise that the atrocities were merely the effect of the root cause – it was the 'whole infernal system of its legal basis, its monstrous claims, its fraudulent accounts and statistics, its gross and enormous profits' which required to be dragged into the daylight and exposed in all its infamy. He stressed that the Congo 'Free State' was neither State nor Protectorate, but a 'personal enterprise thriving upon pillage, necessitating the destruction of innumerable human beings, which began and ended with rubber wrung from the bowels of a helpless people'.

Although as yet he was not entirely sure what action to take, Morel wrote that the need to probe the scandal to its very dregs and take action had become a manifest duty, and his investigations were exhaustive. In order to understand the structural foundations of Congo Free State law, he obtained all the official bulletins of the Congo State from the date of its creation. He discovered, as he had long suspected, that the natives had no rights in law, and that the whole of the land surface of the Congo, except for those parts that were covered by native dwellings or under cultivation with crops, had been declared vacant and ownerless, and the property of the state. He examined the Congo's export returns in relation to the Congo government's budgetary estimates of revenue and expenditure. He turned his attention to the Belgian commercial enterprises in the Congo, where he had a number of useful contacts. He discovered that the Congo Free State's native army was significantly larger in proportion to other native forces maintained by European administrations in their tropical African dependencies. He found out that the concessionaire companies kept large numbers of irregular levies, who were supplied with rifles and guns. In short, he rigorously amassed the facts and figures for which he would become renowned, and on which nobody could fault him.

His main task, as he described it, was to convince the world that the horrors in the Congo were not only indisputable, but being neither accidental nor temporary, were incapable of internal reform. He was determined to show that the policies were deliberate, and that the consequences would be identical in any part of the tropics where similar practices might be introduced. Above all, he wanted to evince that the entire administration was what he described as 'a survival and a revival of the slave mind at work, and of the slave trade in being.'

At the same time, Morel gradually built up contacts with rank and file missionaries and diplomatic and military officials: German, French, Italian and Belgian. He contacted everyone he knew well, and in addition wrote to his acquaintances and their friends, appealing to the conscience of the recipients. He solicited the support of nobility, clergy, academics, journalists and politicians. He was in constant communication with publicists on the Continent, urging them to conduct 'fierce polemics in Belgian and French journals' in order to stir up feeling against Leopold and all his works. He claimed that in order to keep up public interest, hardly a week should pass without several of his letters appearing in the English newspapers, now on one aspect of the controversy, now on another, but increasingly concentrating on native rights. As a result, he started to receive unsolicited correspondence from many countries. Sympathisers in France, Germany, Holland, the United States and even Belgium (among them a disgruntled steamship captain and an office clerk in the Dempster and Company office) consulted him on various matters, and he placed all information on the Congo that reached him at the disposal of the Foreign Office.

An interesting facet of the early days of the campaign was Morel's skill in avoiding charges of sectarianism while condemning the missionary societies' acquiescence to Leopold's regime in the Congo. On one occasion he confessed that 'his heart was hot' on the subject of the missionaries' silence, although after a long interview with the Baptist missionary John Weeks, he quickly recognised that this sentiment was sometimes unjust. 'Against many of them, at any rate, the suggestion that they were shutting their eyes and stuffing their ears would not only have been harsh but untrue.'[37] He himself had no ties with any of the churches in the Congo, believing that Christianity might be the highest religion, but would make no progress in Africa until it recognised that what was 'good and proper and right for one great branch of the human family, may be bad, improper, and wrong for another'.[38] Nevertheless he recognised the need for their cooperation, and continued to seek their support despite rejecting their belief in Leopold's assurances of reform.

Towards the end of 1903 the mission societies were firmly in the camp of the reformers. Morel made sure, however, that they conducted agitation along lines determined by him. He would not permit collections to be taken at meetings, other than those for the CRA itself, and insisted that the welfare of the Congo natives must be their sole objective. He even objected to opening a meeting with a prayer, which he felt gave the occasion a religious flavour. His intentions were to endow the reform movement with an impartial, non-sectarian character, for to be seen supporting a Protestant missionary movement against Leopold's abuses in the Congo at a time of mutual mistrust and hostility between the Catholic and Protestant churches would almost certainly have been offensive to Catholic Belgium. In fact, the Protestant missionaries may have been slow in condemning the regime, but their Catholic counterparts failed to do so at all. It is a great tribute to Morel that nowhere in his work does he say or write anything to offend Catholic sensibilities, despite his personal feelings on the matter. That his own sentiments were far from uncritical is clear from a private letter to Sir Arthur Conan Doyle, in which he observed that 'the Roman

Catholic hierarchy is either incredulous or quietly hostile, quiet hostility having succeeded what at one time was a virulent one and would doubtless have become a more virulent one if I had fallen into the trap of starting a controversy with them.'[39]

It was therefore paradoxical that many years later in his obituary in the *Catholic Herald*, Morel should be accused of being the mouthpiece and spokesman for an alliance forged between the Liverpool gin traders and the British and American missionaries with the intention of starting an anti-Belgian campaign backed up by anti-Catholic forces set in motion by the missionaries. In this piece, the motives of the traders, and the missionaries and philanthropists behind them, were described as 'disreputable'.

Morel soon became the chief figure in the reform movement, and its original pioneers, Sir Charles Dilke and Fox Bourne, found themselves being swept along as its momentum developed on the lines dictated by their erstwhile critic. Morel formed a strong political friendship with Dilke, who opened doors in 'Liberal' society and inspired, edited and helped to place many of his articles. He was slightly more cautious in his relationship with Fox Bourne, not wishing to become subordinate to the APS and its humanitarian aims. Meanwhile Alice Green introduced him to politicians, diplomats and journalists, amongst them the diplomat and explorer Sir Harry Johnston, and Sydney Buxton, the Liberal MP, later Lord Buxton.

Not everything went smoothly; Morel's approach to the Baptist Missionary Society, for instance, was surprisingly unsatisfactory. There were two British Protestant Missionary Societies with missionary stations in the Congo: the Baptist Missionary Society and the Congo-Balolo Mission. Morel, not unreasonably, imagined that these societies would have ample evidence of atrocities, which would help to arouse feelings among the general public. In spite of being warned by Fox Bourne that nothing would come of it, as the society's headquarters in London were determined to keep on good terms with Leopold, he wrote directly to the Director of the Congo-Balolo Mission, Dr Grattan Guinness, who replied that the matter would be brought forward at the next meeting of council. However, further letters from Morel brought only partial and inadequate responses, although Guinness did say that he had personally complained to the King in 1896 about the treatment of the natives.

It was obvious that pressure was being applied to prevent reports being published. Nonetheless, the Reverend John Weeks, who had been sought out by Morel whilst on leave, agreed to send copies of his official reports from the Congo for publication in the *West African Mail*, and a number of prominent Baptists, including Dr John Clifford and Thomas

Bayley MP, protested strongly at the silence of their mission society.

Yet still the society in London remained obdurate. Determined that something must be done, Morel approached the journalist and editor W T Stead, whom he knew to be a personal friend of many prominent Baptists (and who later died in the sinking of the Titanic). In his turn, Stead approached Sir Hugh Gilzean Reid, the newspaper owner and editor. As Morel later remarked, it was an unfortunate choice. Reid was an Officer of the Order of Leopold and held another Belgian honorary appointment as 'Knight Commander of the Crown', and he had virulently attacked Morel's articles in *The Speaker* two years earlier. Instead of support, therefore, Stead received a flood of invective against Fox Bourne, Dilke and Morel. The latter described them as venomous to the last degree and inexplicable, in view of the fact that the Congo Free State and its methods had been pilloried in the most detailed fashion. Gilzean Reid, however, fought hard to win Stead over, ultimately resorting to threats of prosecution under which he would bring to bear 'the utmost rigours of the law.'

Morel was astounded that such a whirlwind of almost hysterical abuse should come from a wealthy and influential Englishman who enjoyed a considerable reputation in the world of journalism, but with so many facts and figures at his fingertips he was not an easy man to intimidate. 'I suppose Mr Fox Bourne and I ought to have felt frightened,' he later observed, 'but if these threats, which were afterwards openly and publicly proffered, were designed to shut our mouths, they signally failed.'

King Leopold Strikes Back

In 1903, Leopold made a further devious effort to undermine the reform movement, provoking a dispute that was to become known as the Burrows Affair. It was announced that a book by a Captain Guy Burrows would shortly be published, giving revelations of fearful atrocities in the Congo Free State. At the same time, it was disclosed that Burrows was to be sued in a British court for criminal libel against a number of Free State officers. If Burrows was found guilty it would be a damaging blow for the reformers. Meanwhile, the allegations remained sub judice, and it was put about that in the event of a guilty verdict the whole case against the Congo Free State would fall. The credibility or otherwise of Burrows, as Morel wrote, was to be the test of the movement's indictment against Leopoldian rule.

In the event, the affair turned out to be something of a propaganda coup for Leopold. Burrows failed to produce any witnesses from the Congo. The British judge at the trial assessed libel at £500 and ordered the book to be suppressed. It is a tribute to Morel that far from being cast down by the affair he regarded the matter with unconcealed contempt, declaring that his condemnations of the Congo Free State rested not upon individual accusations of cruelty, true or false, but upon proving that the policies of Leopold led to the enslavement of the population, in turn resulting in the atrocities that followed. Nonetheless, he appreciated that damage had been done, and that the air was full of scurrilous gossip. He described himself as being thought of as a 'very dark horse', a sinister figure, neither mentioned in *Who's Who*, seen about in London society, nor a member of any club. Amongst the rumours circulating about him was a speculation that he might be part of a conspiracy to obtain a monopoly of the rubber trade for the Liverpool merchants. Although quite untrue, this rumour was perhaps not entirely surprising, in so far as Morel had for many years championed those interests in the press. Besides, the *West African Mail* was dependent largely upon the support of the merchants, amongst whom was John Holt, one of his most prominent allies.

For some time Morel had been pressing for matters in the Congo to be raised in the House of Commons. Dilke had been reluctant to act on this proposal in 1901, but in 1903, at Dilke's suggestion, Morel drew up a resolution to be submitted to the House. It requested that His Majesty's Government confer with the other powers signatory to the Berlin General Act (by virtue of which the Congo Free State existed) in order that measures might be adopted to abate the evils prevalent in that State.

Shortly before the debate in the House of Commons, Leopold made one final attempt to silence Morel, this time through the use of a more persuasive approach than he had employed before. Acting through Alfred Jones, he arranged a meeting in London ostensibly to talk matters over, and Morel accepted Jones's invitation, hoping it would lead to some new move on the part of 'Brussels'. As Morel reported it, there were a number of other officials present, both English and Belgian, and the discussion revolved around the Berlin Act, the legality of the Congo government's proceedings, the exaggerations in the press, and the reluctance of the natives to work.

The divergence of views at this meeting was profound. After dinner, however, Jones suggested that Morel and one of the Belgian members of the party should resume the debate alone, in spite of the awkwardness of the situation. The Belgian was clearly determined to be diplomatic – as Morel put it, 'the Belgian gentleman was extremely suave, eloquent and subtle and possessed of a most insatiable curiosity as to who was behind me.'[40] Asked if no argument would avail him, Morel replied that only the complete reversal of the Leopoldian system, the abandonment of the rubber tax, the cessation of forced labour, the cancellation of the concessions as then constituted, the prosecution, public trial and punishment of individual Belgians guilty of atrocities, and the reopening of the Congo to commerce would suffice. When told that the King would never consent to any such conditions, Morel merely replied that that was not his affair.

> My companion displayed a touching concern for my welfare. I would infallibly fail. Did I expect to be successful against the King, who was very, very powerful?…My health would break down. What were the Congo natives to me?…I was a young man. I had a family – yes? I was running serious risks. And then, a delicately, very delicately veiled suggestion that 'my permanent interests would be better served if…' A bribe? Oh! dear, no, nothing so vulgar, so demeaning…It was a most entertaining interview and lasted until a very late hour. We parted with mutual smiles. But my companion, I thought, was a little ruffled. For my part I enjoyed myself most thoroughly.[41]

Shortly after this meeting, the campaign was given a significant boost by William Morrison, head of the American Presbyterian Mission, who had been speaking out about the abuses in the Congo for some time. Early in May he addressed a large audience organised by the APS at the United Services Institute in London, giving graphic examples of the atrocities practised there. Morel described him as the finest man to set foot in the Congo; one who told his story with a moral force which thrilled all who heard it. The audience included half a dozen MPs, and was a fitting prelude to Morel's resolution which came before the House of Commons on 20th May.

The motion was moved by Herbert Samuel, the Liberal MP for the Cleveland Division of Yorkshire, was supported by Dilke and others, and was carried unanimously. Arthur Balfour, the Prime Minister, admitted that the government 'could not, of course, in any case resist the motion, because it indicated a policy the Government desired to follow.' This meant that Great Britain, on the strength of a resolution proceeding from the manifestation of the will of the entire House of Commons, had become pledged to the cause of Congo emancipation. It was an astonishing achievement for a previously unknown young man of thirty, who came from a modest background, and possessed little formal education and very limited means, and who had initially worked as a shipping clerk.

Morel was at Hawarden when the resolution was passed, and wrote in his *History of the Congo Reform Movement* that it was 'with poignant if pardonable emotion' that he and his wife received the following comment from a friend who was present: 'I do not think you were at the debate on the Congo. The reports do not do you justice. You may like to know your name was referred to in the highest terms...and the reference was warmly cheered. You were referred to as the man who knew more about the subject than anyone else and to whom we should all be grateful.'[42]

This was undoubtedly a great triumph, but it had not definitively turned the tables on Leopold, and the way ahead was far from clear. Morel's journalistic skills were formidable, and by now his network of supporters was extensive, but although he had won many people over, he was still a long way from bringing sufficient pressure to bear on Leopold to force him to abandon his vast fiefdom in Africa and forego the riches it brought him. There also remained much prejudice and enmity to be overcome at home.

The Congo Reform Association

Fortunately, however, the question of how to advance the campaign was soon to be settled. Within a few days of the debate in Parliament, the British government despatched a note to the other signatories of the General Act of the Berlin Conference, drawing their attention to events in the Congo. The note was sent with the full support of both the Conservative government and the Liberal opposition, and committed both parties to the cause of reform. As a result, the Foreign Office sent a telegram to Roger Casement, the British Consul in Congo, ordering him to go to the interior as soon as possible to investigate abuses. Casement was an experienced African hand. He had worked in the continent for twenty years with private firms, the Baptist Missionary Society and the British government, and his despatches had already included criticisms of policies in the Congo Free State. Towards the end of 1903 he returned to England to prepare his report, which contained specific evidence of the brutality of the system.

Morel had been informed by Herbert Ward, the sculptor, that Casement, who was a close friend of his, was due to leave Boma in June for an extensive tour of the Upper River. At this time Morel had neither met nor heard of Casement. In August he received a letter from Ward, in which Casement asked Ward to appeal to Morel not to pause for a moment in his work, and to devote his whole time and energy to the assault upon '...a piratical expedition which was making a holocaust of human victims.' Towards the end of the year Ward wrote to Morel offering to arrange a meeting with Casement,[43] and they finally met for the first time at Ward's house in Chester Square in London.

Morel later described the encounter as 'one of those rare incidents in life which leave behind them an imperishable impression.' And it was indeed a pivotal moment; the coming together of two passionate and driven men, who shared common concerns and interests, and who were both destined to become martyrs to their cause. Even their physiques were unusually impressive. Morel was strikingly good-looking, tall and broad-shouldered, with dark eyebrows and moustache, and piercing eyes. Casement was of similar height, and as Morel described him, was 'lithe and sinewy, black hair and beard, strongly marked features – an extraordinarily handsome and arresting, Vandyck type face.'

Morel was profoundly moved by the meeting. 'From the moment our hands gripped and our eyes met,' he wrote, 'mutual trust and confidence was bred and the feeling of isolation slipped from me like a mantle. Here was a man, indeed. One who would convince those in high places of the foulness of the crime committed upon a helpless race, who would move the bowels of popular compassion as no one else could...if he were unmuzzled.'

They talked long into the December night. Morel paints a vivid picture of the two of them sitting crouched over the fire, in an otherwise unlit room, with Casement speaking for hours, in a language of peculiar dignity and pathos, about a vile conspiracy against civilization and of the difficulties he had to overcome in pursuing his report. Morel was mostly silent as the daily agony of an entire people was paraded before him: hunted women clutching their children and flying panic-stricken into the bush; the blood flowing from quivering black bodies as the hippopotamus-hide whip struck and struck again; the savage soldiery rushing hither and thither amid burning villages; and the ghastly tally of severed hands.

Morel questioned and cross-questioned Casement, finding that his own indictment of the regime was sound in every particular. In his turn, Casement said that he had been amazed to find that Morel, in spite of being so far removed from Africa, had come to conclusions identical to his own on all fundamental issues. He told him that he had long been familiar with his writings, and although he had not doubted Morel's sincerity, he had known the region before Leopold's regime, and had not been able to bring himself to believe that the picture Morel presented of the vast Upper Congo could possibly be accurate until he had seen the horror for himself. It was long after midnight before they retired to bed, Morel sleeping in his clothes on the sofa, with the papers of the report still scattered about the room.

Casement's vindication of his campaign was an enormous relief and solace to Morel. He had immediately recognised the report's significance; that it had potential, as he put it, 'to brand a reigning sovereign, allied by family connections to half the courts of Europe, with indelible infamy, tearing aside the veil from the most gigantic fraud and wickedness which his generation had known.' In addition to discussing the report, Casement had made it clear that some form of organisation must be set up if Leopold was to be overthrown, and as he himself was constrained by his official position in the Foreign Office, only Morel could lead it.

However, although Morel appreciated that this would be the most effective way to proceed, he viewed some of its implications with consternation. The Congo already took up a great deal of his time, and in particular it seriously affected the operation of his newspaper business, generating considerable hostility towards it and threatening its circulation. Moreover, the task of creating an organisation sufficiently well organised and effective to take on Leopold remained extremely daunting. He had already given four years to it, and no longer had any illusions as to the speed with which he could achieve reform. But although he hesitated to take on the role Casement pressed upon him, he also recognised he could not turn his back on the task he had set himself. On his return to Hawarden he was encouraged by Mary's enthusiastic support, and in due course travelled to County Down in Ireland to meet Casement again, at the Slieve Donard Hotel in Newcastle, at the foot of the Mourne Mountains.

At this meeting they agreed that it was necessary to unite the opposition to Leopold under one umbrella, appealing to a wide public, regardless of rank, class or creed. They realised that the matter of Congo reform was not an issue the British government would undertake of its own volition, and that the only way to stir it into action would be to create a great wave of feeling in the country. Morel revealed to Casement that he had no money to pay even for the start-up costs of such a campaign, whereupon Casement wrote him out a cheque for £100, a third of his annual income.

Shortly after his return to England, Morel received a letter from Casement about his proposal to set up a Congo Reform Committee. 'I have been thinking over the suggestion I threw out some days ago in my letter, suggesting the formation of a Congo Reform Committee and the more I think of it the more vitally necessary does the creation of some such body appear to be.'[44] Three weeks later, Morel wrote to Casement that a Congo Reform Association (CRA) was being formed, with Lord Beauchamp as President, himself as Honorary Secretary, and a number of influential names, including John Holt and Grattan Guinness as committee members. On 23rd March 1904, the CRA was formally instituted at the Philharmonic Hall, Liverpool, at a demonstration that attracted more than a thousand people.

Although Morel needed all the support he could get if his new organisation was to succeed, Casement was only able to provide advice from behind the scenes, as his official position prevented him from giving open support to the CRA. Indeed, although he gave Morel both friendship and admiration, he wrote saying firmly that under no circumstances could he be openly identified with him. Nonetheless, he played a very active part, corresponding continuously with Morel during the early days of the CRA, advising him of various ways to enhance its profile, and suggesting numerous contacts who could promote the cause. He greatly respected what Morel had achieved so far, declaring that 'truly if some daylight comes to poor Congoland – it will be you who have brought the dawn and you alone.'[45] Most critically, Morel was able to use Casement's report, with its damning indictment of Leopold's regime, as his principal tool whilst he worked feverishly to enlist support in the brief period between his meeting with Casement and the setting up of the Association.

Casement continued to follow the progress of the campaign assiduously, even from his various posts abroad, passing on encouraging reports: 'I hear on every side nothing but admiration for your pluck, your courage, your persistence.' Morel in his turn was full of praise for Casement when he later exposed the horrendous rubber scandal among the Putumayo Indians in Peru: 'Your two exploits are the bright spots in a record of foreign policy marked by some disgraceful episodes and by a great lack of moral purpose.' They were soon addressing each other in their letters as 'Dear Bulldog' (Morel) and 'Dear Tiger' (Casement). Casement particularly displays considerable affection for Morel, writing mid-letter from time to time, 'mon cher', 'cher Bulldog' or 'caro mio'.

From now on Morel dominated the campaign for reform in the Congo, Casement becoming only a shadowy figure, exhorting and advising in the background. Morel's name is always linked to the Congo, but it should not be forgotten that it was Casement who brought the cruelty involved in making this human sacrifice to the world's attention; and it was Casement who inspired Morel to set up the organisation which eventually prised the Congo from King Leopold's grasp.[46]

Today Morel would surely be at the top of any charity headhunter's list of professional fundraisers and organisers. In just a few weeks he had written to the 'great and good' all around the country. The content of Casement's report was a revelation – an official record of the unrelieved horror Morel had already documented. Here was appalling evidence of the fiendish cruelty, torture, mutilation, flogging, burning, bestiality and massacre that had been perpetrated over a long period of years by the agents of the Congo Free State and the concessionaire companies in the interests of harvesting rubber. When Morel announced the formation of the CRA in the *West African Mail* on 25th March 1904, under the headline 'To Fight the New African Slavery', he was able to list over fifty prominent supporters: 'men of all parties and creeds, joining together to oppose a gigantic evil.' Besides the Earl of Beauchamp, the list included the Earls of Aberdeen and Listowel, Viscount Ennismore, Lords Kinnaird, Ffrench and Denman, five bishops, including the Bishop of Liverpool, and ten MPs. It was an astonishing achievement in so short a time.

Unfortunately, despite their impressive credentials, these prestigious supporters were not notable for dipping into their pockets, and the lack of funds to progress the campaign was still a major drawback. £1,000 a year was considered to be the minimum sum that would be required to fight the Leopold propaganda machine, but in fact the campaign started with a float of less than £400. Casement had already given his £100, Morel could only manage a mere £5. Holt, and William Cadbury of the chocolate dynasty, each gave £100. As Morel complained in a letter to Holt, the majority of the CRA's most influential supporters had not subscribed any money. As a result, there was scarcely sufficient to pay a secretary and meet the expenses of publishing the *West African Mail*. The position was eased in 1905 when Cadbury[47]offered a further £1,000. But while the financial situation was uncertain, so too was the future of the CRA, and this was to remain the case until it was able to enlist the support of the Aborigines' Protection Society (APS).

Before the formation of the CRA, the APS had been the only formal group crusading against Leopold, and Morel's relationship with its most active member, Fox Bourne, was not an easy one. Casement had written to both Fox Bourne and Dilke, putting forward the case for the CRA, but Fox Bourne had campaigned for the rights of native people all over the world and had kept the campaign against Leopold going throughout the 1890s, at a time when Morel had been an active supporter of the regime. He therefore regarded Morel as something of a Johnny-come-lately, and although he recognised Morel's skill and energy as a journalist, he not unnaturally resented what must have appeared to him to be the hijacking of his crusading work. Here was a young man in his early thirties who almost out of the blue had burst upon the scene, and within only three years was responsible for getting a motion passed in Parliament on a matter that had long engaged the attention of seasoned campaigners. Not only had he formed an association within weeks of receiving a report from one of His Majesty's consuls in the Congo, but he also expected the experienced leaders of a long-established association to bow to his will. Fox Bourne wrote angrily to Morel, complaining of the reckless haste with which he was pursuing his plan, and deploring the fact that he expected men who had been working on the Congo question long before he took it up to respect his decisions and submit to his leadership.

There were other contentious issues too. The APS was concerned that the CRA was to be directed from Liverpool by Morel. It considered that Liverpool was not only far from the seat of government, but that the location would arouse suspicion that the movement was associated with the commercial interests of the Liverpool shipping merchants. In addition, it feared that there would be a duplication of effort and a competition for funds.

Another matter that troubled Dilke and Fox Bourne was Morel's ideological insistence that the elimination of the land concessions, and the establishment of free trade, were essential prerequisites to solving the problem. Dilke warned that these measures might well alienate France, since they threatened the similar, though less oppressive, French system of concessions in the Congo. He considered that overt support for this objective in England would make the French (and possibly other European nations) more likely to oppose the campaign as a purely English movement. Although the passage of the resolution in Parliament had ostensibly settled the issue, he felt that the British government would be unlikely to take an active role in a matter that might adversely affect its national interests. This was the first time that Morel was charged with ignoring wider international issues in his pursuit of justice, an allegation that did not deter him in his campaign against Leopold, but was to prove very damaging later in his career. On this occasion, however, Morel and Casement prevailed, and in due course Dilke and Fox Bourne agreed to APS representation on the executive committee of the CRA.

The formation of the CRA was a personal triumph for Morel, but it was only a beginning. It would take many more years of campaigning before the government was compelled to exert further pressure on Leopold to fulfil the conditions under which the Berlin Conference had recognised his sovereignty. Nor could Morel rely on unwavering support from his colleagues. Although himself a crusader and reformer, single-minded in his commitment to the cause, he soon came to realise that the altruistic motives of many of his colleagues were frequently tempered by self-interest. His own idealistic drive now came up against the cautious diplomacy of government and the guarded cooperation of other men of goodwill whose help he sought. The financial problems faced by both the CRA and his paper, the *West African Mail*, elicited a classically frustrated response from Morel, one that would be recognised by many charity campaigners today.

> The funds of the Congo Reform Association are exhausted…I am giving everything that a man can give to this matter, health and time, and any number of minor sacrifices, but I cannot give it financial

support, which I do not possess – if I did I would…it is monstrous
that the entire burden should fall on my shoulders in this country.
I have done the work of six men for the last twelve months, and
have probably shortened my life by several years in the doing of it.
I am telling people soundly here that I would like a little less public
adulation and a little more support.[48]

Morel Visits the USA

Despite the financial problems, sufficient funds were amassed to finance
a trip to the United States in September 1904. It was originally intended
that Grattan Guinness should go, but he declined and Morel took his
place. The purpose of the trip was to give an address to a peace congress
in Boston, sponsored by the Massachusetts Commission of International
Justice. It was hoped that this would arouse American interest in the Congo
and lead to the formation of a branch of the CRA which would support
British efforts towards international action for reform. Morel believed he
would be more likely to get support from the United States than from
the Continent, where there were so many competing concerns. Somewhat
optimistically, he also hoped that the United States, with a large black
population, would have a special concern for people of African origin. He
had found it particularly encouraging that the Board of American Foreign
Missionaries, alarmed by the reports of its missionaries in the Congo, had
already approached President Theodore Roosevelt, the Secretary of State,
and Congress, with requests for diplomatic action by the United States
against the Congo Free State.

The New York Times of 17th October 1904 reported that Morel
had returned to the city after speaking at the Boston Peace Conference. It
also gave an account of his meeting with President Roosevelt two weeks
earlier, at which he had presented a memorandum to the President asking
him to take the initiative for Congo reform. The memorandum had been
signed by a number of Roosevelt's English friends, and Herbert Samuel,
the Liberal MP, had canvassed for signatures in the House of Commons.
The British Ambassador, Sir David Durand, had been persuaded to make
the formal introduction.

Morel denied rumours that the President had refused to appeal for
intervention, and declared that the future course of the United States
government in regard to the matter remained a moot question. He reported
that he had been received by the President within twenty-four hours of
his arrival in the United States, and after giving him the memorial, had a

pleasant talk with him. He added that he had been authorised by Secretary of State John Hay to say that the President was favourably impressed by the memorial and that the matter, far from being dismissed as announced, was receiving the serious consideration of the President and his Cabinet. Morel had emphasised to him that Congo was a world question, not just one for the nations of Europe to settle. The Peace Conference unanimously adopted resolutions endorsing the attitude of the CRA.

When Leopold realised that Morel was visiting the United States, he had immediately gone on the offensive. Unleashing his propaganda machine, he first appointed Cardinal Gibbons of Baltimore as his representative, and charged him with organising a lobby in Washington. The Cardinal duly wrote to the sponsors of the Boston meeting, urging that the Congo question be omitted from the programme. When this initiative failed, two of Leopold's henchmen appeared at the session which Morel was to address, demanding that both sides of the Congo question be heard. The chairman of the meeting rejected the demand, saying that the meeting was assembled not to debate war, but to condemn it and get rid of it. It regarded the iniquities in the Congo, about which it required no further information, as a startling illustration of the kind of evil which kept the world full of conflict.

Notwithstanding the view of the Peace Congress, Leopold managed to get a short article placed in *The New York Times* on 18th October under the headline 'Thanks to Cardinal Gibbons'. The article proclaimed that King Leopold had been gratified by the Cardinal's defence of Belgium's Congo policy, and expressed his appreciation of the nobility of soul and generous impulse that prompted his eminence on this occasion – as always – to espouse the cause of justice and truth. The Cardinal's acknowledgement, included in the article, declared that this was a duty which he had performed with lively satisfaction, since it was executed on behalf of a sovereign who had done so much in the cause of Christianity! [49]

In the long run, the outcome of the trip to the United States was not entirely successful, in spite of Morel's audiences with the President and the Secretary of State. An American Congo Reform Association was formed, but appears never to have been particularly active. Had Morel been in the US to inspire it, its contribution to the cause might have been very different, but one man, no matter how dynamic, cannot be in two places at the same time. However, although there was only a brief flurry of activity on the part of the American branch, Morel managed to maintain his extraordinary self-confidence. It was less than eighteen months since his resolution had been accepted in Parliament and now, within months of the foundation of the CRA, he had actually met President Roosevelt. This seems to have provided enough encouragement to give him hope for the future.[50]

He worked enormously hard, sometimes up to eighteen hours a day, with much of that time spent editing the *West African Mail*. The paper caused him endless worry. From its earliest days it had never made a profit, and at the end of 1903, Sir Alfred Jones, who had continued to be a major stockholder, openly defended the Congo Free State, provoking Morel into public criticism of his attitude. Jones, not surprisingly, withdrew his support the following year, which combined with the loss of advertising revenue he brought to the paper, was a bitter blow. To cap it all, towards the end of 1904 the bookkeeper was found to have absconded with over £100 of the company's funds. Morel described the CRA as being *in extremis* as far as its finances were concerned, and the paper as 'having deep waters closing over it'.

Although Morel deplored his lack of money and considered it 'monstrous' that the entire burden of the CRA should fall upon his shoulders, he never for one moment appears to have thought that he might abandon his crusade. The stress imposed on his family by his workload and his impecunious state must have been considerable, but in fact Mary was his greatest ally, and her support for his efforts never seems to have wavered throughout their whole married life. Until 1908 the CRA had its offices in Liverpool, but Morel largely conducted his campaign from his study at Hawarden. The couple's fourth child, Geoff, was born there in 1904, and with a house full of children to rear and a husband writing an astounding number of pamphlets, newspaper articles and books in his study, life at home must have been busy, to say the least. But Mary appears to have taken the situation in her stride, and her enthusiasm for her husband's cause never faltered. Many years later, Rene Claparède, the philosopher and founder of the International Office for the Defence of Indigenous Peoples, recalled in one of his pamphlets an occasion when he and Morel had walked up and down the railway platform at Dijon and Morel suddenly said to him, 'I should never have done what I have without my wife's help. I was often discouraged. It was she who made me strong again by saying to me, "go on".'[51]

Morel was also popular and well liked locally. Eight years or so later, when he was invited by the Birkenhead Liberal Association to become their MP at the next general election, the *Chester Chronicle* wrote that 'there has not been a resident in Hawarden, not excepting the great Mr Gladstone himself, who is more highly esteemed than Mr Morel...The contest itself will be watched with interest by his many friends and well-wishers in Hawarden.'[52] And yet he was, to all intents and purposes, a one-man band. He had many friends, admirers and supporters, but he brooked no interference with the direction of his campaigns. As Seymour Cocks put it, who knew him personally and admired him greatly, he was not a 'pliable man'.

It has occasionally been said of Morel that despite his achievements he essentially remained uncritical of colonialism in general and of Britain's role in Africa in particular. In his recent *History of the Congo*, for instance, Didier Gondola writes that although Casement and Morel deserve full credit for their international effort to expose the near extinction of the Congolese and awaken European opinion from its ignorance and apathy, they also remained strongly attached to the colonial ideas of the period. As far as Morel goes, however, this assessment appears manifestly unjust. Although it is true that he stopped short of calling for the European powers to leave Africa (a demand that would not be made, let alone heeded, for another fifty years) he incessantly condemned their administrative policies, including the sequestration of land, the imposition of Christianity and the unfair trading practices that bled the continent of its resources. The wide range of issues he addressed during his many years as editor of the *West African Mail* (later the *African Mail*), and in particular his book on Nigeria, bear witness to his intense disapproval of the imperialist attitudes of his day, and show a remarkable grasp of the way in which Africa was being exploited by those who had seized possession of its territory. That he focused his immense energy on a country where all the very worst practices of a dominant and invading power were abundantly evident (most particularly in the seizure of native land) is hardly a reason to deny or doubt his wider concerns about the behaviour and ethos of the prevailing hegemony.

However, despite all his expertise, Morel did make an unfortunate and serious mistake shortly after his return from the United States. He became involved with Antonio Benedetti, an Italian employee of the Congo Free State. Benedetti was a commissioner of police at Boma who claimed that he was outraged by the atrocities, and approached the British Consul offering to speak out with official evidence if he could be provided with enough money to resettle in Europe. The Consul refused to help, but Morel got news of the Italian's proposal. Using a British subject, H A Shanu, a native of Lagos and successful businessman living in Boma, as an intermediary, he got in touch with Benedetti, who finally came to meet Morel and Holt in the Exchange Station Hotel in Liverpool in the middle of November

1904. The trio conferred for several hours over the documents brought by Benedetti, which included warrants for the arrest of Belgians and senior officials accused of atrocities. It was agreed that the documents should be incorporated into a pamphlet to be published under Morel's supervision, and a contract was signed. Benedetti then returned to Brussels.

This turned out to be a blunder, and was quickly exploited by Leopold. On 1st December, the journalist Roland de Mares published a charge in the *Interdependence Belge* accusing Morel of procuring and even paying for evidence when he found that such a cause would serve his purpose. Roland de Mares alleged that Morel and Holt had promised bribes of up to £450 to Benedetti if he was prepared to provide information that would support both the imperialist ambitions of the British government and the trading interests of the Liverpool shippers who regarded the Congo as easy prey. Benedetti in his turn now claimed that he had agreed to the scheme only to trap the reformers, saying that the documents he had shown Morel were trumped up and imaginary. Unfortunately, Morel had handed them back to Benedetti so that he could prepare his pamphlet, leaving him with nothing to counter the charges. Unsurprisingly, the Congo Free State press used the case to make much of the deviousness of British imperialism.

It is not clear whether the whole scheme was set up by Leopold's officials or whether it was concocted by Benedetti acting on his own, appreciating that he would be well rewarded in Brussels for his plot. Apart from damage in the short term to Morel's reputation, the tragic outcome was Shanu's suicide, prompted by economic reprisals and other humiliations in Boma, a death that could arguably be regarded as a sacrifice to the Congo Reform Association.

The Janssens Report

Following the Casement Report, Leopold forestalled demands for reform by setting up his own Commission of Inquiry to investigate the alleged maladministration of the Congo State. This was established in July 1904 and led by a Belgian judge, Émile Janssens. The Foreign Office provided the Commission with a more detailed copy of Casement's report, including the names, dates and places which had been suppressed in the original. Morel, not unnaturally, thought the inquiry would be a whitewash, a mere apologia for the policies of the regime. However, when the Commission's findings failed to appear by the middle of 1905, and the British government refused to exert further pressure on Brussels, suspicion grew that its conclusions might in fact prove critical of Leopold's regime.

Rumours about the testimonies being given made their way back to Brussels, but Leopold remained unaware of the impression they were making on his appointees. A forewarning that all might not be progressing to his satisfaction came when the territory's acting Governor General, Paul Costermans, a man of some integrity and principle, was informed of the Commission's findings. Costermans became deeply depressed and shortly afterwards, having penned a number of farewell letters, cut his throat with a razor.

The Janssens Report was received by Leopold in March 1905. To his consternation and fury it proved to be an indictment of his system of rule. Instead of whitewashing the regime as he had hoped, it confirmed the worst suspicions of the numerous people who had not previously been persuaded of the regime's guilt. He refused ever to meet Janssens again, would not discuss any of the issues with him and ensured that he was politically and socially ostracised. He also dismissed out of hand a proposal to award decorations to members of the Commission. The report was not permitted to be made public until November 1905, when Morel reported the evidence given by the missionaries in the *Official Organ* of the CRA. Although it was suspected that at least one of the Commission's members was under some form of obligation to Leopold, and despite attempts to sidetrack the report, sabotage its proceedings, and intimidate witnesses, 'doubters could no longer withhold judgement.'[53]

The outcome was a great moral victory for Morel, justifying the immense amount of work he had put into the campaign over the previous years. It was also something of a surprise to him, confounding his suspicions that the report would be nothing more than a cover-up. Even the explorer, Sir Harry Johnston, 'entering the arena of strife with great reluctance,' came over to the side of the CRA. In the introductory chapter to *Red Rubber,* Morel's blistering attack on Leopold and the Congo, Johnston had written of his unwillingness to chair a meeting of the CRA in June 1905. This was largely due to his belief that Leopold wouldn't face up to the results of his commercial activities and the methods used by his officials to exact revenue from the peoples of the Congo. However, Johnston now accepted that creditable testimony tended rather to show that the evils complained of in the Congo had intensified, whilst 'the direct utterances' of the King of the Belgians on the subject of his work on the Congo were 'deplorable in their sardonic indifference to the real condition of the natives of the great African dominion which Europe had entrusted to his charge.'[54]

Nonetheless, Johnston's support for the CRA was provisional upon the Association's adoption of what came to be called the 'Belgian solution'

– in other words, the transfer of the Congo Free State to Belgium. Morel himself never believed in such a solution, but was aware that he did not have enough support to oppose it, and that it would therefore be impolitic to do so. His own preference was for a partition of the country between France, Germany and Britain. Johnston, on the other hand, felt that such a proposal would only create suspicion amongst the other European powers that the reform movement was a front for the heavyweights in Europe to get their hands on more of Africa.

The Belgian Solution

Most critically, however, and in spite of Leopold's every effort to suppress news coming out of the Congo, there was now no doubt about the extent of the atrocities. The Belgians themselves were shocked, and when the question was eventually debated early in 1906, the Congo administration was fiercely attacked in the Belgian Parliament. In the course of this debate M Lorand, a Liberal, said that the information he had been able to obtain about Morel showed him to be 'a thoroughly honest man and absolutely sincere…inspired by humanitarianism, earnest and enlightened principles, guided by a desire for the salvation of the natives, and for the freedom of their commerce, whom he has seen handed over to the horrors of forced labour.' In spite of such tributes the five-day debate concluded with a resolution praising the Congo administration's activities and 'rendering homage to all those who have devoted themselves to this civilising work'. There was no question that Leopold still called the shots.

The Belgian solution was officially adopted by the CRA in June 1905, at a meeting chaired by Johnston at Holborn Town Hall. During the debate Dilke moved a resolution urging the people of Belgium to take on the administration of the Congo, and it seemed that the prospects for reform were to be realised at last. Morel hoped that, following the fall of the Conservative government, the incoming Liberal administration would usher in a more reformist political climate. Sir Edward Grey, great-grandson of the younger brother of the British Prime Minister Earl Grey who had sponsored the bill abolishing the slave trade a century earlier, had become Foreign Secretary, replacing Lord Lansdowne who, in Morel's opinion, had cared little about the whole matter. As it turned out, however, Leopold's hold on the Congo was tenacious. He managed to block any measures for the annexation of the country for several years, and even then no major reforms could be enacted until after his death a year later.

As a result, there was no remission, and the campaigning continued.

In August 1905 Morel wrote to John St Loe Strachey, editor of *The Spectator*: 'If civilization allows this Leopoldian system to take root, and become recognised as a practical and right system for the development of tropical Africa by the white races, the whole of European thought with regard to Africa will become gradually poisoned, and will in fact sanction the revival of something which is infinitely worse (as Joseph Conrad has truly said) than the overseas slave trade with all its horror.'[55]

Red Rubber was published the following year, and had the widest circulation of all Morel's major works on the Congo, running into five editions. Johnston wrote to Morel saying, 'You have a great hit with *Red Rubber* – greater than perhaps you realise. I have heard it discussed in high political circles, and even by prominent officials who are not wont to be moved by appeals of this kind.'[56] The *Daily Mail* described it as 'the most appalling indictment of personal rapacity, cruelty, expropriation of life and labour, maladministration and tyrannical atrocity ever recorded on irrefutable proof against any one man in any country or any age.' The *Evening Standard* wrote, 'Mr Morel has done more than any man living to expose the foul blot on the reputation of certain Belgian financiers... For every shift and wile, for every specious argument, he is ready with facts and proofs.' Even the Brussels newspaper, *Le Peuple*, noted that 'Mr Morel understands clearly the difficult position in which Belgium finds herself in her relations with the Congo State. Annexation appears to be the best solution, because, as he says, it would free Belgium from an intolerable moral situation.'

The publication of *Red Rubber* brought the unexpected support of the author Arthur Conan Doyle, who was moved to volunteer his services to the CRA. He wrote to Morel, 'I have just finished *Red Rubber*. I am horrified, as anyone must be, by the facts disclosed. If there is any possible way I can help I shall be glad to do so. I enclose a mite for your funds.'[57] Conan Doyle was perhaps the only person in England to take a more extreme view of the Congo question than Morel. Two years later he wrote, 'I sit embedded in Congo literature and trust that it may result in some good to the cause – your own efforts put us all to shame.' Shortly afterwards he wrote that he had started on a book, proposing a title, *Hell on Earth*, later suggesting, however, that it should be *The Congo Hell*. He remarked that Morel's work was wonderful: 'I am lost in amazement at its quantity and quality.' In no time he wrote again: 'I have finished my book. 45,000 words in eight days, one of which I spent in London.' He arranged for distribution to all French and Belgian papers and all Belgian senators and deputies, and inquired about sending it to all French deputies as well.

It seemed as though a prodigious writer had almost met his match. Conan Doyle was to prove indefatigable. His correspondence included a 'man to man' letter to the President of the USA, and one to Mr Curtis Brown the publisher, in which he remarked that the latter could 'plant an article in fifty or sixty American papers simultaneously'. Of a letter written to *The Times*, he declared, 'if it is too strong for them I will get it in somewhere.' He made direct approaches to various literary figures, including Rudyard Kipling, J M Barrie and Joseph Conrad, enlisting their support. Morel himself was particularly struck by Conrad's work, writing to Conan Doyle that he had 'always thought Jacob Conrad's *Heart of Darkness* was the most powerful thing on the subject.'

Conan Doyle also suggested paying for a leaflet covering all the ground and appealing directly to the person to whom it was sent, and at one point stated that he was working thirteen hours a day on the Congo. He addressed the question of remuneration too, observing that 'the money part of this affair – it has always seemed to me that the Association might be better run in this respect. First of all it is obvious that you (Morel) should not be *Honorary* anything. You should be official organiser with an honorarium of at least £250-£350 a year, which would pay for itself by allowing you to turn to the work without any money worries, especially to the work of collecting funds.'

The two men frequently appeared together as speakers at public meetings. In October Morel wrote to Conan Doyle that since sending his last letter he had fixed up to be in Edinburgh for 25th November, thus filling every day of the week except Saturday. 'I'm afraid we shall have to leave Edinburgh at midnight to be in Manchester for the meeting at 3.00pm the next day…we shall both be very nearly dead at the end of that week.'

Meanwhile, there was increasing tension on the international scene as the new Liberal regime took power towards the end of 1905, with Sir Henry Campbell-Bannerman as Prime Minister and Sir Edward Grey as Foreign Secretary. The threat of war hung over Europe – the result of a clash of interests over Morocco instigated by Germany. King Edward VII had visited the Kaiser in Kiel in 1904, and during their time together the King had been assured that Germany had no territorial interests in North Africa. But when the Kaiser was staying in Tangier a few months later in March 1905, he announced that all the powers had equal rights in an 'absolutely free country', making it clear that Germany intended to exert 'its great and growing interest' in Morocco. There was no military commitment to support France, but Grey emphasised to Count Metternich, the German minister in London, that if Germany invaded France the series of written and partly secret agreements made between Britain and France in 1904 (known as the Anglo-French Entente Cordial) would oblige the British government to come to its support with land and sea forces. This agreement was to become a primary focus of Morel's anti-war campaigning in the years to come.

Under the circumstances, and while the government recognised the need to demonstrate Britain's role as the champion of the weak and oppressed in places like the Congo, its actions also had to be balanced against the realisation that it could not upset a country of such strategic importance as Belgium. Grey disliked Leopold and all that he was doing in the Congo, but it was difficult to attack him without wounding the pride of his people and driving him into the arms of the Kaiser. Nonetheless, and to his considerable credit, Grey announced his support for the Belgian solution and endorsed the official policy of the CRA in April 1906.

In many respects Morel had achieved his objectives. Leopold's control and exploitation of the Congo Free State had been revealed for what it was by the Casement Report and his own commission of inquiry. The House of Commons had unanimously passed a resolution calling on the British government to confer with the other signatories of the Berlin Act, and the Belgian Chamber had debated the issue. Yet Morel remained, as he wrote in a letter to Cadbury, as 'Congo possessed' as ever. The Belgian solution was very far from what he had hoped to achieve, and he was well aware that there was little enthusiasm in Belgium for taking on the economic burdens of governing the Congo. Much had been accomplished, most of it entirely due to his own tireless work and commitment to reform, but for him the continued presence of Leopold as the final arbiter of the fate of the Congo and its people was impossible to tolerate.

Leopold's actual power, however, remained undiminished. As he himself described it:

My rights to the Congo are indivisible. They are the result of my toil, and the expenditure of my money. It is essential that I should proclaim these rights aloud, for Belgium does not possess any in the Congo except those that emanate from me. If I am careful not to allow my rights to elapse, it is because Belgium, without them, would have no rights at all. The Powers accorded their good will to the birth of the new state, but not one was called upon to participate in my efforts, hence none has the right of intervention, which nothing could justify.[58]

It was Morel's drive and energy that gave force to the continuing activism. He told a rank and file supporter that the movement for reform was now sweeping through the country like a whirlwind. 'For six years I have appealed to the head and I'm now appealing to the heart, the head having been captured.' In May 1906 he wrote to Cadbury, 'I'm not usually optimistic, but I believe we are progressing rapidly, and I think the next twelve months ought to see either international control of the Congo or Belgian annexation with guarantees.' He went on to say that mass meetings were planned for the 25th May at the Sun Hall in Liverpool, and on the 29th at a town meeting in Sheffield. In another letter to Cadbury later in the same year he wrote that he had 'returned last night from a week's campaigning. Leeds on Monday, Sunderland on Wednesday and Jarrow on Thursday, I stayed with Dr Hodgkin at Barmoor Castle on Tuesday.'[59] Towards the end of the year he had a meeting for over half an hour alone with Grey at the Foreign Office. Early the following year he spoke at London, Hull, Plymouth and Devonport. At the Leeds annual meeting of the Council of Free Churches he received a tremendous ovation. All 4,000 leaders of the British nonconformity rose when he got up to speak.

There are not many people who can boast of attracting an audience of thousands, and the sheer number of people who habitually turned out to hear Morel vouches for his charisma as a speaker. He had a fine voice, his arguments were carefully marshalled and supported by convincing evidence, and his words were delivered with a passionate sincerity. After a quiet exposition of the facts he would throw up his head, fixing the audience with his eyes, and appeal for their support. Although his speeches appeared to be spontaneous and he seldom used notes, he was said to be terrified that his memory might fail him,[60] and the contents were in fact written out and memorised by him in advance. Notwithstanding this anxiety, he appears to have impressed all who heard him, and commentators compared his oratory to that of Lloyd George.

During this time, his friends and colleagues became increasingly concerned about his health and workload, and Morel himself complained that his home life was 'reduced to microscopic proportions'. This must have been deeply stressful for him; he was very much a 'family man' and the increasingly skewed balance between his campaigning work and the time he could spend with his wife and children must have caused him considerable distress. Holt begged him to take it easy, declaring that nobody should be as 'weary and worried' by an attack of sciatica, which seemed to have plagued him for some time, and was most probably brought on by mental strain over the Congo affair. Morel, however, found it virtually impossible to relax his efforts. He was very conscious of the centrality of his role in the campaign, recognising that he was the first person to whom many looked for advice and guidance. In an unusually self-deprecating letter he wrote, 'What I mean about advice – not that I am a Lord high nabob who knows everything and to whose penetrating gaze no door is closed! But simply I have been at the Congo affair for six or seven years.' [61] Emmott, Cadbury and others advised him to take a salary for his work in order to reduce his worries, but he declined such suggestions, arguing that he should remain independent of outside direction by those less competent than himself.

E D Morel and the Archbishop[62]

If flair and precision ranked high among Morel's many attributes, dogged perseverance was not far behind, and his three years of correspondence with Randall Davidson, the Archbishop of Canterbury, is a classic example of the almost alarming tenacity with which he could pursue the support and approval of a key establishment figure. It also serves as an illustration of the extreme reluctance that such dignitaries frequently displayed when invited publicly to endorse a controversial cause.

In October 1906, when Morel first wrote to the Archbishop asking him to support the objectives of the CRA, his Grace was obviously disinclined to get involved, and his response was distinctly cool. 'In making our feelings clear upon terrible matters of this kind' he wrote, '…we should avoid the temptation of yielding to what I cannot but regard as a subtle sort of selfishness…the satisfaction, that is, of making our sentiments public without ascertaining that by so doing we may be aggravating rather than diminishing the evils which we so cordially detest.'

Morel was not in the least put off, and responded immediately with a five-page letter, in which he observed that 'it is, I suppose, a characteristic, and an inevitable one of all governments, that when no great material interests are involved, a reluctance should be manifested to grapple with great moral responsibilities.' He continued at considerable length (for which he apologised), emphasising that the problem of the Congo differed in several radical aspects from the somewhat similar moral problems that confronted civilised opinion elsewhere. In addition to an account of the campaign for reform and a listing of all his contacts, he detailed the background to the emergence of the Congo from the time of the Conference of the Powers, and described Leopold's management of the country. He referred the Archbishop to his book *Red Rubber*, and in particular to the chapter 'What can Britain do?', whilst at the same time asking his Grace if he would be good enough to accept a copy. Finally, he suggested a joint appeal, on the part of the established and nonconformist churches, to convince the government that the forces of public opinion could not be ignored.

A few days later the Archbishop responded in a letter marked 'Private'. He had already contacted Sir Edward Grey who had replied that he had 'always avoided saying anything which would justify the last paragraph of Mr Morel's letter…It is often the case that reticence publicly, and pressure brought to bear privately, is both the more effective and the more courageous course.' Now quite uncertain what to make of the whole affair and obviously feeling rather harried, the Archbishop informed Morel that he was 'under some misapprehension in supposing that he (Grey) had encouraged the publication of such a memorial (the joint appeal) as you suggest, signed by the heads of different religious communities.' He also enclosed an anodyne letter which he said could be for public distribution. In it he expressed his support for every effort made to ameliorate the terrible condition of affairs in the Congo State, but also noted that it was a very difficult question and that he had no wish to upset the Belgians! Morel replied the next day, perfectly politely but in a tone of some exasperation, saying that the Belgian people had been reduced to impotence, and the view of the CRA was that the matter could not be allowed to rest.

Possibly discouraged by his initial efforts to lobby the Archbishop, Morel then appears to have fallen silent for a while, and the correspondence lapsed. However, some months later the Archbishop wrote to say that he had signed a letter to the press, but that he was still very concerned not to offend the Belgians. He still seemed most reluctant to commit himself to any radical criticism. 'Further, I am myself always unwilling to say too much about the details of controversies in which I am bearing no part and I feel that the Belgians might fairly resent any endeavour on the part of English critics to describe and comment on the action of different parties in Belgium itself. My line is rather the general one, and about that I am in private communication with the government. I doubt the advantage of my endeavouring to master the details of the internal situation in Belgium.'

In spite of this equivocation Morel took up the cudgels again, sending a volley of articles to the Archbishop. These appear to have placed considerable demands on his Grace's time. On one occasion in February 1908 he responded with weary resignation. 'I will certainly read the article to which you have diverted my attention.' On receipt of yet another letter from Morel he concluded 'be sure that I am as anxious as man can be to aid if it be possible in what I am certain is a true and righteous cause.' On this occasion he noted the possibility of war in Europe and mentioned Morel's letters to *The Times* and *Manchester Guardian*.

This particular letter evoked another, and lengthy, response from Morel, this time running to eleven pages. In it he flattered the Archbishop, 'Your Grace's moral position is such, and your reputation for wise statesmanship...so clearly established in the land, that the importance of your ultimate decision can hardly be over estimated. Can I then ask you to bear with me?' The Archbishop had to bear with him for another ten pages, which covered a wide range of subjects: white rule in Africa, British statesmanship, Sir Edward Grey, the Belgian solution, relations with Germany, the feelings in the country, Leopold, the possibility of war, the position of France and the terrible woes of the Congo people.

By now the Archbishop was obviously wilting under the onslaught, replying gloomily 'I thank you for an extremely important letter – as weighty as it is interesting.' He expressed his sorrow at the depressing nature of the issue and the impotence of those who wanted to end it. 'I think you can rely on me to do my best.' However, towards the middle of 1908 he appeared to have gathered sufficient strength to respond to a letter of Morel's saying that he proposed to raise the question of East Equatorial Africa in the House of Lords. He now wrote, 'I can take the occasion to refer emphatically and prominently to the keen interest with which we are watching and waiting in the development of the Congo story.'

What is interesting about this correspondence is the Archbishop's obvious reluctance, even in the face of Morel's persistence, to get involved in any prominently active way with the Congo reform movement. He recognised he could not ignore it, but there is a strong sense that he simply wished Morel would go away. At the end of 1908 he wrote to Morel about talks he had had with the Bishop of Southwark, concerning a proposed letter to the press on the Congo. Aware that any such letter would carry his name at the top of the list of signatories, he wrote, '...and so weighty a lot of signatories but...on the whole it would be better if I did not sign the letter...There is a real danger in my at present having my finger in too many matters at once. I honestly believe I can do more for the Congo by speaking and acting *behind the scenes* in your support.'

Characteristically, Morel was not deflected by the Archbishop's attempts to remain a shadowy supporting figure. He thanked him politely for 'listening to me so patiently', informed him of a private meeting he had with the Foreign Secretary, Dr Clifford and the Bishop of Southwark, and sent him a copy of *Great Britain and the Congo*. In early October 1909 he wrote again, this time about the resolution to be adopted at a meeting at the Royal Albert Hall, which the Archbishop eventually agreed to attend. But the resolution itself did not meet with his approval, and he declared that he could not support so detailed a statement as that which Morel had drafted. 'The resolution should be brief, grave, simple, and in some sense general.'

Morel responded, 'I quite agree with your Grace's views. I am sending your Grace nearly every day various matter which I'm writing in the papers, and I hope I am not unduly troubling you.' History does not relate how troubled the Archbishop may have been, but he was certainly accorded little respite. Morel wrote again later in the month, twelve pages this time, reiterating much of what he had previously said and once more offering profound apologies to his Grace. Once again, the letter covered a wide range of issues: trade and trading relationships, native rights to their own produce, the economic ruin of the African tropics, honour, the Foreign Office, Treaty obligations, and the measures that should now be taken regarding the future of the Congo. In reply, the Archbishop said that he had read the letter with the greatest care, and accepted its two premises on trade and administration of overseas territories, but added that he did not feel that he possessed adequate knowledge to justify expressing an opinion which would be of any value.

Eventually, however, the barrage of correspondence resulted in a degree of capitulation. The Archbishop found himself unable to brush aside the pressure brought to bear upon him by Morel, and in spite of all his protestations about adopting a public role in the campaign, and his emphasis on public reticence and private pressure, he found it impossible to remain completely 'behind the scenes'. Although his desire not to rock the boat of state was very deeply engrained, and while he remained reluctant to upset the Foreign Secretary, and still expressed concern about giving offence to the Belgian people, he did eventually chair the CRA meeting at the Royal Albert Hall, thus officially adding his support to Morel's campaign.

Move to London

During the Hawarden years it appears that the Morel family lived frugally; Mary reported that they existed 'very cheaply' at Stafford House, spending about £35 or £40 per annum.[63] At this time, both the costs of running the *West African Mail* and Morel's living expenses were very largely financed by two men, William Cadbury and John Holt.

Cadbury was a Quaker and a member of the long-established chocolate manufacturing company. He had first responded to the CRA's appeal for funds at the time of its foundation, with two contributions totalling £200. His company had major economic ties with the cocoa-producing regions of Africa, and he appears to have felt a particular concern for the welfare of Africans. Morel rightly recognised that a benefactor of Cadbury's stature would turn out to be of great benefit to his campaign, and they first met in Liverpool in June 1905, after corresponding for some eighteen months. At this meeting Cadbury was so appalled by Morel's moving account of the horrors of the Congo that he offered to contribute £1,000 to the CRA.[64] £600 of this sum was paid directly to the CRA, and the balance of £400 was to be used over the next two years to subsidise Morel's salary as editor of the *West African Mail*. In his letter of thanks Morel apologised for taking so calmly Cadbury's 'extraordinarily generous statement that you wished to give £1,000 to the cause. The fact of the matter was that I did not quite know what to say – I felt rather overwhelmed.' In the event, Cadbury's contributions continued throughout the Congo campaign, and he supported Morel until his death nearly twenty years later.

As the campaign intensified, occupying all of Morel's time and energy, it became obvious to him that the 200 miles that separated Liverpool from London was a distinct disadvantage for the CRA. Acquiring an office closer to the seat of government was becoming an essential if the campaign was to be pursued more effectively and its influence maximised. Morel's decision to move premises was also driven by his increasingly acrimonious relationship with the Reverend John Harris of the Congo-Balola Mission.

John Harris, who had been stationed at the Anglo-Belgian India Rubber Company (ABIR), had given one of the most significant testimonies provided to Janssens's Commission in the Congo, and the native witnesses he had persuaded to appear had corroborated his evidence. When Harris and his wife returned to England in 1905, Morel had quickly taken advantage of their experience and arranged for them to give a series of lectures, which helped to keep the Congo in the public eye.

With the agreement of Grattan Guinness, the Harrises joined the staff of the CRA in the following year, and shortly afterwards embarked on a further lecture tour of the US arranged by the American branch, during which they addressed over 200 meetings. On their return the couple were put in charge of a newly established London office at Queen Victoria Street, EC4, and John and Alice Harris were appointed as joint Secretaries to the London Branch of the CRA. It was perhaps inevitable that being closer to the centre of power, the new London branch should quickly come to rival its northern counterpart, particularly when it was manned by two such dynamic campaigners. Morel initially welcomed the assistance that the Harrises gave to the campaign, but despite, or perhaps because of the fact that that the three of them brought comparable energy, experience and commitment to the cause, tensions soon arose.

One source of discord was the fact that Morel was strongly against any fracturing of the campaign. He was probably right in thinking that different groups campaigning for comparable aims would only dilute the force of the CRA and, equally correctly but with a certain degree of hubris, he also identified himself with the whole of the campaign from its inception. When Harris wrote in April 1906, saying that the Baptist Society wanted to form a committee of its own, Morel replied in a most forthright tone:

> If the Baptist Society want to form a Committee of their own to fight the Congo, let them do it. I don't care. They won't help on the cause, and they won't do themselves any good. If Guinness likes to strike out on an independent line of his, with them, and leave the CRA, let him do so, I don't care. I think it would be very foolish of him to do it. But the idea that the Baptist Society or Guinness are going to dictate to me, shows if they entertain it, that they don't know what they have to deal with. I thoroughly appreciate your loyalty…No branch of the CRA ought to be run by the Baptists any more than any other section. It would be a fatal mistake for the CRA to allow itself to be swamped by any denomination; this would never do. [65]

On this occasion Morel's advice was heeded and the CRA retained its wholly secular constitution, but it soon became abundantly apparent how much Harris was at the centre of affairs in London. Among other engagements, he attended debates in the House of Lords and the House of Commons. In one letter to Morel in September 1906 he reports that 'the other movement I have been carrying on is to increase our hold over the Common-Councillors of the City of London so that should a time ever arrive when we would wish their assistance they would have already been secured for Congo Reform.'

Harris also campaigned to get Grey invited to the Lord Mayor's Banquet as the principal guest. When he went further, informing Morel of efforts to set up a meeting with Grey, Morel responded expressing considerable concern about the lack of liaison between them. On 6th November he wrote 'Do *absolutely nothing* about this deputation yourself…I must be most careful, and if any mistake is made the fact of my being alone responsible for it will make it easier to bear.' And later in December he addressed the subject more generally, '*Meetings:* I think it is time we came to some understanding as to these meetings; which reminds me that I sent you a form of resolution the other day, as a suggestion, to be adopted at future meetings and which you have not acknowledged.' Despite this kind of snub, however, Harris pursued a progressively higher profile. In a letter at the start of 1907 he described how he had visited Berlin and met with leading dignitaries, including the Vice President of the Reichstag, before going on to Brussels to learn more about the Janssens Report.

Relations between the two men became more acerbic. Morel clearly felt that he was losing control of the CRA and being marginalised and overshadowed by Harris, and by the middle of the year the association between the two offices had deteriorated sharply. A row blew up when confusion arose over a donation to the CRA in response to an appeal from the London office which appeared to give the impression that the headquarters of the CRA had moved to London. Harold Brabner, solicitor and Honorary Treasurer of the CRA, wrote to Harris complaining that he was… 'going beyond the scope of fair play in trying to imagine/lead others to imagine the London Branch is the headquarters of the Association…I do not know how you propose to rectify this, but I certainly think you should take steps to attempt to do so; at any rate to refrain from filling people's minds with a false idea.' Harris, in letters to Brabner and Morel, denied the assertion and asked both to remember all that he had achieved. He ended his letter to Morel writing, 'I am quite satisfied in my own mind that you *would* not, and Brabant *does* not, really think me guilty of such conduct, otherwise there would only be one course open to us.'

Morel remained dissatisfied, however, and responded with further forthright criticism of Harris's failure to liaise with him. The following month finds him admonishing him again, writing on the 8th August that 'for my part I must demur most strongly to your making public statements on the international scene without discussing with me beforehand.' It is not clear whether or not Harris decided to ignore these diktats; he certainly went ahead and set up an interview with the *Westminster Gazette* on 24th August, in which he called into question whether the Powers, which guaranteed the neutrality and integrity of Belgium, could continue to do so if the administration of the Congo was conducted in violation not only of international goodwill but of all treaties.

The atmosphere of increasing rivalry between the two offices became steadily worse, and Morel complained that Harris was openly hinting of competition between them. He wrote to Harris that when the creation of a London office was discussed he did not imagine it would be necessary to draw up and publish a sort of moral balance sheet of his activities, or the activities of other people connected with the work. This was rather rich of Morel, who appeared to want to keep the reins of power in his own hands, and was exceptionally aware of anybody who threatened his role. Harris and his wife cared passionately about the people of the Congo and endured Morel's rebukes with apparently uncomplaining stoicism, but the fractious climate between them, and Morel's feeling that the London office was out of his control, convinced him that he and his family should move to London.

Harris too may well have felt that their relationship was becoming difficult to endure. He wrote to Morel of his intention to return to the Congo, and was later offered a position with the Anti-Slavery and Aborigines' Protection Society. Morel had originally planned to move Harris and his wife out of London to a provincial office as organising secretaries, since it would have been impossible arbitrarily to dismiss two people who had many supporters and were obviously a huge asset to the CRA. Their proposal to return to the Congo therefore came at a most fortuitous moment. Morel was able to write to Brabner that the CRA should break off its relationship with Harris if he accepted the offer, and ensure that he had no further connection with it.

Mary Morel, unsurprisingly, put rather a different gloss on the situation. She recalled that:

> After five years at Stafford House, Hawarden, we decided that EDM (sic) was wanted at the centre of the Congo Reform movement in London. Harris was making difficulties. I hunted for a week and we found 96 Talbot Road, Highgate. EDM made our little town garden lovely in front and at the back. We had games with the children (Stella, Roger, John and Geoffrey) in Highgate Wood, which seemed very dirty after our country life.[66]

Morel himself found that the move placed some constraints on his behaviour. '*Must* I be respectable in London?' he asked in a letter to Casement. 'I have not been respectable for seven years. None of us have. We are Bohemians and frightfully unorthodox, and recluses and all sorts of impossible things.' But on the whole he seemed pleased with the new arrangements, despite the area's lack of sophistication. 'Henceforth,' he went on, 'please address me to the highly unfashionable 96 Talbot Road. However, it is a ripping little house, with no room to swing a cat in, and horrible expense, but a nice strip of garden.'[67]

Despite this claimed lack of refinement, once settled the Morels clearly pursued a busy and varied social life. They went to House of Commons dinners, attended prestigious meetings, and got to know a great many people, among them the historian Alice Stopford Green, the Gilmours, and the Wedgwoods. But the house had one major drawback – it was noisy in the extreme. It stood less than fifty yards from the Great North Road, or the A1 as it is now known, and later on, when Morel returned from his six-month trip to Nigeria and the Gold Coast and was endeavouring to write a book about his experiences, he found the noise of trams and carts particularly trying. Several years were to elapse, however, before the family moved out of London to Hertfordshire.

The End of the Congo Campaign

At the end of 1906 the US announced its support for British diplomatic action on the Congo. This decision, combined with growing parliamentary pressure in Belgium, forced Leopold to drop his opposition to annexation, although in the short term it was clear that he had little intention of relinquishing control over his vast African territory. The development drove Morel to return, though with little enthusiasm, to a discussion of the Belgian solution.

It had been reported that Grey was taking action to promote the Belgian annexation after consultation with Charles Trevelyan, Ramsay MacDonald and Sir Gilbert Parker, but Morel was extremely uneasy about the future of the country under Belgian rule. The distinguished Belgian socialist Emile Vandervelde, had told him that only British pressure would compel reforms, and that Belgium alone would make no changes of its own volition, but the Belgians were insisting that the administration of the Congo was a question of internal sovereignty, and should not be the subject of criticism on the part of a foreign power. This stance greatly disturbed Morel, who remained convinced of the need to restore native rights to forest produce and open the Congo to foreign trade, as guaranteed by the Berlin Act; anything less would mean that the long campaign by the CRA had been in vain. 'Only the introduction of real, normal trade into the Congo is going to wrest the natives from the slave system under which they are perishing.'[68] He was therefore convinced that more positive action was needed to persuade the British Foreign Office to demand appropriate guarantees from Belgium before annexation.

These hopes were abruptly dashed when on the 20th August 1908 the Treaty of Cession and the Colonial Law was passed by the Belgian Chamber on substantially the original terms. There were no guarantees either of the abolition of forced labour, the dissolution of concessionaire companies, the restoration to the natives of rights to land or disposition of produce, or the institution of the freedom of trade. Leopold was granted £20m, payable in fifteen annuities, 'in testimony of gratitude for his great sacrifice in favour of the Congo created by him.'

As far as John Holt was concerned, this was the end of the matter, and following the Treaty he wrote to Morel advising him to wind up the CRA and turn his attention to finding some other project that would afford him a living wage. But Morel was not to be deflected. He simply reckoned that the campaign must be redirected towards opposing the Belgian government instead of Leopold. This change of focus was admittedly challenging; it would necessitate pitting the CRA against the government, against Belgian delaying tactics, against flagging enthusiasm for Congo Reform, and against the possibility of wavering press support.

Later in the year, however, the situation appeared to improve when Morel's previous meeting with Grey bore unexpected fruit in the form of a Foreign Office memorandum asking for 'definite assurances' that Belgian annexation would revise the system of the Congo Free State to suit the imperatives of the Anglo-Congolese Convention of 1884 and of the Berlin Act. Britain asked for native lands to be extended for trade and cultivation, for free labour and free trade, and for the establishment of some system of arbitration should Belgium and Britain disagree on procedure. It was suggested that tribal land rights, alienated by the Free State, be restored on the pattern of the British systems in Africa and in the South Pacific, Europeans having rights only in territories unoccupied by natives. Equal rights for missionaries of all Christian denominations were requested.

As a result of this encouraging memorandum, the CRA Executive, which met in October 1908 to consider its future, agreed to carry on with the agitation at the current cost of approx £2,000 per year. Three days later the 'Appeal to the Nation' appeared, signed by the Archbishop, the Presidents of the Free Church Council, the Church Missionary Society and many others. Although Holt remained pessimistic, 'The Congo has no chance, what with the German Emperor, Lord Roberts, Austria, Turkey etc.', the signatories expressed 'deep satisfaction' with Grey's memorandum. Later, a letter appeared in *The Times* affirming the importance of the full restoration to native races of their communal rights to land, with the power to trade freely in the produce of the soil. This letter suggested that the settlement of native rights in the Congo would prove a turning point in future dealings between the white and black populations in the vast tropical regions of Africa. It was signed by Lord Cromer and ten other peers; by nineteen bishops; many other ecclesiastics; by seventy-six MPs; by all the lord mayors in the country and thirty-two provincial mayors; by thirteen editors and by miscellaneous famous writers, scientists and Congo Reform colleagues.

Casement, delighted by this positive response, wrote to Morel:

Do you remember the coffee room in the Slieve Donard Hotel, at Newcastle, Co. Down, in January 1904? How we planned and plotted – and said that if the Congo question was to be made a living one, it must be taken out of the hands of the FO effort and made a people's question? – and how I said to you 'Thou art the man!' Well, you have proved yourself indeed this man.

But unfortunately, the public outcry that Morel had so successfully generated proved to have little influence on the Belgian government. The country had finally been transferred to Belgium in November 1908, with the Congo Free State renamed as the Belgian Congo, but its answer to Grey's memorandum of 4th November, communicated to the Foreign Office on 13th March 1909, rebutted Grey's points and asserted Belgian independence of action in the Congo. Its tone was one of righteous indignation – 'how painful it is for the Belgian people to see their intentions called in question, after the innumerable proofs which they have given of their love of civilisation, and after the great progress which they have made and which has won for them a position of such respect'. Belgium was resolved 'to develop and to advance the great work accomplished by the founder of the Independent State, despite the slender means at his disposal.'

Germany also recognised Belgium's annexation, a decision which particularly troubled Morel, who felt it left Britain isolated as the only country critical of the conditions of the transfer. It also confirmed a suspicion that had been circulating within the CRA for some time – that Belgium was playing the two power blocs off one against the other. In an attempt to clarify the situation, Morel visited the Continent, submitting a preview of his itinerary to the Foreign Office and asking if officials wanted to brief him. He was told that this was not necessary, but that Grey would like to hear about his visit on his return. During the trip, he worked hard to dispel the Continental notion that the CRA was a beachhead for an imperialist invasion of the Congo. He met Clemenceau and many other distinguished politicians, and spoke at the Sorbonne and at the University of Geneva, but it became increasingly obvious that there was only one person who could bring any significant further pressure to bear, and that was Sir Edward Grey himself.

Morel was now convinced that Britain was determined to back Belgium's annexation of the Congo in order to offset Germany's growing, and potentially threatening power. He also felt that the British government's habitual weakness was responsible for the present dilemma. 'The whole policy of the Foreign Office since 1903, under Lansdowne and Grey, in this Congo business has been one of incomprehensible pusillanimity, a missing of chance after chance, a general exhibition of incompetence which is perfectly appalling.'[69] As a result, there was now no indication that the system would be changed. Instead, it appeared that annexation had consolidated, rather than alleviated the state of affairs in the Congo. It seemed as if all the CRA's heroic efforts to rouse public disquiet had come to nothing.

Although Grey's expressed sentiments about the situation were broadly in tune with his own, Morel had little confidence that his new attempts at arbitration would be any more robust or successful than they had been in the past. Such efforts, he felt, should now be backed up by some form of physical sanction that would impact upon Belgian interests, and he hoped for more support from the US, believing that Anglo-American unity would overcome the fear of Germany. At one point, he suggested that the US might join Britain in imposing a trade embargo, using a naval squadron to intercept Belgian ships leaving the Congo with cargoes of rubber and ivory (the products of slavery, as far as he was concerned) and confiscating their wares. By this time, however, the US had to all intents and purposes abandoned any further agitation against the Congo.

The CRA's official policy rhetoric reflected these views, and Morel articulated them in his usual flamboyant way. Writing in the CRA *Official Organ* in June 1909, he declared 'England today is hovering about the borderland which separates greatness from decadence…On then, to the final assault with arquebus and halberd, with pick and shovel, with battering ram and scaling ladder – the Citadel of Infamy lies before us. Before that edifice of abomination and fraud, of greed and slavery, our battle cry rings out anew: '*delenda est Carthago*'.

To his disgust, however, Grey remained opposed to any form of physical intervention, holding that such a course would only increase tensions in Europe. Others, including John St Loe Strachey, also regarded Morel's approach to the foreign aspects of the case as 'simply childish… hopelessly amateurish and unwise,' while the Bishop of Southwark begged Morel not to create a definite breach between Grey and himself, lest it turn the Congo issue into a catalyst for European strife.

Morel nonetheless kept up the pressure. He wrote to Grey in August 1909 that according to the information received, the state of affairs in Katanga was 'altogether incompatible with the Berlin Act of 1884'.[70] The letter detailed some of these reports: there were terrible conditions of poverty; Katanga was subject to strict monopolies; the governing body was virtually acting as a sovereign power. It appeared that the Comité Spécial du Katanga had claimed to own the whole of the land, together with all the products of the soil of commercial value. This had been confirmed by the Belgian government by Act of Transfer, and the Comité now maintained its own armed forces and excluded newcomers, thereby making it impossible for merchants to settle in the territory. Morel therefore suggested that Britain ensure the establishment of a proper administration for justice towards foreigners to prevent such incidents arising in the future.

There were of course many other interests at stake at the time, most particularly the position of British capital. London was enjoying a rubber-stocks boom and plantation rubber was gradually replacing wild rubber as sources of the latter became scarcer. The shares of ten rubber-plantation companies with a capital value of £1.3m had risen in market value from £11.8m to £16.2m, whilst many other non-rubber securities were losing ground. Any change in the Congo's rubber production and exports would therefore have carried significant implications for the British economy. Morel and his supporters had access to these details, but surprisingly they did not feature in the arguments used in their campaign.

Belgium Assumes Administration of Congo

Morel published his fifth book, *Great Britain and the Congo* in 1909. The book effectively summed up the outcome of King Leopold's possession of the Congo, and was described by Conan Doyle as 'the most terrific indictment against a man and against a system which has ever been drawn up.'[71] In June of the same year, an extract from the Despatch of the British Government to the Government of Belgium read:

> The ravages of sickness and the results of the System of Administration pursued by the authorities during the last twenty years have swept away altogether the population of some districts and greatly reduced that of others. Under the previous government of the Congo, in large districts, if not in the greater part of the whole Congo state, the forced labour extracted from men, and in many cases from women, amounted to nearly, if not quite, the whole time of an adult year after year.[72]

A glance at the minutes of the proceedings of the Common Council of the City of London in April 1885 illustrates how far attitudes had altered as a result of the campaign. In these minutes the Mayor reported that a deputation appointed by the court had attended his Majesty King Leopold to offer, '…our most respectful and earnest congratulations on the great work you have performed in the interests of civilisation by the creation of the Congo Free State in the heart of the dark continent of Africa.'[73] By 1909, such a eulogy would have been impossible. However reluctantly, eyes had finally been opened and public opinion changed.

Yet although the Congo campaign rumbled on, there was an increasing sense that it was coming to a conclusion. By now talk of war in Europe was much higher up the agenda of European statesmen than the humanitarian issues of the Congo. As time went on, Congo reform became increasingly an academic issue, and the 'final assault by arquebus and halberd' never materialised.

Belgium itself was not at all enthusiastic about the acquisition. It certainly wasn't persuaded that it should fulfil any moral or political obligation to its new possession. This reluctance was largely because of the administrative burden, the Congo being some eighty times Belgium's size, but on the other hand, the Congo's enormous resources also made it potentially one of the wealthiest mining countries in Africa. The succession was therefore motivated by the hope that the Congo might provide a lucrative economic opportunity.[74]

It was rubber that had filled Leopold's coffers, but had he lived longer and continued freely to exploit the country, he would doubtless have turned his attention to the other sources of wealth with which it is richly endowed: oil, cobalt, diamonds, copper, copal, tin, rubber and palm oil. (Morel recognised, for instance, that the future of Katanga would lie in its copper mines.) The enormous cost of harvesting rubber without a shred of moral concern for the brutalities inflicted had already left an indelible legacy, and within a few years the Belgian Congo would again become one of the main suppliers of strategic resources, particularly rubber, in the war that was soon to break out in Europe.

However, once the Congo passed into the control of Belgium, it was largely assumed that the Belgian government would no longer permit the continuation of the abuses of Leopold's regime. Morel for his part imagined that Britain would take an active role in persuading Belgium to act on reform, and in 1910 wrote to the Archbishop of Canterbury asking what was to be done. He explained that the CRA could now do little more than 'hang on, as long as annexation is not recognised, intervening here and there when opportunity offers…I have done my best and I think there is no doubt the back of the system is broken, and it is undoubtedly true the worst form of cruelties have disappeared. But owing to the disgraceful pusillanimity and ineptitude of the Foreign Office, the only guarantee which the natives have in the future is the self-interest of the Belgians.'[75]

For now, however, he was held in the highest regard by his many friends and admirers. There were presentations, a cheque for £4,000, £3,000 of which was raised from public subscriptions, with a further £1,000 contributed by John Holt; a bronze statuette of a Congo chief, the gift of the sculptor Herbert Ward; and widespread praise for his courage, determination and compassion. Silvester Horne, MP asserted that 'Mr Morel has represented and saved the reputation of Europe, the honour of England and the soul of the church', while Fabian Ware of the *Morning Post* declared that 'the one feature of Mr Morel's mission which has impressed me more than anything else was his glorious fighting qualities. He was always calm, always genial, even in moments of the greatest depression always debonair.' In short, the teenager who had begun his career in the north of England as a shipping clerk had become a national hero. He had faced down King Leopold and made his influence felt in the highest echelons of government.

Encouraged by this continued support, he now kept up the pressure on the government, even as his interests turned to other matters. In 1911 he wrote a memorandum from the CRA to the government, addressed to the Foreign Secretary,[76] setting out in detail the CRA's many misgivings concerning the progress being made in the Congo following the transfer of power to Belgium. In it, he reiterated the conditions on which the CRA had supported the policy of Belgian annexation. These were the suppression of both the claim by the Congo State government to the negotiable wealth of the land, and the force exercised by government to collect it for its own revenue.

The condition of the people in both the 'reformed' and 'unreformed' areas was reviewed. In the former, the memorandum expressed concern at the retention of officials compromised by the old system, and the appointment of persons (sometimes ex-soldiers) with no authority and no hereditary claim to chieftainship over native communities. It also pointed out the difficulty the natives experienced in paying their taxes in silver coin. In the 'unreformed' areas, the state of affairs was described as extremely grave, justifying the CRA's predictions of what would happen in the event of the Belgian government being allowed to annex the Congo on the basis of the old system. Even the British Consul spoke of the situation as amounting to a 'direct system of slavery, created and maintained by the Government.'

The other matter for deep concern was the arms traffic carried on by the Belgian government. The British Consul reported that the sale of arms and ammunition by the Belgian government had reached 'alarming proportions'. The majority of these were given in exchange for ivory. Nearly all freemen in every village had guns, and chiefs sometimes as many as 150. In a sentence that carried depressing premonitions of the escalation of future conflict, the Consul described this as a positive menace to the tranquillity not only of the Belgian Colony, but also of the neighbouring colonies in the region.

Overall, the memorandum considered twenty-two issues concerning the future outlook for the Belgian Congo. Amongst these were native rights to land and control over their produce, in particular their position in the European trade in rubber and ivory; the practice of natives being called upon to furnish labour; the size of the army and the employment of 'armed ruffians'; and numerous other obstacles to development and plantations. It expressed deep disquiet and doubt as to the role and future intentions of the Belgian government with regard to all but three or four of these issues.

It has been said recently that the Congo campaign, 'once a blazing bonfire, a subject that moved the world like no other for more than a decade', was now an international human rights movement that had simply ended.[77] Morel, however, was not easily put down, and in answer to his own question, 'What's to be done?', he kept up the effort and remained firmly committed to campaigning on those issues that most troubled him. Thus it was fitting that the memorandum from the CRA, and his consistent emphasis during the Congo campaign on the importance of Africans maintaining their rights in land, were recognised by the government in 1911 when he was invited by the Secretary of State for the Colonies, Lewis Harcourt, to become a member of the West African Lands Committee (WALC). The Committee was charged with examining and reporting upon the system of land tenure among the people of Britain's West African Protectorates, and was finally appointed in June 1912.

By this time the huge increase in the rubber trade and rapidly rising demand for vegetable oils had encouraged a wave of entrepreneurs and speculators to descend on West Africa, which in turn prompted tribal chiefs to barter away their rights to land over vast areas. This issue typified the exploitation that had so often driven Morel to take the side of indigenous peoples in the face of rapacious foreign companies, and as a member of the WALC, he managed to get questions asked about the matter in Parliament where, as usual, he did not mince his words. His indignation was evident in a letter to Lord Crewe, who had preceded Lewis Harcourt as Secretary of State for the Colonies, in which he declared, 'I cannot believe that His

Majesty's Government, who have given so many proofs of their desire to pursue a wise and just policy towards the native races of West Africa, can be consenting parties to the process whereby the economic future and consequently the social rights of the natives (of the Gold Coast) are being seriously jeopardised.'[78] He also wrote a report in the *African Mail* in October 1912 in which he roundly condemned the Manchester Chamber of Commerce for proposing to give evidence to the Land Committee suggesting that the system of short leases was holding back the development of the Gold Coast with respect to crop production and the enhancement of trading infrastructure.[79] The Chamber of Commerce hoped to persuade the Committee to appoint an independent land evaluator to enforce the sale and transfer of land and buildings from local people in the country to foreign investors.

The Committee was charged with producing a report and the final draft was almost complete when war broke out.[80] It was described as a charter of native rights for the tropical regions of Africa, and the chapter by Morel on the occupation of land by native communities was considered to be one of the most valuable papers ever to be written on the administrative policy appropriate to those regions.[81]

The CRA finally dissolved itself in June 1913, holding its last meeting on 16th July at the Westminster Palace Hotel. The meeting, chaired by Sir Gilbert Parker, was attended by the Archbishop of Canterbury, Sir Harry Johnston, the Bishop of Winchester, and various other luminaries, including peers, editors and MPs. Praise was heaped on Morel from all quarters, with messages from British and Continental supporters unable to attend, including Casement, Ramsay MacDonald, Holt and Cadbury. A resolution was proposed, placing on record the invaluable services rendered by Morel, not only to the natives of the Congo but to the British people, by his unflagging and disinterested exposure of the evils of the Leopoldian system of government. Before putting the resolution to the meeting, the chairman read out a telegram from Lord Aberdeen, the Lord Lieutenant of Ireland. Regretting his own absence, Aberdeen wrote, Morel 'has earned a notable place in the true roll call of fame, and the name of E D Morel will be held in grateful admiration and esteem with a permanence that no titular distinction could secure.'[82] With Morel at the zenith of his power, the tribute stands in poignant contrast to the opprobrium and obscurity that were to come.

But in truth, the tragedy of Morel's Congo Reform Campaign was that the years of activism, the thousands of letters, articles and books, the hundreds of meetings and speeches, had ultimately achieved considerably less than had been called for. Rather, the Congo had exchanged a brutal, deeply authoritarian master for rule by a ruthlessly exploitative state, the missions and the major commercial enterprises. With Belgium now in command, this vast colony was set to experience one of the most draconian colonial regimes in Africa. The 'back of the system' was far from 'broken', even if the worst of the atrocities – the casual killings, the hostage taking, the burning of villages and the amputations – had abated. At the time of the public presentation to Morel, many of the aims of the CRA had not been realised. It was true that Leopold had been ousted, but the Congolese had been granted neither free labour, free trade, nor recognition of tribal and communal rights to the land. The new government continued the exploitation of the Congolese population by forcing people to work through the imposition of taxes. A heavy head tax forced able-bodied men to migrate to work areas, plantations, mines, railways, and white residential areas.[83] Farmers were made to grow cash crops which they sold to the government at set prices.

Morel, however, appeared unable to fully face up to this bitterly disappointing situation. Although the transfer of the Congo to Belgian administration had clearly fallen short of his objectives, and despite his memorandum to the government less than two years earlier, he was able to make a speech to the Executive Committee of the CRA in 1913 asserting that, 'We have won, gentlemen. We have won a victory which, in my humble opinion, has saved the African tropics from the permanent yoke of slavery...and rescued generations yet unborn from a cruel and destructive fate.'[84] At the same meeting, Sir Gilbert Parker, MP claimed that the people of the Congo had at last 'got a decent government for the whole of the natives.'

This exercise in wishful thinking was echoed in valedictory declarations by other commentators. Seymour Cocks, for instance, devotes a chapter to Morel's 'victory'. He states that the atrocities had ceased, the reforms demanded were being conceded, a responsible government had replaced an irresponsible despotism, the rubber tax had been abolished, freedom of trade over most of the country had been reinstated, and the rights of natives to free access to the land for gathering its natural product had been restored. The chapter continues in much the same vein, citing articles from the *Evening Standard* and the *Daily News and Leader*: the one suggesting that Morel's name should go down to posterity with that of Wilberforce, and the other claiming that the CRA abolished the system of forced labour.

Although it is surprising to find such a cloud of unverified hyperbole swirling around the new Belgian Congo, it is easier to understand why

Morel was loath to recognise that to some extent his efforts had failed. He was only too aware of power politics and alliances, and must have known that when Belgium took control of the Congo his ability to further influence events would be minimal. But for someone who had toiled so persistently and been deeply committed to reform over many years, it must have been almost impossible to admit that the enterprise had come to a far from satisfactory conclusion.

Yet sadly that was the case. There was little, if any, truth in Morel's assertion made in 1913 that 'The native of the Congo is once more a free man. His elementary rights have been restored to him, he is once more free to gather the natural products of his soil and dispose of them in legitimate trade…and free to cultivate his land for his own sustenance and for the planting of products of economic value for his own enrichment.'[85] Indeed, this assessment can only be described as delusional, and it seems profoundly tragic that a man who was renowned for his mastery of facts and figures, and who had devoted so much energy to describing how he felt the African territories should be administered, was eventually reduced to making exaggerated claims about the success of his endeavours.

While Morel's statements in this regard reveal an unexpected facet of his character, it is also interesting to consider why he had made the Congo such an exclusive focus of his campaign. At the time, other European nations – the Germans in South West Africa (now Namibia) and the Cameroons, the Portuguese in Angola, and the French in French Congo, to name but a few – were plundering their colonies' resources with total disregard for the lives or rights of their native populations. Yet no other major reform movement of any significance arose in mainland Europe over this period. To quote Adam Hochschild, 'we live in a world of corpses, and only about some of them is there a hue and cry.'[86]

Possibly Morel's decision to concentrate single-mindedly on the Congo was simply driven by an appreciation of campaigning realities. By focusing on the largest country in Africa, and one that was entirely in the possession of a single individual, he was able to arouse the indignation of the nation. To a great extent, his success was determined by the fact that Leopold was the target – a tyrant and ogre free of European alliances, who indulged himself personally in the extraction of wealth from the Congo at the expense of a defenceless people. Above all, no sacrifice was necessary from the people of Britain. At the time, the country was not dependent on any products coming from the Congo; all that was asked of the public was their moral outrage at the abuses perpetrated. Morel succeeded remarkably in arousing that disgust, but once the main focus of indignation had been toppled the campaign ran out of steam.

In the event, the seeds of the ruin of the country today known as the Democratic Republic of Congo (DRC) were sown by Leopold, and it has never recovered. Indeed, the situation there has recently been described as the worst human catastrophe of our time. In a report reminiscent of Morel's campaign, and entitled 'Turning a blind eye to killing and rape in the DRC', the United Nations High Commissioner for Human Rights wrote recently of seeing ample evidence that ignoring egregious human rights abuses is a recipe for disaster. The report points out that the resulting impunity only emboldens perpetrators to commit further crimes and encourages others to join their ranks, and that with no resource to justice, victims are left to fend for themselves. This enables the state to disregard two of its primary responsibilities: the duty to protect civilians in all circumstances, and to provide justice when violations occur.

Morel's description of the Commission of Inquiry's experience in Maringa, including the reports of murders, torture, rape, mutilation, impoverishment and depopulation, foreshadowed these depressing conclusions. The overall mortality figure for the period of Leopold's reign is still disputed, but the best authorities appear to agree that the population stood at some 20 million when Leopold acquired the Congo, and had declined by 50% by the time he ceded power. The Baptist missionary John Weeks wrote of the population in one district dropping over a period of thirteen years from 50,000 to 5,000.[87] Today millions of lives are still being lost. It is estimated that 4-5 million people have died from the effects of war, starvation, disease and rape in one of the bloodiest conflicts since the Second World War.

Post-colonial denial of responsibility for this ongoing catastrophe nonetheless remains persistent. A visitor to Tervuren, a small town outside Brussels, where Leopold commissioned the Royal Museum of Central Africa, will find little evidence today of the atrocities perpetrated by its creator. The entrance hall of this huge triumphalist building is dominated by Herbert Ward's life-size African sculptures, but otherwise it appears empty of life, and there is virtually no mention of the African peoples whose artefacts are on display, often with no explanation of their provenance, age or purpose. Nor is there anything but the most cursory reference to the horrors perpetrated on the Congolese during Belgium's colonial past, let alone any acknowledgement of the deadly legacy that still tortures the country.

A recent guidebook to Brussels and Bruges[88] also notes that the Royal Museum contains the complete archives of the 'controversial' explorer

Henry Morton Stanley, who helped to secure Central Africa for Leopold, but makes only a passing mention of Leopold's controversial exploitation of his fiefdom. Instead, it describes his reign as memorable for its rapid industrialisation and the enrichment of Belgium through the industrial revolution, the country's massive coal reserves, and the Belgian Congo. At the same time it notes that the museum is working hard to create a modern ethnographical collection that 'judges history fairly'.

The Lever Affair[89]

Just as the Congo campaign was drawing to a conclusion, William Lever approached Morel requesting his support for a proposal to establish a palm kernel crushing mill in Southern Nigeria. Lever was one of Britain's leading industrialists. He had made a vast fortune in soap manufacture, and his name lives on in the multinational firm Unilever. He was regarded as an enlightened employer, and Port Sunlight in Cheshire was a monument to his care for his employees. His approach to Morel led to a lengthy correspondence between the two men, which allowed them both to set out their views on European economic investment in Africa.

In view of Morel's uncertain financial position, he may have seen some chance of remuneration from working with, or advising Lever. It is clear that Lever felt that Morel had influence in the Colonial Office (CO) which he could use to obtain support for his project. Earlier proposals put to the CO for a mill had been rejected.

Morel wrote to Sir Walter Egerton at the CO, putting Lever's proposals to him, and Egerton responded saying that he had no objection in principle to Lever's plans, but declared himself 'strongly against concessions – I hate the word.' In a further letter to Egerton, Morel writes, 'Lever comes to me (Why, goodness only knows) and says, in effect, "I shall be greatly indebted if you will get to know for me [sic] the mystery of this opposition to my beautiful scheme"'. In a further letter to Charles Strachey, another official at the CO, he repeats this, writing, 'I may be a simple person, and Mr Lever may be a very astute one. But, even so…I should still fail to understand what conceivable object Lever would have in coming to me.' This seems curiously disingenuous of Morel, as he must have known exactly why Lever had got in touch with him. Perhaps he hoped to appear reluctant to support a major British industrialist, in a relationship that might turn out to be financially advantageous to him. Later he would write to Lever, 'You have immense financial power. I have a certain amount of public influence.'

Contrary to what he had opposed in the Congo, Morel thought that such a mill would be an addition to the economy of Southern Nigeria. It did not seem at this stage that Lever was asking for a concession of land or of palm-bearing trees, and Lever could not understand why there was opposition to his proposal. Morel appeared to feel it was eminently reasonable, and that the introduction of a crushing industry into Southern Nigeria would be an excellent thing for the country. He himself was planning a trip to Nigeria around this time and seemed eager to act as the intermediary between the CO and the British merchants. He also asked if he could be of assistance to Lever during his journey.

The relationship appeared to prosper, and Morel and his wife were invited to dine at Lever's house, 'The Hill' at Hampstead, in October, prior to Morel's departure for his tour of Nigeria. In a letter to Lever before leaving, Morel asked Lever if he had read Mary Kingsley's *West African Studies*.

Lever responded to the mention of Mary Kingsley in the most patronising, supremacist terms. 'It would serve no useful purpose for the white man to go and try to reverse the Divine order under which intellect and mental power rules and develops, protects and benefits inferior nations.' Morel for all his good works for Africans should not '...build a halo round the black man and convert him into a kind of being which it will take him hundreds of years of intercourse with the white man to become.'

Not be put down, Morel responded strongly, writing to Lever, '... while I understand your point of view, it is quite clear to me you do not understand mine.' In a long and detailed letter he sets out, in forthright terms, his opinions based on his knowledge of West Africa, on how Europeans should engage with local populations, and how economic relationships should be conducted. The policy of:

> ...rooting the people in the land: assisting them by technical knowledge to develop the land and its resources for the benefit of themselves and their descendants. That policy entails the fundamental administrative and legislative basis that the land of West Africa belongs to the people of West Africa whose trustees we are...That policy by no means excludes individual economic enterprise in West Africa...But it does exclude the conferring upon individual European companies of exclusive territorial or other privileges calculated to interfere with what, in my view should be the first duty of Government, namely: preserving the land for the people.

Regrettably, Morel's hopes for rooting native people in the land and giving them control over their own resources remain unrealised. In a renewed scramble for Africa and Asia today, multinational companies are being granted concessions over huge parcels of land, which are frequently described as 'neglected'. Recently, the DRC granted rent-free, renewable, thirty-year leases over an area the size of West Yorkshire to South African farmers, in the hope they will be able to improve the country's farming industry. Other countries, among them China, South Korea and India, have all made major investments in African land and raw material reserves. In Asia, a massive transmigration programme of Javanese aims to make Papuans a minority in their own lands. At least 100,000 Papuans, according to Amnesty International, have been murdered with weaponry provided by British and American companies in lucrative arms deals.[90]

Morel has been accused of serious misjudgement in associating himself with Lever, who was described by Vandervelde as 'a man without education and without sensibility, a commercial genius, enormously, fabulously rich, probably good-hearted but also hard, who sees humanity as a vast engine of production without souls nor desires or ambitions other than the accumulation of money, authoritarian, rarely thwarted.' If Morel thought he might benefit financially through some tie-up with Lever, it is apparent that he was not prepared to sacrifice his principles. He certainly had no intention of ingratiating himself with one of Britain's most powerful industrialists. It has to be said that Lever responded most civilly, and further correspondence between the two men continued over a number of months.

In due course Lever wrote to Morel confirming his intention of commencing operations in the Congo. He said they would be conducted in an area where in all probability the population would not have been spoiled and contaminated, and where, as far as African civilisation went, the natives seemed to be very industrious and fairly civilised beings!

Morel, sticking to his principles, expressed his satisfaction with Lever's proposals as long as the native peoples retained possession of their land, and had the free and unfettered right to buy and sell the produce thereof. He said he was reassured that Lever's intentions towards the local population were just and humane.

Morel later declared that Lever Brothers concessions in British West Africa were 'minor privileges which do not infringe the rights of third parties, which have been given in exchange for the initiation of enterprises in British West Africa involving considerable risks and which, if successful, will probably rebound to the prosperity of the dependencies in question.'[91]

In the event, Lever eventually got his concessions in the Congo. Harris reported from Africa at the end of 1911 that Lever apparently had optional control over some 2 million acres of oil-producing areas. Harris held that this was worse robbery than Leopold's rubber extraction, as the palm nuts provided local people with many of their necessities. He foresaw another future of coercion, reprisals and punitive expeditions.[92]

Somewhat astonishingly, Morel voiced no objection to this agreement. Instead, he declared that he now regarded Lever's concessions as a fait accompli. If Vandervelde had found it impossible to oppose the concessions, it would only be quixotic for the CRA to make an open stand against them. Yet his encounter with Lever had clearly tested his principles. Hoping to advise the industrialist and perhaps profit from his dealings with him, he had found himself in the company of a ruthless capitalist, who may have cared for his workforce at home, but regarded Africans with patronising contempt. In view of his long battle with Leopold, it is surprising that he did not realise from the outset that his own views and those of Lever's corporate interests were unlikely to coincide.

The postscript to the Lever affair appeared in the *Liverpool Journal of Commerce* at the end of 1911. The paper reported that Sir William Lever presided at a lantern lecture on 'The Congo of today' in the Gladstone Hall, Port Sunlight. 'Sir William said that under the guidance of an enlightened Belgian Government the Congo region – a region of perpetual warmth, unlimited productiveness of soil, enormous rivers and teeming millions of population was about to enter upon what he ventured to say would be a glorious dawn for the inhabitants, and an era of great benefit also to the peoples of Europe.'[93]

Nigeria: Its Peoples and its Problems[94]

If I were a poet I would write an ode to the African carrier.

E D Morel
Nigeria: Its Peoples and its Problems, 1911

Morel had been barred by Leopold from visiting the Congo, and must have felt his lack of personal experience of the country was a hindrance to his campaign, particularly when others, such as Harris, Casement and Holt had travelled so extensively in the Congo and other parts of the continent. The idea of a trip to West Africa was therefore very attractive, and in March 1910, whilst still living at Talbot Road, he told Holt of plans he had made to visit Nigeria. He had agreed contracts for articles with *The Times* and the *Morning Post,* which combined would pay for the cost of the visit. Cadbury had also contributed.

Although the CRA was not officially disbanded until 1913, by 1911 it was already clear that its work was drawing to a close, and Morel set off in November of that year, arriving by sea at Warri in the middle of the month and travelling inland to Northern Nigeria. During this visit, he appeared able to escape his campaigning and polemicist role for the first time, and write freely about what he saw around him. For a brief period, it was as if the dark shadow of the Congo campaign had been lifted, allowing suppressed emotions and interests to emerge.

The articles that he sent back to the two newspapers are gathered into his book, *Nigeria: Its Peoples and its Problems.* The book has been described as a statement of his philosophy and a guide to how the colonial powers should manage their territories, and it certainly plays this role, but it also bears all the marks of a man fascinated by his surroundings and absorbed by all he sees, and possessed of a clear vision of the implications of Western Europe's impact on the continent.

Morel travelled widely throughout the country, and among other expeditions, took a boat for 400 miles on the River Niger, from Forçados on the coast to Baro in Northern Nigeria. Throughout this time, he was acutely aware that he was moving within cultures of great anthropological interest, and that a knowledge of the inhabitants' numerous religious beliefs and philological structures would greatly enhance any understanding of the country and its history. The book contains much florid descriptive writing on the topography and beauties of Nigeria, with many lyrical passages describing what he calls 'the kaleidoscopic varieties of scenic effects, enchanting the eye'. There is even a page or two about his great hobby, butterflies. 'A sight for the dear gods, I tell you – is the *Euphaedra* sunning himself on a Niger forest path.'

He writes that after trekking on horseback for 500 miles or so, he acquired the philosophy of this sort of locomotion.

> One day holds much – so much of time, so much of space, so much of change. The paling stars or the waning moon greet your first swing into the saddle, and the air strikes crisp and chill. You are still there as the orange globe mounts the skies…lighting some fantastic peak of granite boulders piled up as though by Titan's hand. You are still there when the rays pour downwards from on high, strike upwards from some dusty track and burning rock, and all the countryside quivers and simmers in the glow. Sometimes you may still be there (in the saddle)…when the shadows fall swiftly, and the cry of the crownbirds seeking shelter for the night on some marshy spot to their liking, heralds the dying of the day.

He was delighted by the people, and gives vivid descriptions of their courtesy and modesty.

> Nature seems such an open book here. She does not hide her secrets. She displays them; which means that she has none; and, in consequence, she is as she was meant to be. The trappings of hide-bound convention do not trammel her every stride like the hobble skirts of the foolish women who parade their shapes along the fashionable thoroughfares of London…The Kukuruku girl, whose only garment is a single string of beads round neck and waist is more modest than your Bond Street dame clad in the prevailing fashion, suggesting nakedness.

Later on, on his journey home, he deplores the influence of European fashion and the discarding of national dress. 'Clad in his national dress, the

African has a dignity which in most cases he loses entirely when he attires himself in a costume totally unfit for the country, and hideous at best.' In Lagos there was 'every variety of dress from the voluminous robes of the turbaned Mohammedan to the latest tailored monstrosities of Western Europe. The Yoruba lady with a Bond Street hat and hobble skirt; her sister in the infinitely more graceful enfolding cloths of blue or terra-cotta.'

He found the contrasts were a continual fascination:

> Here a happy African family laughing and chattering in a tumble-down old shanty within close proximity to a 'swagger bungalow' gay with brilliant creepers; there a seminary where a number of young ladies, looking supremely uncomfortable in their European frocks, their short hair frizzled out into weird contortions, are learning as fast as their teachers can make them those hundred and one inutilities which widen the breach between them and their own beautiful and interesting land.

The charge that the Africans are uncivilized produced an angry riposte.

> The sacrificial knife of the Nigerian negro may seem more repulsive to the modern eye from the setting of black forms framed in the deep shadows of primeval forest and foetid swamp, and a double dose of original sin may with complacency be assigned to him by the superficial. But in itself and in the motive which raises it quivering over the bound and helpless victim, it differentiates not at all from the story of Abraham and Isaac handed down to us in the sacred writings, and not certainly, in a light other than commendable, given the setting.

He went on to say that 'If some of those who are so ready to pass shallow judgment upon the social and spiritual habits of the West African *chez lui* and who are responsible for so much misapprehension in the public mind as to his true character, would study the book of Genesis, they might approach the subject with an exacter sense of proportion.'

He deplored the lamentable intolerance displayed by Christian proselytizers towards one another, asserting that it led to a confusion of beliefs amongst their African converts. Indeed, the whole missionary effort worried him. 'There is much that is dark and dismal about it...inwardly I mean. All the African world is black to it, black with sin, black with lust, black with cruelty. And there is this besetting misfortune – it is alien.

It preaches an alien God; a White God, not a Black God. The God that is imported here has nothing African about him. How can he appeal to Africa?' He also heard that there was to be a crusade against Islam in Nigeria, '…emissaries are to come and check this poisonous growth. This is very strange to read…out here, as one listens to the call of God in the evening, and in the morning, pealing out to the stars. These people are worshipping the God of Africa. It seems they ought to worship the God of Europe; and yet there is more evidence of spiritual influence out here, than in our great congested cities.'

He had made a trip to Kano, a city that lay in the far north of the country at the head of the river Tubo, which he said held him in the grip of a fascinated interest. Here he had visited the Emir, who expressed a wish that the propagandizing of Christianity should cease, as it disturbed his people, making them suspicious and afraid, and undermining their cultural empathy. Islam, on the other hand, had not resulted in this destabilising outcome.

Morel expanded considerably upon this theme, stressing the differences between Christianity and Islam. Christianity:

> …remains for the people of Nigeria, and all West Africa, an alien religion taught by aliens who cannot assimilate themselves to the life of the people. Islam on the other hand has long ceased to be an alien religion. It is imparted by Africans. It is disseminated by Africans. It has its roots in the soil. One might be permitted, perhaps, to suggest that those who are disposed to regard the condition of the Nigerian forest-dweller in these matters as calling for hard and rigid regulation are prone to forget what Lecky describes as 'the appalling amount of moral evil, festering uncontrolled, undiscussed and unalleviated under the fair surface of a decorous society'.

As he saw it, Christianity destroyed racial identity in West Africa, whilst Islam preserved it. He wrote:

> Family bonds are threatened by Christianity. Christianity, as propounded to the Nigerian at the opening of the 20th century, presents itself to him in the light of a hurtful and disintegrating influence. This creed is proffered, either by aliens between whom and the inner life of the people there yawns an unbridgeable gulf, or by denationalised Africans who have become, in the eyes of the people, strangers well-nigh as complete as the alien himself, part and parcel of the alien's machinery.

One can hardly escape the thought that if the West was to show comparable humility today, it might go a long way towards resolving the so-called 'clash' of these two great religions in our own particularly troubled times.

Indeed, Morel consistently proved a perceptive critic of many aspects of his own cultural heritage. Commenting on the weakening of the Fulani dynasty in North Nigeria and the disorder that followed, he reflected that it could hardly have been worse than the condition of Western Europe at sundry stages in its history, when the weakness of the paramount authority, and the foraging and strife of the rival barons, combined to desolate the homesteads of the people and lay waste to the countryside.

Equally, he recognised that West African polygamy contained many ugly features, but observed that the European system did so too. Morel appreciated that the Christian missionary's insistence upon an acceptance of a monogamous sexual relationship, contrary to what he described as 'the promptings of Nature', must present the greatest barrier to the acceptance of the Christian faith. Sexual relations, he observed, whatever their character and the conditions of society surrounding them, could never be free from abuses.

Unsurprisingly, much of the book is a reflection on the British administration of Nigeria. He describes the administrators as a 'handful of quiet men with a strong sense of duty, keen on their sense of right and firm in their sense of justice'. However, the issue that most concerned Morel, as it had in his Congo campaign, was the ownership and working of the land. He was passionate about the principle of a sustainable and productive agriculture operating hand in hand with an artisan sector. Among other things, he hoped that 'civilization' would not seek to stamp out the native ironstone industry. He writes that land tenure should be secured:

> ...not only against a certain type of European capitalist who covets this rich soil for his own schemes and, under the pretence of industrial expansion, would cheerfully turn the native agriculturalist, farmer and trader into a "labourer", but against the class of native who for his own ends, for speculative purposes mainly, seeks to undermine native law and to change the right of user, into that of owner at the expense of the community at large.

Morel denounced what he saw happening in the Egba district in Yorubaland, where Egbas were beginning to buy and sell land among themselves in complete violation of their own customs and laws, thereby letting in land monopolists and speculators. Huge sums were being made from the exploitation of raw materials; for example, from oil palm plantation. In 1910, Nigeria exported 173k tons of kernels and 77k tons of oil with a value of over £4 million (approx £360 million in today's terms) – wealth that was being expropriated by foreign investors. This process was also evident in commercial and mining development, and demands for prospecting licences and concessions were already in the pipeline, with the tin industry in particular attracting investment and fly-by-night speculators. There were also profound problems brought about by the intrusion of a cash economy into an economy still extensively using barter – and in all this, there was little evidence of the proper treatment and protection of the native people.

There was also an abundance of other resources. Morel recognised the importance of forestry conservation to safeguard forest resources for the benefit of the state, and had strong views on their protection. In practice, he suggested that the native communities and their descendants should own the land, but that the administration should be charged with its guardianship, thus preventing the wholesale exploitation of its resources for the benefit of individuals, white or black. 'The welfare of an agricultural community,' he wrote, 'demands for many reasons scientifically substantiated, that a stop should be put to the reckless destruction of timbered areas such as has been proceeding all over Yorubaland.' Historically, the inalienability of land had been the cardinal principle of Yoruba land tenure.

In principle, Morel praised 'The Land and Native Rights Proclamation', which declared the whole of the land, whether occupied or unoccupied, to be 'native land'. This proclamation put the land under the control of, and made it subject to, the disposition of the Governor. But the Governor's power had to be exercised in accordance with the 'native laws and customs', which resulted in a structure of indirect administration through the native rulers of the communities, the chiefs and their executives.

This was a policy that had been followed by Sir Frederick Lugard and his successors, and Morel regarded it as a genuine endeavour to rule through the native chiefs on native lines. However, he realized that it was now being overridden by the insidious assaults of interested, or prejudiced, or ill-informed opinion. It was especially contested by European capitalists in a hurry to push on 'development', and those missionaries who regarded it as a stumbling block to Christian propaganda.

Morel placed great emphasis on the importance of establishing a national system of education that included the preservation of native language, customs and character through the establishment of schools managed by the Africans themselves. He feared that the predominant characteristic of the current administration's educational methods, both official and unofficial, could be summed up in one word: denationalisation. He was aware of the irresistible power of the new forces sweeping through the country, and was desperately concerned that it should be wisely exercised in the future, and not thoughtlessly allowed to impact upon the existing structures of the people.

He had four main aims for education policy: firstly, to train men who would later be able to administer the country, understanding the needs of the people and the methods of British administration; secondly, to train teachers for branch schools throughout the country; thirdly, to train native artisans; and fourthly, to teach the improvement of agriculture and stock-raising. These principle aims would be included in an overall objective of educational training in literacy, the three R's and hygiene.

There were few aspects of Nigerian life that escaped Morel's attention. He was horrified to observe that the introduction of Western consumption habits, which in practice caused mayhem in Africa, was hailed as a moral and commercial triumph in Europe. 'People at home,' he wrote, 'are prone, in approaching problems connected with the coloured races, to place themselves exclusively from the subjective point of view.' He roundly condemned such ethnocentrism, and was shocked by its effects on the local population. As he put it, 'the European individualistic social system grafted upon the communal life of a coloured people – these things may produce widespread human misery and immorality.'

He considered that many Western ethics and practices (including marriage laws, sexual mores, and consumerism) not infrequently resulted in what he described as a 'holocaust of human victims'. The damage done by the liquor trade was one example of this terrible outcome, and he devoted an entire chapter to the issue, and to the effect it had had upon the communal life of West Africans, who had previously been only moderate drinkers. He was both shocked and depressed by the blindness of those who imposed their way of life on peoples unsuited to adopt it, writing sorrowfully of the 'God-fearing, Christian men and women in Europe who judge other countries by their own, other peoples by their own people, other needs by their own needs, with the best of intentions and with the purest of motives.'

On his homeward journey to Lagos he visited the Bale of Ibadan and the Alake of Abeokuta. In Lagos he was received by the native community and lodged in Government House with Sir Walter Egerton. He noted that most of the white men there refused to meet a man who fraternized with black men, but does not mention whether this majority included the British administrators whom he had praised for their fairness and justice at the outset of the book.

Morel was obviously captivated by Africa, and was intrigued and exhilarated by his visit to the continent. But although the trip gave rise to numerous recommendations specifically focused on his experiences in Nigeria, it is interesting that his general conclusions – on imperialism, cultural supremacy and the exploitation of indigenous inhabitants, for example – were wholly unchanged by the situation he found there. It is remarkable that a man who had never left Europe had already developed such an accurate and comprehensive grasp of the impact of colonialism on a continent of which he had no first-hand knowledge. It is a testament to his extraordinary powers of imagination and empathy that he had been able to do so.

European Alliances

On his return from Nigeria, Morel continued to be deeply concerned about the fate of Africans in the face of European colonialism. His reflections on his journey had clearly demonstrated the way in which he considered the colonial powers should administer their territories, but as relations between the powers worsened, he turned his attention increasingly from Africa to Europe. From campaigning on a largely single strand issue which received almost universal support, he began to involve himself in much more contentious matters and murkier waters, a course that both challenged his powers of judgement and imperilled his reputation.

A trip he had made to Paris in 1909 seems to have been influential in changing his tactics, and to have acted as the catalyst for his subsequent attack on the Anglo-French Entente. During this visit, he had been persuaded that the Entente was a serious obstacle to Britain's capacity to act forcefully on the Congo issue, an assumption that arose largely because the French were deeply concerned to suppress revelations of widespread abuse emerging from the French Congo. It appeared that the pressure of Franco-Belgian financiers was enough to prevent French officials from making any progress towards Congo reform.

Morel had been aware for some time of the influence of these factors in France, but being faced with what he described as a 'mass of intrigue... corruption and incompetence,' and 'moral cowardice which is literally abject,' he seemed to be profoundly cast down.[95] His despondency regarding the French position made his hopes that the British government would take serious action on behalf of the people of the colony all the more surprising, for it must have been clear to him that such a course would simultaneously embroil it in controversy with France, Germany and Belgium.

However, he was by no means exceptional in turning his attention towards the prospect of war in Europe. From the end of the 19th century, following Edward VII's accession to the throne, there had been a flood of fictional accounts of a future Anglo-German war. Prominent politicians, leading servicemen, defence analysts and journalists had speculated for years on the possibilities and outcomes of war in Europe. If there was any agreement amongst them, it was that a war between the great powers of Europe would be militarily, politically and socially devastating.[96]

Morel's years of lobbying the government and the Foreign Office had left him with no illusions that Britain would jeopardise its alliances in Europe to humour the Kaiser, or act in secret if it felt it desirable to do so. Furthermore, the photographic evidence accompanying the Congo campaign recording the atrocities (possibly the first photographic campaign in support of human rights) must have left him intensely aware of the physical brutality that humans could inflict upon each other. For a man driven by compassionate concerns for the natives of the Congo, the thought of a major war must have been deeply repugnant. Later he would write: 'These men who sit in the seats of the mighty in every belligerent state…they know what it means – this orgy of blood, this riot of bestiality, this nerve shattering fury of sound which bursts the drums of ears, drives reason from its tenement and sight from the eyes with its withering blast.'[97]

Morel's relationship with the Foreign Office had always been somewhat fractious, but on the whole he had remained uncritical of Sir Edward Grey, who had been forthright in his attitude to Leopold and his administration of the Congo. Grey recognised that only the government of Belgium could take over the Congo, and that Britain must work to make it possible for them to do so. In February 1908, Grey wrote to Sir Arthur Hardinge, British Minister at Brussels:

> My own personal feeling is that we are justified in any measures which will result in taking the Congo out of the hands of the King. He has forfeited every claim to it he ever had; and to take the Congo away from him without compensation would be less than justice, for it would leave him still with all the gains he has made by his monstrous system.[98]

He went on to say that the system of forced labour, a flagrant violation of the conditions on which Britain had recognised the Congo State, must cease, and that in future the monopolies and concessions in the Congo must accord with the Treaty obligations by which the Congo was bound.[99]

Nonetheless, as the campaign for Congo reform began to be influenced by his concerns about the prospect of war in Europe, and the secret diplomacy that gave rise to it, Morel's criticism started to be increasingly focussed on the Foreign Secretary.

In *Great Britain and the Congo* he now wrote contemptuously of:

> ...anxious Ministers holding innumerable and mysterious strings of the greatest delicacy; of a Government department harassed, but steeped in wisdom, searching with sagacious eye the bye-ways of world politics, bending a penetrating gaze upon the mystic recesses of dark intrigue, moving only when assured of absolute success, loftily indifferent in the profundity and all-embracing sweep of its trained outlook, to these rash and clamouring voices from outside, beyond the pale of official sapiency.[100]

This change of tone caused the admiration Morel had enjoyed for so long from so many supporters to give way to a considerable degree of disquiet. He was rebuked by a number of his friends, including Gilmour, who wrote that he had read reports of a speech he gave in Redditch in *The Times,* and felt that he was committing a very grave error in taking such a hostile attitude to the Foreign Office.[101] The Archbishop of Canterbury and the Bishop of Southwark both lined up to express their concern, the former not surprisingly expressing the 'delicacy of the diplomatic situation.' Even Casement, no friend of the Foreign Office, weighed in with a lengthy letter.

> I fear that you have not done wisely in that attack on the FO. I do not think you have advanced the Congo cause by traversing FO policy as a whole and censuring their general control of foreign affairs. People will not accept your judgement on that, while everyone would accept your guidance and judgement on Congo matters...Leave the Entente Cordiale alone. John Bull won't drop that for anything just now, with the German Airship and Dreadnought Nightmare on his stomach.[102]

Morel cannot have been blind to the many complex issues that the Foreign Office had to juggle with at a time of rising tension in Europe, or to the particularly unenviable position of the Foreign Secretary, and it is not entirely to his credit that he chose largely to ignore the importance of dealing sensitively with the situation. Years later, in his biography of Sir Edward Grey, G M Trevelyan summed up the risk that he had faced during this period. He wrote:

> Rather than let the evil system continue in the Congo, Grey ran the risk of a serious, possibly a fatal check to his general policy, perhaps risking England's safety by the line he took. Belgium might have been

driven into the arms of Germany, if the matter had been conducted with less than his skill, tact and consideration, or by a British Minister whose character did not, like Grey's, half persuade the cynical Europeans that he was not a hypocrite but an honest man.'[103]

Morel, however, appeared to find it quite impossible to admire such diplomacy, or allow for any hint of deviation from what might be called 'the path of righteousness', and the next six years were to see him emerge as an implacable opponent of the impending war. The uncompromising nature of his criticism, directed as it was at the heart of the establishment, was to prove a significant factor in his ultimate fall from grace.

It is difficult to view the run up to the First World War in any fully objective way, and this is not the place to discuss the causes of the conflict. Many millions of words have been devoted to examining the subject from the combatants' various perspectives, and it is only now, nearly a century later, that any generally agreed consensus has been reached. However, it is necessary to consider some of the pressures that were pushing the European nations towards such a catastrophe, particularly in so far as those issues engaged Morel.

Morel's views in the pre-War years were obviously deeply influenced by the Congo campaign, and the role of the French and British governments as colonial powers in West Africa. The First Morocco Crisis[104] in 1905 had alerted him to the Anglo-French Entente Cordiale, and made him aware that Britain's largely secret treaty was a principal driver of its policies in Europe. Following the incident, representatives of the two countries' respective armies had held secret talks in 1906 about how they might cooperate in the face of German aggression. In violation of democratic institutions, neither the public, Parliament, or full Cabinet were informed of the existence of such military arrangements with France.[105] The Treaty of Algeciras in the same year resulted in Britain standing firmly behind France, in a determined move to keep Germany out of the Mediterranean, leaving Morocco securely under the influence of France and Spain.

In 1911, shortly after visiting Britain, the Kaiser again announced his interest in North Africa. Moroccan tribesmen had risen in revolt against the Sultan, and French troops were sent to occupy Tangier. Germany asserted that this amounted to a full annexation for which she should be compensated. The Kaiser ordered a gun boat to be deployed to Agadir, and German troops were landed. For a brief spell the Great Powers hovered on the brink of war. However, in this instance Germany withdrew, having been faced with an aggressive ultimatum from the British government warning Berlin 'not to treat Britain as if she were of no account in the cabinet of nations.'[106] Nonetheless, there was little diminution in the tension within Europe.

The Agadir crisis was the first time that the Cabinet learned of military staff talks with France, and the more radical members were appalled. In spite of Grey agreeing formally that no communications between staff should commit Britain to military or naval intervention, those who were opposed to a collision with Germany became wary of Grey. If military talks with France had been kept secret what else was the Foreign Secretary concealing?[107]

These two 'incidents' provided the stimulus for Morel to publish a number of articles towards the end of 1911, and with the book that followed, *Morocco in Diplomacy*, they constitute his critique of Britain's pre-war foreign policy. As usual, his approach was unequivocal and sharply defined. As Catherine Cline would later write in *The Strategies of Protest*, 'Morel's temperament required him to discover fundamental, total explanations for the evils which surrounded him. In the Congo he found the answer in the system of landownership; in Europe, in the system of diplomacy'.[108]

In *Morocco in Diplomacy* he attempted to analyse the differences that existed between the two countries. He believed that 'no greater disaster could befall both peoples, and all that is most worthy of preservation in modern civilisation, than war between them.'[109] He studied the British, French and German interests in Morocco, reviewing the Act of Algeciras; the Anglo-French Declaration of 1904 and its secret articles; the Kaiser's 1905 visit to Tangier; and the 1911 gun boat incident and its repercussions. He concluded that it was the Entente Cordiale that had provoked Germany's justifiable reactions, which had been misrepresented by anti-German press and Foreign Office influence.

During these pre-war years, Morel was also seriously entertaining the idea of a career in politics, and as the Congo campaign drew to a close, he increasingly felt that this might be an appropriate way to employ his talents. He was not alone in holding this view, and as early as 1907 William Cadbury had expressed a wish that he might enter Parliament. Four years later he had written to Morel, whilst he was still in Nigeria, indicating that he thought he should stand, offering him £800 a year and a guarantee of £400 for any parliamentary election he might contest. Furthermore, in the event of Morel's death, he agreed to give Mary £500 a year until her youngest son became twenty-one, and subsequently £300 a year.[110]

In October 1912, Morel took up Cadbury's generous offer, and was invited by Birkenhead Liberal Association to be their candidate at the next general election. His adoption speech is particularly interesting, as it clearly displays that his awareness of colonial injustice had not blinded him to the vital problem of social inequalities at home. Morel's words of a hundred years ago could well be addressed to Parliament today at a time when the Office for National Statistics July 2012 bulletin on net wealth in the UK shows that 'In 2008/10, the least wealthy half of households in Great Britain had 10 per cent of the total wealth (including private pension wealth), while the wealthiest half of households had 90 per cent of the total'.[111]

> To my mind, of all the problems which confront our national life, and go right down to the root of our racial power and prosperity, the gravest…is the problem which presents itself through the terrible inequalities in well-being and opportunity which divide various classes of our population…What, after all is the social phenomenon of our age? Wealth piling up more and more every year, more and more concentrated; luxury more and more pronounced; and, beside that wealth and luxury, a vast, increasing, unchartered desert of human discomfort and distress. A more equitable distribution…of socially produced wealth should, and must be, the ultimate, constant, perpetual aim of Liberalism.[112]

In the same speech he referred to the issues that would obsess him in the years to come, international and Anglo-German relations, and to the importance of solving the friction between the two powers. He felt strongly that the greatest national interest of the British people was, and would continue to be, the establishment and maintenance of friendly relations with Germany.

He also believed that if war broke out, the secret diplomacy and treaties existing between France and England would be largely responsible for the disaster. There was a pressing need for the democratisation of foreign policy and the disclosure of the real Anglo-French relationship. With considerable percipience he foresaw that the victorious conclusion of a world war would not be the end but the beginning of a legacy of hatred – of which no man could estimate the final reckoning.

The Approach to War

The first edition of *Morocco in Diplomacy* was dedicated to those who believed that the establishment of friendlier relations between Britain and Germany were essential to the prosperity and welfare of the two nations, and for the maintenance of world peace. The dedication also included all those who appreciated that the acceptance of national liabilities towards foreign powers, if entered into under secret agreements withheld from the British people, was both a menace to the security of the state and a betrayal of the national trust.

In a foreword to the book, Ramsay MacDonald wrote that he well remembered the unpleasant effect it had upon him when he first read it. He hadn't wanted to believe the contents, yet the facts were so authoritative and the conclusions so logical that he had to believe them despite himself.

Following shortly on the heels of his book on Nigeria, *Morocco in Diplomacy* was another example of Morel's extraordinary command of the facts surrounding very complex issues. He can be credited with reconstructing the background and evolution of the crisis with a high degree of accuracy, at a time when the documents available were still incomplete. The book is all the more remarkable when it is borne in mind that it represents a total change of tack, from an intensely focussed campaign (albeit one which was affected by European alliances) to a multi-faceted, international arena. Morel has been described as the first radical of the 20th century to take up foreign affairs as a full-time interest, and in keeping with his personality, his attention was concentrated. Unlike many activists of his day, until he became a prospective parliamentary candidate and later an MP, he was not distracted by other issues such as social reform, women's rights or the situation in Ireland. He worked with the radicals solely because they accepted his views on foreign affairs.[113]

Extracts from a number of reviews by both the British and Continental press were inserted at the beginning of the book. Unsurprisingly, *Le Temps*, the organ of the French Foreign Office, and *La Dépêche Coloniale*, the paper of the French Colonial Party, were critical. One declared that the book was an effort to destroy the Entente Cordiale. The other claimed that the book was a tissue of the basest calumnies, and Morel was the unofficial agent of the new German Ambassador, endeavouring to mislead his countrymen to please the merchants of Hamburg. However, at this time most other reviews were complimentary. This would be the last time that Morel received such general approval for promotion of Anglo-German friendship, and his opposition to the impending war.

Morel had said that *Morocco in Diplomacy* was written 'in the hope of helping to avert a catastrophe', but by the time it was published tension in Europe was rising fast. British officials regarded Germany's construction of battleships – fourteen were built between 1900 and 1905; a rate unmatched by Britain – as a serious threat to peace and stability. The newly appointed First Sea Lord, Reginald McKenna, proposed that the increasing disparity in numbers between the German and British fleets should be met by the immediate construction of eighteen 'Dreadnoughts' over the next three years. His proposal was eventually negotiated down to four battleships to be built with immediate effect, but the reduction did little to divert the drift to war.[114]

Morel, on the contrary, dismissed the German naval programme as a precautionary defensive measure on the part of a country more threatened than threatening. The menace to European peace, he argued, came not from Germany, but from those parties in France who wished to take their revenge for their humiliating defeat in the Franco-Prussian war of 1870, before Germany's expanding population and industrial strength would make victory difficult, if not impossible. By 1913 Germany's iron and steel production had overtaken Britain's, and its national income was greater than that of France.[115]

Morel claimed that Britain's alliance with France, in the face of an imaginary German threat, had merely encouraged reactionary forces to seek redress in conflict. He believed that Germany not only considered itself threatened by Great Britain, but that Britain intended to take the first favourable opportunity to force a war. 'The *entente cordiale* was founded, not on the positive basis of a defence of common interests, but on the negative basis of hatred against the German Empire…It is the *entente* which has revived the spirit of revenge in France which had largely subsided.'[116] At the same time, he was convinced that Germany's supreme need was 'not war but peace, not military conquest but trade, not the acquisition of colonies peopled by a German-speaking race, but unfettered access to overseas markets.'[117]

In the preface to the second edition of *Morocco in Diplomacy*, written a few months after the outbreak of war, Morel defines his main object of criticism. It had now become evident that secret diplomacy designed to preserve a balance of power had not saved Europe from a catastrophe of unprecedented proportions. The old-fashioned methods of safeguarding peace by preparing for conflict had proved an utter failure. Years of international intrigue had been largely ignored by an indifferent public, and the nation had been led blindfolded into war as the result of liabilities secretly contracted by its diplomats without its authority.

So too, nearly a century later, would Britain be led into another war under a false premise. Martin Kettle, writing in the autumn of 2010, draws the analogy particularly clearly:

The broad parallels with today are very strong. A war that was widely opposed; a traumatic generational experience; a collective belief that people were deceived; a conviction that public inquiries and the opening up of documents would reveal the incriminating evidence; and a desire to change the rules, above all by making them more democratically accountable, to avoid the same thing happening again. All these were present in the generation that lived through the First World War. All are present in the generation that has lived through the Iraq and Afghan conflicts.[118]

However, while a concerted effort towards official anti-war protest and political reform has been lamentably absent in the past decade, the early years of the 20th century produced a more spirited resistance. The Agadir crisis provoked the first attempt to organise dissent against the official line of foreign policy, and the Foreign Affairs Group of the Liberal Party in Parliament was set up with seventy-five members, who met regularly and tried to plan a concerted campaign. Noel Buxton, its originator, was mainly concerned to meet the 'legitimate aspirations of Germany', whilst others had a more general grievance against secret diplomacy.

The group sought for a friendly approach to the German government, more publicity about foreign affairs, and better parliamentary control. It got off to a good start, with sufficient funding and a secretary, but never gained momentum. A J P Taylor suggests that it was perhaps too tied to the Radical Intellectuals, and lacked 'the mass support it might have got from associating with Labour men.' He also remarks that most of all 'it lacked a dynamic leader. Yet he was waiting in the wings.'[119] In the event, however, it would be the Union of Democratic Control (the UDC as it became known), that secured Morel as Secretary, and he would come to be intrinsically identified with the movement. In the words of Helena Swanwick, sister of the artist Walter Sickert and historian of the UDC: 'EDM was the UDC, and the UDC was EDM'.[120]

Shortly after completing *Morocco in Diplomacy*, and before Morel became Secretary of the UDC, he and Mary decided that it was time to move from Talbot Road in Highgate. The noise of the traffic was presumably proving too much to bear, and besides there were four children now, and the house was not large. In a letter to Holt, Morel wrote, 'We are in a lively pickle at Highgate; all our pipes are frozen and we have got no water, the inconvenience is horrible; and I haven't had a cold bath for four days, which to me is purgatory.'[121]

There was also the children's future education to consider. The eldest, Stella, was now fifteen; the others, Roger, John and Geoffrey were, respectively, thirteen, eleven and eight. Mary went to look at several boarding schools including Bedales, near Petersfield in Hampshire, and Marlborough in Wiltshire. Eventually they settled for Berkhampstead School in Cheltenham for Roger, and Coombe Hill Junior and Senior School in Surrey for the other children.

They decided to return to the country, and to move to Kings Langley in Hertfordshire. There they bought a plot of land for a house, and whilst it was being built they lived with a farming friend at Balls Pond Farm. According to Mary's written recollections, it seems that the money left by the de Horne family paid for the new house, and it was to be Morel's home for the remainder of his life. It was a large, gabled building in the neo-Tudor style, with an extensive garden and a tennis court, and it appears to have been much loved. Morel was always a keen gardener, and it is evident from family photographs that the children enjoyed playing tennis. Later on in 1916, the couple's fifth child, Oliver, was born. He was the only one of the children to live on into the 21st century, and died in 2003.

In July 1914, just before the outbreak of war, Morel went on holiday to Dieppe with his daughter, Stella. Describing this trip, he would later write:

In the last days of July the West African Lands Committee, on which I was working at the Colonial Office, broke up for the holidays. We said good-bye – some of us for the last time as it turned out – and spoke of whither we were respectively bound. I mentioned that I was crossing to Dieppe for a few days with my daughter, Stella. The secretary of the Committee…took me aside and endeavoured earnestly to dissuade me. I asked him why. The answer was to the effect that the international situation was very serious – more serious than the public was aware. This was on Wednesday July 26th. We crossed on the Thursday. The storm clouds were gathering fast, but somehow it seemed impossible they could burst. On the Saturday morning I was swimming in the sea before breakfast and heard a Frenchman shout to his neighbour that Jaurès had been assassinated, 'Enfin, on lui a fait son affaire.' I hurried back to the hotel. The news was only too true. On Sunday morning the walls were covered with the General Mobilization Order, and there were many heart-rending scenes in the narrow streets of the old town. Its irregular, ill-paved streets full of men, women and children, mostly weeping… At every door stood little groups of people with faces drawn and pitiful…Above all, permeating all, a consciousness of some invisible, irresistible presence, inhuman, pitiless; some monstrous, unseen hand stretched out, tearing son from mother, husband from wife, father from children. And one realised with an icy chill at one's heart that the inevitable had already happened; that because one of the great ones of the earth had fallen beneath the hand of the assassin in a far-distant country, because the other great ones of the earth had quarrelled as the result of that crime, because the rulers of Christian Europe had for years been squandering the substance of their peoples in piling up weapons destructive of human life until all Europe was one vast arsenal, and had planned and schemed against one another through their appointed agents; that because of these things, these humble folk in this small town in which I moved, were stricken down, their lives rent and shattered.

We decided to leave by the one o'clock boat, which was crammed. It was a horrible feeling waiting for the gangplank to be lowered – the anxious crowd, the confusion, the sense of impending disaster; and all the while one's brain throbbed with the knowledge that the calamity so long feared, so long predicted, had fallen at last… We had an awful crossing. There was no room to move on deck, and the seas came over drenching us.

At home I found letters from Trevelyan speaking of some contemplated effort on the part of Radical and Labour members for peace and asking my help. I called on him early on Monday. At a few minutes to three he and I and his brother walked through the empty House of Commons. I recalled Bright's phrase: The Angel of death has been abroad throughout the land; you may almost hear the beating of his wings.[122]

Morel's profound abhorrence of war, his foresight and his compassion are all evident in this letter, and these qualities never left him. Nor did he moderate his loathing of what he saw as the deceitful political intrigue that had led to the conflict. Later in 1914, he wrote in *Truth and the War* that:

A painstaking investigation of the whole diplomatic history of Morocco revealed a record of treachery and deceit towards the British and French peoples, towards Morocco and the rest of the world, by the French and British Foreign Offices, with few parallels even in the annals of diplomacy…the mischief is that the detestable system of intrigue in which diplomats live, move and have their official being is such that it sets up wholly false ethical values, and imposes a standard of morals which would not be tolerated for a moment among decent men in social life.

The Union for Democratic Control[123]

It was clear before war was declared in 1914 that a platform for those who did not support the conflict would have to be found outside Parliament. As already mentioned, the Radicals had formed an unofficial Liberal Foreign Affairs Group in Parliament after the Agadir crisis of 1911, and had established a Foreign Policy Committee outside it. These activities clearly demonstrated that a considerable number of Liberals, including at least seventy-five MPs, were prepared to criticise the government's direction of foreign affairs, but the groups had made little headway.

At the same time, there were resignations from the government amongst those opposed to the war, including a number from senior positions. Charles Trevelyan, elder brother of G M Trevelyan, then Parliamentary Secretary to the Board of Education, was one of them. Early in August, Trevelyan, aware that Morel had wound up his work on the CRA, wrote to inform him of the proposal to set up an organisation, the Union of Democratic Control (UDC), to represent those against the war, and asked him if he would become Secretary.[124]

Morel was still the Liberal Candidate for Birkenhead and continuing his work on the West African Land Commission, but responded immediately that he would be honoured to do so. This decision again reflects Morel's extraordinarily focused sense of purpose. He must have known that accepting the post possibly entailed the sacrifice of his prospective parliamentary career, and ran the risk of destroying his reputation, but the aims of the UDC coincided with his own objectives, and his choice was clearly dictated by a passionate dedication to their mutual cause. His position, as both Secretary and Treasurer, was initially unpaid, until in 1915 he began to draw a salary for his secretarial duties and relinquished the role of Treasurer.

The name given to the UDC is obviously indicative of its principal purpose: to secure proper control of foreign policy by Parliament. That need had been highlighted throughout the years leading up to the War, in particular by the questions surrounding the Entente and the extent of

Britain's commitment to France, and consequently to Russia. Questions had repeatedly been asked in Parliament, with a view to discovering exactly what Britain's responsibilities were with respect to both countries. Was Britain bound by any military or naval agreement to come to France's support if attacked by Germany? France was committed to Russia. If Russia threatened Germany would France be drawn in, and if so would Britain become involved?

In March 1913 the government was asked if it was under any obligation by assurance or treaty with the French to send armed forces to support them in the event of European hostilities. The Prime Minister, Mr Asquith, replied that the country was not under any obligation unknown to Parliament, which compelled it to take part in any war; 'there are no unpublished agreements which will restrict or hamper the freedom of the government or of parliament to decide whether or not Britain should participate in a war.'[125]

Much the same assertions were made over a year later in June 1914, when Sir Edward Grey, replying to similar questions by the same MPs, reminded them of the Prime Minister's response the previous year. He said that it remained as true as it was a year ago. No negotiations had been concluded with any power that would make the statement less true. As late as 3rd August he assured Parliament again that if any crisis arose, the government would come before the House of Commons and say that it was free to decide what action Britain should take. He described the organisation of Britain, France and Russia – the Triple Entente – as a 'Diplomatic Group', to distinguish it from the Triple Alliance, and declared that the government had given no promise of anything more than diplomatic support.

Grey emphasised that he did not consider conversations between French and British military and naval experts following the Algeciras Conference in 1906, or the further conversations of a similar nature after the Agadir Crisis in 1912, as binding engagements. However, in 1912 he had expressed in writing his view of the implications of such 'conversations'. At that time, he had made it clear that if either government had any reason to expect an unprovoked attack by a third power, or by some other event that threatened peace in Europe, it should discuss with the other what action to take in order to preserve peace.

Accordingly, on 2nd August 1914, days before the outbreak of war, and with the French fleet in the Mediterranean, Grey gave an assurance to the French Ambassador that if the German fleet came into the Channel or through the North Sea to undertake hostile action against the French coast or shipping, the British fleet would provide all the protection it could. He told the Ambassador that he had informed Parliament of this, not as a declaration of war, or entailing immediate aggressive action on the part of Britain, but 'as binding us to take aggressive action should that contingency arise.'[126] To the UDC and its members it was quite clear that, apart from violating Belgian neutrality, the Foreign Secretary considered Britain bound to take aggressive action against Germany as a consequence of obligations incurred in 'conversations'.

The UDC's first step was to write a private letter in August, addressed to those known to be favourable to its objectives. In this letter it stated three principal aims: to secure parliamentary control over foreign policy, so that it could not be formulated in secret and sprung upon the country as accomplished fact; to open direct negotiations with democratic parties on the Continent, in order to form an international understanding depending on popular parties rather than governments; and to achieve such terms that the war would not merely become the starting point for new national antagonisms and future wars, either through the humiliation of the defeated nation or an artificial rearrangement of frontiers.

Some months later the UDC decided to alter these statements of its objectives, in order to embrace a general principle of peace. The four Cardinal Points, as they came to be known, were: no transfer of territory without a plebiscite; no treaty or undertaking without parliamentary sanction; drastic reduction of armaments and nationalisation of the arms-traffic; and a rejection of the aim of creating a balance of power.

The letter also proposed the organisation of meetings and speakers, in addition to the preparation and issue of books, leaflets and pamphlets. It further asked for the names and addresses of those likely to share the views it expressed. The letter was signed by Ramsay MacDonald, who resigned his chairmanship of the Parliamentary Labour Party; Charles Trevelyan, who had resigned from the government; Arthur Ponsonby, an outspoken critic of Grey's diplomacy in Parliament; the journalist Norman Angell, and Morel.[127] While MacDonald had commitments outside the UDC which were of great importance to him, Morel had only his editorship of the *African Mail* to claim his attention, besides his devotion to his family and garden. He was free to focus the greater part of his formidable energy on pursuing the objectives of the Union, and in the words of Marvin Swartz, he was soon to become the 'heart and soul' of the organisation.[128]

It was a taste of things to come that the *Morning Post* somehow got hold of the letter, which it published together with an editorial claiming to have unearthed a conspiracy, insinuating that the authors had acted at the instigation of the German government. A number of other newspapers followed suit, taking up the cry of treachery. In view of this, it was decided that the movement should be made public, and another letter was sent to the press. For the first time the letter carried the title of the new organisation, 'The Union for Democratic Control'. This letter noted that leaflets putting forward arguments in favour of the policy would be issued as soon as a favourable situation arose.

At much the same time, Morel had been asked to speak to his prospective constituents on the 'Irish Question'. In spite of his preoccupation with foreign affairs and the UDC, he presented a lengthy and informed address on Irish Home Rule and the problem of Ulster. Although it appears that he had never previously given significant thought to the matter, this speech again shows a remarkably comprehensive grasp of the details and issues surrounding a complex political problem.[129]

His views on the Irish question were much in keeping with those that determined his outlook on peoples subject to colonial rule. He vigorously supported the Liberal government's proposals for Home Rule for Ireland, strongly condemning the stance of the Conservative and Unionist Parties. There is a light-hearted ribaldry about this speech, a feature not often manifested in his writing:

> What we are virtually asked to do – and upon every imaginable instrument of discord, from the trombone of Mr Bonar Law (Leader of the Opposition) to the shrill flute of Mr Balfour; from the double-bass of the joint proprietor of the *Daily Mail* and *The Times*, to the penny whistle of Mr F E Smith and the primitive war-horn of Sir Edward Carson – what we are adjured to do on these cymbals of brass and on these Orange drums, is humbly to admit that we Liberals and our Irish friends have been endowed by nature with a double dose of original sin.[130]

He lambasted the idea that half the population of one province of Ireland (Ulster) should demand the right to impose a permanent veto upon the aspirations of the Irish people. He attacked all talk of Ulster's 'loyalty' as an 'odious appeal to sectarian passion which belched from Belfast pulpits, carrying people back to the dimmest, dreariest, darkest days of the middle ages.'[131] He ended by saying that the covenanters were backed by a caste and class conspiracy in England that pursued its own ends and cared nothing for Ireland except as a peg on which to hang its ambitions and hates. If Britain were so misguided as to allow such a movement to defeat

Home Rule, the upshot would not merely be revolution at home but doom for the British Empire.

Morel regarded Ireland as a test case. If England was unable to crush the forces of reaction in its midst, the 'hundreds of millions of men and women who were watching, waiting and wondering from afar' would see that England's authority to give Ireland the freedom it had demanded for centuries had been flouted. With hindsight, it is plain that this was a very accurate prediction. The British Empire would soon be discredited and consigned to history, while a divided Ireland would lead to thirty years of bitter internal conflict at the end of the century.

Six months after Morel had given this speech, the Executive Council of Birkenhead Liberal Association declared that their selection board was now finding his anti-war views unacceptable, and asked him to resign his candidacy for the seat. Morel had placed considerable store on becoming a Member of Parliament, and the fact that he had been selected as a Liberal candidate meant a great deal to him. The Executive Council's decision was a severe rebuff to his hopes and aspirations, and the loss of confidence of its members must have been extremely distressing. He expressed considerable bitterness over the decision, but in fact he can hardly have failed to anticipate it, and it is difficult to see how he could have pursued his work with the UDC while under the constraint of a Liberal whip in Parliament.

The first General Council meeting of the UDC was held in November 1914, and a simple and democratic constitution was adopted. At the meeting it was reported that 5,000 members had already joined nationally, including various bodies, Trade Union organisations, branches of the Independent Labour Party and cooperative societies. Four editions of a pamphlet explaining the four cardinal points of the UDC's campaign had already been published, and editions of 10,000 were sold out in a fortnight.

With his speaking and literary skills and over a decade of campaigning experience, Morel was perfectly equipped for the formidable task ahead. 'It was to be a very big thing indeed,' he wrote, 'a far bigger thing than the Congo.' Within two weeks of agreeing to accept the post of Secretary, he had drawn up a plan of campaign. The strategy has a distinctly military ring to it, perhaps affected by the pervasively warlike atmosphere in the country. The campaign was designed to take city by city and town by town systematically, using any existing organisation which could be captured for distribution work and the subsequent organisation of public meetings. Various groups such as the existing Labour organisation, National Peace Society, Brotherhood Union or Free Church Council would be brought together to arrange for the systematic distribution of literature, without overlapping.[132] Morel also knew where to look for rich sympathisers, taking their money without compromising the democratic nature of the UDC, and plunged into the fray with his usual intensity.

This time his supreme objective was to achieve the democratic control of foreign policy; his target was secret diplomacy, and his bête noire, Sir Edward Grey. His pen, now put to the service of the UDC, was to be his principal weapon during the war years, as it had been during the Congo campaign. *Morocco in Diplomacy* was reissued in 1915 by the *National Labour Press*, with a foreword by Ramsay Macdonald, and was retitled *Ten Years of Secret Diplomacy: An Unheeded Warning*. It went through five editions between 1915 and 1918. The *National Labour Press* also published *Truth and the War* in 1916. 10,000 copies sold in three months; a further edition of 5,000 also sold out, and a third was published.[133]

A hundred years later, the conduct of Britain's foreign policy during the years leading up to the First World War continues to attract analysis by historians, academics and politicians, and Grey, the longest serving Foreign Secretary in British history, was in office from 1905 to 1916. He therefore played a central role during this period, and it was against Grey and his policies that Morel directed the greater part of the UDC's opposition.

Morel had held a grudging respect for the Foreign Secretary in the years leading up to the transfer of the Congo to the Belgian government, but that respect had diminished rapidly as it became obvious that Grey would not, and could not, enforce the reforms the CRA wished to see. By the time Morel turned his attention to exposing the ramifications of Britain's foreign policy, Grey had come to personify the deceit, ineptitude, and abuse of power against which he was protesting.

Morel was not alone in doubting the qualities of the Foreign Secretary. In an unflattering sketch in 1908 the editor of the *Daily News*, A G Gardiner, described Grey's 'lack of flexibility of mind, unqualified by large knowledge, swift apprehension of events or urgent passion for humanity' as constituting a peril to the future. 'His aims are high and his honour stainless, but the slow movement of his mind renders it easy for him to drift into courses which a more imaginative sense and a swifter instinct would lead him to question and repudiate.'[134] Later in 1918, Lloyd George asserted that he was one of the two men primarily responsible for the war.[135]

Although it is sometimes said that Grey was not an ardent imperialist, and shared the Radicals' desire to pursue a European policy without keeping up a great army, from as early as 1902 Grey had also held a dominant belief that Britain should align itself against Germany.[136] At that time he wrote 'I have come to think that Germany is our worst enemy and our greatest danger…I believe the policy of Germany to be that of using us without helping us: keeping us isolated, that she may have us to fall back upon.' He went on to declare that if any government dragged Britain into the German net, he would oppose it openly at all costs.[137]

The charges that Morel laid against Grey were largely based on Grey's Germanophobia and his commitment to the Entente with France. On both issues, Grey's position was at odds with the views of the Liberal Parliamentary Party. In order to avoid discord within the party, Grey strove to limit its influence over, and awareness of, foreign policy, a practice which eminently suited the officials at the Foreign Office. Indeed, Grey complained in 1906 that Liberal MPs had acquired the art of asking questions and raising debates when there was so much in foreign affairs which attracted attention and would be better left alone.[138] He was quite unashamed about this; writing in 1908, following some unsolicited advice given by Sir Thomas Sanderson, his erstwhile permanent Undersecretary at the Foreign Office, he declared that 'one of the difficulties that exists with colleagues is to convince them there are such things as brick walls; the most certain way of doing this is to let them run their own heads against them.'[139]

Grey's desire to keep foreign policy out of the public realm was tacitly supported by the Opposition, who imagined that it should be lifted out of party politics and placed on 'a higher and different plane…not to be deflected from its course by the eddies of party political opinion.'[140] It appeared that there was more agreement between Grey and the Opposition front bench than there was within the Cabinet itself, to say nothing of the Liberal Party as a whole.

The result of this attitude was that Grey's policy was subject to minimal parliamentary scrutiny, giving him considerable freedom of action.[141] The axiom he adopted, however, was exceptionally rigid. Indeed, it has been said that the avoidance of isolation and his lack of confidence in Britain's self-sufficiency was the only principle upon which Grey based his foreign policy.[142] This restricted aspiration and the secrecy that surrounded its implementation totally disempowered the electorate, although their fate rested entirely in his hands. So pervasive was Grey's determination to keep control that the Prime Minister, David Lloyd George, could say in a private conversation with C P Scott in 1917, 'If people really knew the truth, the war would be stopped tomorrow. But of course they don't know and can't know.'[143]

It was, of course, primarily this cavalier attitude to the public and their elected representatives, and the secret treaties and lies that accompanied it, that drove Morel to channel all his extraordinary energy into building the UDC into a formidable organ of wartime dissent. His voluminous writings were informed by outstanding research and a clear analysis of the cause of the war. As well as outlining a path to peace to prevent a recurrence of the conflict, they helped to influence the attitudes of the British public towards both the war and the peace, and in many ways these years represented the height of his influence in public life.

At the same time, many of his supporters advised him to moderate his tone, but he remained impervious to their suggestions. In the preface to *Red Rubber*, he had quoted William Lloyd Garrison's testament – 'I will be harsh as truth and as uncompromising as justice. I am in earnest; I will not equivocate; I will not excuse; I will not retreat a single inch; and I will be heard. Posterity will bear testimony that I was right' – and had adopted it as his own. Now he brought its inflexible principles to bear on his work for the UDC. 'He was more than a critic;' wrote A J P Taylor, 'in his own mind, he was from the first the alternative foreign secretary, the foreign secretary of Dissent.'[144]

The determination to forego any attempt at nuanced debate may be of great advantage in certain circumstances, serving to cut through smokescreens designed to conceal deceit, corruption and abuse of power, but rigid conviction, stridently upheld, can sometimes prove counter-productive. Morel's exposure of Leopold during the Congo campaign certainly benefited from his refusal to equivocate, but aspects of the delicately balanced power structure in Europe arguably required more subtle handling. His refusal to hold Germany wholly responsible for the war was perhaps too forcefully expressed, and certainly it later led to much vilification, even to allegations of treason.[145]

These accusations might have carried less weight if his campaigning approach had not been so dogmatic, for in fact he was far from blind to the failings of Germany. As he put it in *Truth and the War*, 'German diplomacy has been as immoral, as short-sighted, as treacherous as any other. And it has added to those defects…a brutality of manifestation peculiarly its own, combined with an almost phenomenal incapacity to understand, still less to appreciate, the psychology of the nations with whom it has to deal.'[146] But this damning indictment appears to have been almost entirely obscured by the militant way in which he pursued his resolve to 'assist in destroying the legend that Germany was the sole responsible author of this war, undertaken by her to subjugate Europe'. Indeed, Morel's campaigning over these years was distinguished by a fanatical zeal and passion, as if he could no longer bear man's inhumanity to man. He burned with a furi[...] sense of outrage against the policies that he considered had aided anu abetted the drift to war.

It was partly as a result of this vehemence that the UDC was often accused of being a 'pro-German' organisation, although it vigorously denied that it was anything of the sort. Indeed, it emphasised that the majority of the Executive Committee were better acquainted with the French people and language than with the German, and it kept in close touch with like-minded Frenchmen. This was especially true in the case of Morel, with his French background and fluency in the language. From the outset, the UDC simply pursued the line that Britain must bear a share of the blame for the war, and that France and Russia were also partly responsible.[147] The Union's principal goal, throughout the conflict, was a lasting post-war settlement.

It is also fair to say that by 1914 Morel had already been largely vindicated in his earlier predictions that the Anglo-French Entente would ultimately involve Britain in a wider conflict. Indeed, in view of the widespread criticism of Grey and his foreign policy, it is remarkable that he survived in office. In a later conversation with C P Scott, Lord Loreburn, the Lord Chancellor, remarked that 'it was impossible for the Cabinet to control Grey in detail, yet everything depended in diplomacy in the handling of detail.'[148]

Unfortunately, such 'details' were incessantly withheld or distorted. Grey continually deceived his radical colleagues, evading their questions with actual falsehoods. On one occasion, he placed an alarmist report on German naval developments before the Cabinet. The rumours contained in this report proved totally fallacious, just as the recent reports on Weapons of Mass Destruction were shown to be unfounded in the run up to war in Iraq in 2003. In the former case, however, less damage was done by the misinformation, since Asquith, the Prime Minister, refused to sanction Grey's unjustified allegations.

There were many other similar incidents. On one occasion, Grey's permanent Undersecretary accused him of resorting to subterfuge in withholding the truth about Russian action in Persia from the House of Commons. For over five years he also kept secret from the Cabinet the fact there had been conversations between the British and French naval authorities regarding joint operations for war. Nor were Grey and Lord Haldane, the War Minister, authorised by Parliament to issue the ultimatum that they delivered to the German Ambassador on the 3rd and 4th of December, at the time of the second Morocco incident.[149]

This disdainful abuse of proper democratic procedures continued in spite of the turmoil in Europe. Grey left Britain in July 1914 for the first time during his lengthy tenure of office, and accompanied by King George V, travelled to Paris where a concerted attempt was made to transform the Entente between France and Russia into an alliance. Subject to the approval of his colleagues, Grey consented to allow 'conversations' between British and Russian experts similar to those which had taken place between London and Paris since 1906. The Cabinet agreed to this, and plans for naval cooperation were still under discussion when war broke out. To the annoyance of Grey, who had 'returned a studiously ambiguous reply to the House of Commons', it quickly leaked out that these discussions were taking place, but in the end they turned out to be successful. Russia declared itself satisfied by 'the substitution of something more substantial for the too theoretical and pacific foundations of the Entente.' [150]

Grey continued to display an extraordinary level of legerdemain, even on the very brink of war. On 31st July and 1st August, as the Austrians attacked Serbia, and Germany, Russia and France prepared for war, Grey conveyed intimations of Britain's intent to the German and French governments, each consisting of contradictory information that neither can have been pleased to hear. On 31st July he hinted to the Germans that Britain would be compelled to support France. A day later he denied to the French Ambassador, Cambon, that Britain had any obligation to help France and said it was up to her to decide for herself.[151]

None of these actions on its own is comparable to the enormity of Leopold's crimes in the Congo. However, when taken collectively, and in view of the fact that they contributed to a European-wide war that shattered a century of peace, they can be seen as a critical part of the process that led to a cataclysmic disaster of a scale never before seen in history. They also formed the precondition for further calamities, including the Second World War.

Morel was far from alone in sensing the 'angel of death' abroad in the land. Some monarchs, politicians and servicemen may have imagined the war would last only a few months, but most were perceptive enough to appreciate the fearful outcome of a major clash between the most powerfully armed industrial states in the world. General staffs appreciated that a European war would be extremely bloody and was unlikely to be short. Amongst them, Lord Kitchener, the conqueror of Sudan, who was brought in as Secretary of State for War, was sufficiently farsighted to foresee a conflict that would last for two or more years,[152] but regrettably these professionals concealed their misgivings from their political masters.[153]

As the UDC's campaign progressed and Morel became its principal, and often vilified, spokesman, it is easy to forget that he had considerable support for his analysis of the events leading up to the war. Even Austen Chamberlain, looking back on the crisis in December 1914 from a Conservative perspective could comment that:

> There had been nothing beforehand in official speeches or official publications to make known…the danger that we ran to prepare them for the discharge of our responsibilities and the defence of our interests. Those who knew most were silent; those who undertook to instruct the mass of the public were ignorant, and our democracy with its decisive voice on the conduct of public affairs was left without guidance by those who could have directed it properly, and was misled by those who constituted themselves its guides.[154]

There is general agreement today that Morel's crusade against the secrets and lies surrounding important foreign policy issues was justified. Grey was undoubtedly guilty of distorting the democratic political process, just as it has recently been perverted by the falsification of the facts leading to the Iraq War. In a remarkable repeat of past events, this recent conflict saw Parliament sidelined during the negotiations that led to war, and then placed in a position where opposition appeared at best disloyal, and at worst almost treasonable. In exposing the secrecy behind the international agreements of his own time, Morel's aim was to demonstrate that a similar lack of transparency in issues of European-wide importance only made relationships with Germany much worse. His description of the second Moroccan 'incident' in 1911 illustrates this unhappy causality. The Moroccan International Treaty included four directly interested European powers. Three of them – France, England and Spain – had concluded a secret pact providing for the political and economic partition of Morocco. This made their signatures at the foot of an international treaty proclaiming the independence and integrity of Morocco a 'more than usually dishonest farce'. The pact was concealed not only from Germany, which was the fourth interested party, but from their own parliaments and people. When Germany intervened, public opinion in France and England, unaware of the true facts and misinformed by much of the press, not unnaturally regarded German action as grossly provocative and designed to force a war, or at least break up the so-called 'Entente'.[155]

Morel's investigation, the results of which have never been contested, revealed that the whole diplomatic process surrounding the Moroccan affair had demonstrated a record of treachery and deceit by the French and British Foreign Offices towards the British and French people, and towards Morocco and the rest of the world. He maintained that this duplicity had few parallels in the annals of diplomatic history, and although he recognised that the German reaction was also immoral and short-sighted, he felt that the only possible way to save the situation was to make the true facts known to the British public, in the hope that it would lead to a clearer understanding of the German case. In its turn this would bring about a proper debate in Parliament, clarifying Britain's relations with France, and thereby revealing the implications of France's alliance with Russia.

Today it is impossible to do more than speculate on how Germany might have reacted had it been more fully engaged with the machinations of European foreign policy. There is no doubt that it felt hemmed in by France in the west and Russia in the east. The large alliance blocs in Europe were the key to any calculation of deterrence and strategic advantage, and the core partnerships were the Austro-German alliance, signed in 1879, and the Franco-Russian alliance, negotiated between 1891 and 1894. These agreements were directed against Russia and Germany respectively, while Britain was loosely connected to the second through its 'Entente Cordiale' with France.

For many years these alliances provided mutual deterrence, but although it was known they existed, their terms remained secret. Nonetheless, their existence implied that any conflict between two powers could ignite a showdown between the two coalitions. Institutional strategic planning, a new phenomenon, was a significant feature of these alliances, and this approach was demonstrated by Germany in particular during the unification wars of 1866 and 1870. These wars were not only triumphs of technology, but also of superior preparation by the Prussian general staff. The other powers in turn imitated the Prussian model; in future, military forces would be larger and more complex, and their control and coordination more challenging. The underlying assumption was that if deterrence failed it would be appropriate to use them.

The foundations of the principle of deterrence gradually collapsed between 1905 and the outbreak of war, as the two major alliances moved closer to military equality. At the same time, armaments competition intensified and political antagonism worsened, fuelled by a succession of diplomatic crises, amongst them the Morocco affairs. Although neither side viewed war as inevitable, both were increasingly prepared for it, both militarily and psychologically.[156] In the case of Germany, Alfred von Schlieffen's 1905 memorandum, or 'think-piece' for an invasion of

France,[157] and Von Moltke's adjustments to it, had been planned years before the final outbreak of war.

In view of Grey's fear of Britain's isolation, and well-founded concerns about German militarism and increasing industrial power, it was not unreasonable that he should have looked to France as an ally. But it is indisputable that alliances with France, however informal, should have been properly put before Parliament, and obligations and commitments clarified. The interesting question is whether it would it have made any difference if they had been – in other words, if the 'true facts' had been laid before the public, as Morel demanded.

In an article published in the *New York Tribune*, nine months after the start of war, Morel wrote, 'Germany's supreme interest is peace, and when you have said all that there is to be said about her national faults and of her conduct of the war, the solid fact remains that this powerful nation had for forty and four years kept the peace when war broke out last August.'[158] However true this may have been it is not unreasonable to feel that Morel was remarkably naive in placing so much emphasis on Germany's peaceful intentions, in view of von Schlieffen's 'think-note' on the invasion of France, the increasing militarisation of society and the significant increase in armaments which indicated that by then the situation had deteriorated. In fact, the two opposing coalitions were fundamentally unstable and an increasing source of tension, and the devastating power of the technological advances in naval and military weapons gave them special credence, as adjuncts to the political process. The operational planners in the German General Staff had never abandoned the idea of war, but its outbreak was determined by the political agenda of all the participating nations. Even this most frustrating and intractable of conflicts conformed with Clausewitz's dictum that 'war…is a true political instrument, a continuation of political activity by other means.'[159]

The UDC was convinced that if there had been a more open and measured foreign policy, hostilities could have been avoided. Morel's pamphlet, *How the War Began*, published in 1914, and later included in *Truth and the War*, developed his private verdict that 'you are all guilty – everyone.' As we have seen, his main task was to show that there had been nothing in German policy before 1914 to indicate that it wished to engage in a pre-emptive war to subjugate Europe. To represent it as the sole aggressor was therefore unjust; rather the five major European powers all bore responsibility for the conflict.

Morel also felt that a fair settlement at the end of the war, leading to a lasting peace, could only be achieved if this analysis was accepted. In 1915 he wrote:

> The more deeply rooted becomes the belief that Germany is the sole responsible author of the war…the more will public opinion gravitate towards the 'unconditional surrender' policy; and that policy means an indefinite prolongation of the war and, consequently, an immense loss of life…and is a policy which means a bad settlement, a settlement which would settle nothing…which would pave the way for fresh convulsions, and which, both in its external and internal implications, would, in the ultimate resort, bring disaster upon the British Commonwealth.[160]

In this judgement he showed remarkable foresight; in the event, the Treaty of Versailles, negotiated on the premise of Germany's sole culpability, was to have a devastating impact on the future course of history in Europe.

The rapid manner in which opposition to the war disintegrated across Europe in the weeks before its outbreak was particularly galling to Morel. Governments were able to bring an end to peace only because of the weakness of the anti-war political forces, and because the majority of the population acquiesced. Up to the beginning of August, opposition to British involvement had been widespread, and all the Liberal newspapers opposed intervention, as did the majority of Liberal MPs. However, once Germany threatened Belgium and France, and the Cabinet had committed itself, the Commons speedily fell in behind, leaving the opposition leaderless, and with no time to organise a response.[161]

The UDC's persistent campaigning eventually opened a gulf between the Unionists and the Liberal Party, and significantly contributed to the rise of Labour during the First World War. Lloyd George, Prime Minister of the coalition government from 1916-22, was the last of the Liberal Prime Ministers, and the party itself entered into a long and protracted decline. It would be all but a century before it again played any significant role in national politics, this time as the Liberal Democrats in a coalition with the Conservatives.

Support for the goals enshrined in the UDC programme essentially came from the far left of the British electorate, and although the Labour Party officially defended the war, internationalism remained a strong force within the ranks of Labour; for instance, British delegates had voted enthusiastically for various anti-war resolutions adopted at meetings of the Second International. As a result, the UDC liberals transferred their loyalty to the party which embraced their foreign policy views, and the founders of the UDC gradually came to the conclusion that their best interests lay in association with the Labour Party.

Morel's own relationship with the Liberal Party was particularly painful. As we have seen, he had been selected as its candidate for Birkenhead, but once his views on the war were expressed in public he had been forced to resign his candidature. For some time he probably continued to imagine himself a Liberal, as did a number of his associates, but as he became increasingly disenchanted with the party's policy and leadership, he too began to contemplate an alternative allegiance.

Meanwhile, a dedicated staff helped him to run the UDC office, which at various times moved between locations in Central London. Morel's early biographer, Seymour Cocks, was one of the Union's London organisers, and received an annual salary of £260. On William Cadbury's advice, and to ward off suspicions that he was subsidised by Germany, Morel requested that the UDC should pay him as well, and it subsequently granted him a stipend of £350 a year from the beginning of August 1915. As the UDC expanded, it also hired additional organisers on a part-time basis, paying them up to £3 a week. Between three and six women secretaries worked in the office, which Morel managed with ruthless efficiency, opening all correspondence himself. Marvin Swartz writes that his zeal for the cause of the UDC affected the girls, producing an admiration for their demanding chief and generating an enthusiasm which resulted in long hours of overtime, often unpaid. Later, when Morel was imprisoned for five months in 1917, the UDC was described as 'a ship adrift without power or rudder until its captain returned.'[162]

If Morel's organisational accomplishments were impressive, his written contributions to the UDC's activist campaign were even more critical to its success. His prodigious output was undoubtedly repetitious, but the relentless regularity of his polemic was precisely what upset the authorities, for it provided an unwavering focus for anti-war sentiment. In his introduction to *Thoughts on the War*, Robert Smillie, founder member of the Independent Labour Party and later MP for Morpeth, wrote that he had probably read Morel's articles and speeches as they appeared, but on sitting down to reread them found that 'every sentence, every line, almost every word shone out with greater clearness. They brought home with increased force the full meaning of Morel's aims and his simple truth, the bedrock on which he founded the structure of his faith, "There never has been and there never will be a just war."'[163] As always, it was acknowledged by both friends and critics that Morel's work showed remarkable integrity.

After his death in 1924 the philosopher and pacifist Bertrand Russell wrote, 'I respected and loved him as much as any man I have ever known.' And a decade later, 'No other man known to me has had the same heroic simplicity in pursuing and proclaiming political truth'.[164]

During the war years, Morel worked so unremittingly that that his friends worried that he would ruin his health. In 1916, Ponsonby confided to Trevelyan, 'I do wish EDM could absorb himself in other subjects and have other writing on hand quite unconnected with the war. It would be an advantage for his own peace of mind. It is fatal to be *l'homme d'une seule idée*.'[165] It is questionable whether Ponsonby can actually have known Morel very well if he thought it possible that he would distract himself from his appointed task by giving his attention to a little light reading! Unfortunately, however, his anxiety turned out to be entirely justified, and around October 1916 Morel's doctor ordered him to take a month's rest. As Morel described it, he had experienced a fainting fit and gone down like a poll-axed bullock, 'an awful crash: most absurd.' This appears to be at least his second collapse; he had also passed out on a train some six months earlier. This is the first time that Morel's health appears as a matter of serious concern.[166]

The End of the *African Mail* [167]

John Holt died in June 1915 at the age of seventy-four, shortly before Morel ended his long association with the *African Mail*. In a letter to Casement written two years earlier, Morel had described how he and Mary had been to visit him in Lincolnshire after he had had a stroke, and found him badly affected, paralysed all down one side and confined to a wheelchair.[168] And now he was gone. Morel had been closely associated with Holt for over twenty years, and the loss of one of the most influential and loyal people in his life, who had provided both moral and financial support over such a long period, must have caused him extreme sadness. He had held Holt's views in great respect, and had placed considerable weight on his knowledge of Africa. In his obituary in the July edition of the *African Mail* he wrote with admiration of the fortitude Holt and his generation had shown in the early days of trading enterprise on the continent:

> Before the European Governments had begun the process of partitioning Africa and 'civilizing' the natives, he and his prototypes were living amongst the latter, trusting them and being trusted by them; alone and unprotected, dealing fairly and justly, else indeed

their lives had not been worth a day's purchase. For who was to come to their rescue if trouble arose? There were no punitive expeditions in those days to avenge the real or imaginary wrongs of [suffered by] the white man.

By the time of Holt's death, however, Morel's editorship of the *African Mail* was becoming increasingly incompatible with his role in the UDC. In October 1915, after eight years of publication, the paper's advertising manager, Nolan, wrote to Brabner, the Honorary Treasurer of the CRA, telling him that the paper was now running at a loss. He suggested a general meeting should be called to explain the position and convince the shareholders voluntarily to pass a resolution to wind up the paper. Nolan also made it clear to Brabner that advertisers had withdrawn their support on account of Morel's opposition to the war and his work with the UDC. In fact, Brabner learnt subsequently that Lord Scarborough, chairman of the Niger Company, had been putting it about that the company should cease supporting the paper because of Morel's attitude to the war.

Nolan described himself as being at his wits' end to find a job, and suggested that Morel might give him a letter of introduction. 'My only regret will be,' he wrote, 'that I am severing my connection with the one man in the world that I could always be proud to serve.' Alternatively, he thought there was a chance that he might be able to keep the paper going under a different name as a trade organ if he could persuade the West African traders in Liverpool that Morel had cut all his connections and no longer had anything to do with it. Brabner, for his part, was doubtful whether the Liverpool traders would entrust Nolan with such a task.

Morel wrote to Brabner saying that he now felt aloof from the whole thing and was no longer interested one way or another in the paper's survival; his only concern was for the future of Nolan. In his reply to Nolan, Morel made it clear that he was willing to withdraw from the editorship and leave the field clear for him to do what he thought best. Otherwise his letter offered little comfort, although he provided Nolan with a glowing reference. In the event, Morel resigned the editorship of the paper at the end of 1915, and Nolan stayed on in the post of Business Manager, having convinced the shareholders of his ability to keep the publication going.

Morel's resignation from the *African Mail* was the most obvious indication that he had moved on decisively from the Congo campaign and all that was associated with it. By the time he gave up his editorship, he was concentrating almost exclusively on his work with the UDC.

After more than a year of conflict, the war in Europe had already claimed hundreds of thousands of lives, and the struggle had descended into stalemate. The combatant armies' offensive forces were exhausted and a huge barrier had opened up in Europe. As John Keegan puts it, 'the new frontier resembled the *limes* (fortifications) of the Roman Legions, an earthwork barrier separating a vast military empire from the outside world. Nothing indeed had been seen like it in Europe since Rome – not under Charlemagne, not under Louis XIV, not under Napoleon – nor would it again until the outbreak of the Cold War thirty years into the future.'[169] This enormous fortification, which was both offensive and defensive, stretched for nearly 1,300 miles, and the Western Front settled into a battle of attrition along a trench line that was to change little until 1917. Between them the Western and Eastern fronts would claim millions more lives.

British Society and the War

The entire mechanism of international relationships is based upon the permanence of the institution of War...Let us change all this. We have it in our power to do so if we will.

E D Morel

Thoughts on the War: the Peace – and Prison, 1920

Morel's book, *Truth and the War*, which was described as 'poisonous' and caused a massive furore, is in fact a collection of speeches, articles and letters, concluding with a lengthy peroration in a form of blank verse to the 'Belligerent Governments'. It is dedicated to Morel's sons, 'in the hope that they may help to free humanity from the curse of militarism and war,' and covers a period of around eighteen months following the outbreak of the conflict. The text addresses a wide variety of issues, ranging from the question of German responsibility for the war to secret diplomacy, from an appeal to President Wilson to Russian military preparations, and from the interests of Belgium to a plea for sanity.

In his report to the first annual meeting of the General Council of the UDC, given towards the end of 1915,[170] Morel recognised that the atmosphere in the country was far from conducive to the promotion of the UDC's cause. Indeed he declared that opposition to the aims of the UDC was sufficient to depress even the most committed campaigner. Nonetheless, in spite of the calumny and misrepresentation that had been heaped upon the organisation from all quarters, it had become, as Morel described it, 'a plant of vigorous growth'. Sixty-six members were present at the council meeting. They included five MPs, amongst them Ramsay MacDonald, three members of the aristocracy and five clergymen. Towns and cities from all around Britain were represented: Glasgow, Liverpool, Newcastle, Bradford, Portsmouth, Bournemouth, Letchworth, London, and Manchester among them. There were also delegates from Ireland, and ten other branches sent their apologies for absence.

The first edition of the UDC's monthly paper, somewhat confusingly also called the *U.D.C.*, included an article on Bulgaria joining the war and entering 'into the ranks of our enemies', another on 'The Voice of Reason in Germany', and a review of two books: one fiction and the other non-fiction by Charles Trevelyan, MP. The first, *The Human Slaughter House*, 'only takes a hundred pages to strip the mask off the horror, and the reader is made to feel how little a thing is the virtue of heroism compared with the brutality of fear and cruelty, and writhing flesh and death and insanity.' The second, *The Soul of War*, described as 'partly a simple narrative, and partly an impression of Belgians, French and British under the stress of war,' deals with war as 'all men see it who are not poring over maps at the end of telephone wires at headquarters.'

The next eleven editions of the U.D.C., published over the 1915/16 period, continued in much the same vein, reporting on the organisation's campaign and the progress of the war. In the tenth issue Trevelyan reviewed Morel's *Truth and the War*, remarking that although the form of the book was not altogether perfect, its message was coherent and pertinent. 'It is principally a collection of all the articles and pamphlets which Mr Morel has written since the war began. But it has essential unity and a single spirit. Everyone who wants to form a just judgement of the war ought to read the last chapters on the "Betrayal of the Nation".'[171] Governments, newspapers, and most of the writers of the belligerent nations, he continued, were still united in an unqualified denunciation of their enemies. It was still official heresy to suggest that partial, even if secondary, responsibility for the outbreak of war rested with Britain. It was depressing to find that the mass of people in the country was almost unaware of a peace movement in its midst, in spite of much fine writing, investigative journalism, meetings and speeches, and the commitment and passion of Morel, the UDC and its supporters.

This insensibility was relatively recent. The idea that British society was strongly jingoistic in the run up to the war, and that the population was longing to 'have a go' at the Germans, has largely been refuted in recent literature on Britain during the war years.[172] In fact, strident nationalistic rhetoric was a late development in Britain, and until hostilities actually commenced there is little evidence to suggest that British people had harboured any enthusiasm for entering the war. To the contrary, anti-German feeling was not as rampant as might have been expected. On the eve of war the *Manchester Guardian*'s London correspondent could still write that, 'What seemed almost unanimous was that no one seemed to want war. There were no war songs or war talk except by way of a joke or forecast. The "we don't want war" that we hear so often should be made into a song to counter the jingo one.'[173]

Much of the provincial press, both Liberal and Unionist, also demonstrated a strong preference for neutrality. Liberals and socialists agreed that the only purpose served by an Anglo-German war would be to place Europe at the mercy of Russian autocracy. Most organised manifestations of public opinion towards the war were pro-neutrality and anti-war as well. The *Daily Chronicle* described the large socialist demonstration in Trafalgar Square on 2nd August 1914 as being 'completely unanimous in passing a resolution deploring the impotence to which the democracy of Germany had been reduced, and called on the British government in the first place to prevent the spread of war, and in the second to see that the country was not dragged in to the conflict.'[174] At the same demonstration Robert Smillie even promised that his miners would back any European-wide commitment to try and stop the war.

All this was changed when Germany invaded Belgium. It had long been acknowledged that the defeat of France would be disastrous for Britain; as Asquith, the Prime Minister, put it, 'It is against British interests that France should be wiped out as a great power…we cannot allow Germany to use the Channel as a hostile base.'[175] The Foreign Office, however, had always considered that the decision to intervene on behalf of France would be 'more easily arrived at if German aggressiveness entailed a violation of the neutrality of Belgium', since such an invasion would make the possibility of a German attack on Britain an immediately threatening prospect. The German assault on Belgium therefore provided an excuse for the Liberals (and most particularly for Lloyd George, who had already decided that Germany had to be resisted) to take the country to war. At this point the TUC and the Labour Party fell in behind the government and also declared their support for the conflict, but it was primarily Liberal politicians and, to a lesser extent Liberal newspaper editors, who guaranteed that anti-war sentiment remained marginalised after the outbreak of hostilities.

However vigorous Morel's 'plant' had become, it was fortunate to survive at all in this environment. Although the UDC was considered to be the most successful organisation in uniting the diverse disaffected groups, it is difficult to disagree with the view that political dissent was carried out by mainly fringe ideologues who maintained a lonely and futile opposition to the government.[176] Bertrand Russell summed this up many years later in his autobiography:

> When the War was over, I saw that all I had done had been totally useless except to myself. I had not saved a single life or shortened the War by a minute. I had not succeeded in doing anything to diminish

the bitterness which caused the Treaty of Versailles. But at any rate I had not been an accomplice in the crime of all the belligerent nations, and for myself I had acquired a new philosophy and a new youth.[177]

This 'lonely and futile opposition' consisted of a group of dedicated and committed people, largely made up of pacifists, socialists and feminists, and later joined by some members of the Labour Party, when Labour became part of the coalition in March 1915. But its existence ensured that political protest was kept alive, despite the prohibition against spreading dissent, and the terms of the Defence of the Realm Act passed on 8th August – an act that amply demonstrated how swiftly an otherwise liberal and anti-interventionist government could establish strong mechanisms for social control.

Nonetheless, all opposition soon became the focus of widespread animosity and public hostility, and many of Morel's closest friends and admirers who had previously felt his pre-war stance to be imprudent, now considered that it was positively reckless. In Seymour Cocks's opinion, they thought that the position he had adopted, particularly in his criticism of Grey and the Foreign Office, would raise 'an unyielding wall of prejudice and passion, incurring a storm of unpopularity, the extreme violence of which he might perhaps have mitigated had he taken a more discreet and diplomatic course.'[178] Dr Scott Lidgett, Methodist minister and long-time supporter of Morel and the CRA, expressed what many of his friends felt when he wrote to Morel at the end of 1915, shortly after one of the UDC's meetings had been broken up.[179] He said how sorry he was to hear of the disruption of the meeting but he could not help feeling that 'you only weaken your case and discount your influence in advance by statements like that about diplomats'.[180] Surely, he went on, Morel recognised the gallant fight which the British and French diplomats made in the summer of 1914 to avoid war!

Even Conan Doyle, who before the war had been a member of an Anglo-German Society, withdrew his support, although he declared that he didn't think there was much use in arguing with Morel, as it would only deepen a growing rift between them. 'I am convinced,' he wrote, 'Britain will be nearly ruined in this war. But she will preserve her honour and her self-respect. On any other hypothesis she would within a little time have lost her place in the world and the rest as well…I am truly sorry about it, but I have said and done all I could, so will bother you no more.'[181] C P Scott, editor of the *Manchester Guardian* wrote, 'You have said what you thought about the origins of the war – that's over –

now we have got to deal first with the prosecution of it, which is not in controversy, and then with the time and the terms for stopping it, which is a new problem and the one for which we must next prepare.' He urged Morel not to send out further copies of the pamphlet outlining the UDC's manifesto, or take any action at the present time, and to wait until he saw how the war was going. Finally, he wrote towards the end of September, saying that he could not join the committee: 'I agree with your objects but I should be apt to part company with you as to the methods – so I'm better out of it.'[182]

Ramsay MacDonald, in a letter from his home at Lossiemouth, also expressed caution in the light of what appeared to be a series of impending calamities. 'I was quite convinced (by C P Scott) that should they happen it would be a great mistake to run the risk of continuing to issue the pamphlet, so urgently required as it is from other points of view...I also found that some of the most important people who were willing to cooperate with us were viewing the publication of the pamphlet with grave concern.' In the same letter he wrote that a friend had come to see him recently who was not well known locally. A report, which was believed, went round that he was the German Emperor, who had arrived secretly by aeroplane. 'If someone had said that he was Morel of the Congo my house would have been blown up. The Kaiser's wickedness is known, Morel's would have been supplied by imagination.'[183]

As the war progressed, the UDC began to be attacked continuously as 'pro-German', 'defeatist', an exponent of 'peace at any price', and there were times when its meetings were met with heckling and disorder, possibly incited by officers and recruiting authorities. There were other occasions when gatherings were stormed by soldiers who 'were invited to break the heads of "pro-Germans"'.[184] The authorities reacted to these incidents simply by describing them as outbreaks of popular indignation, although some protested to the Prime Minister that the UDC was aiding and abetting the enemy. Under political pressure, local authorities and the police denied the UDC access to halls and meeting places.

Anger against individuals perceived to be active in the anti-war movement intensified. The District Council of Elland, Charles Trevelyan's Yorkshire constituency, was reported to have gone so far as to pass a resolution 'that Mr Trevelyan be taken out and shot.' Trinity College, Cambridge, deprived Bertrand Russell of his lectureship, and the headmaster of Eton, who had spoken of the advantages of a compromise peace, was forced to resign. But soon such senior casualties became little more than the tip of an iceberg. As the government propaganda machine gathered momentum, public opinion in defence of the war hardened, and patriotic fervour became widespread. Dissidents and conscientious objectors alike were excoriated as cowards, and scorn and loathing was increasingly directed towards them. Ramsay MacDonald, who himself had been barred from his golf club, wrote to Trevelyan that people believed the UDC was selling the country, and that members of the UDC were tainted as with leprosy.[185]

During the ensuing years of the war, there were few who would be as reserved in their judgement of Morel's activities as Doyle, Scott and Ramsay MacDonald. The *Daily Express*, under the editorship of Ralph Blumenfeld, made continuous 'pro-German' allegations against Morel and the UDC. The *New Witness* likewise constantly denigrated the UDC and particularly Morel. Sir George Makgill, professional patriot and Honorary Secretary of the Anti-German Union, pursued Morel remorselessly. Indeed, although Morel's total integrity, honesty and sincerity were widely acknowledged by all who knew him, his enemies employed every means they could find to revile him, amongst others attacking him for changing his name and his 'foreign birth', overlooking that he had been born in an allied country. The *Daily Express* went so far as to carry a headline 'Who is Mr E D Morel? And who pays for his pro-German union?'

The charge of 'traitor' began to be used against him. Early in 1915, for example, he received two postcards, one addressed to Mr E D Morel (The Democratic Union of Dirty Sneaks and Traitors). 'How much,' it asked, 'does the German Emperor pay you and the other traitors for your dirty work?…cowardly hounds…' The message on the second anonymous card read, 'It is to be hoped you and your dirty colleagues will be shot as traitors after the war is over. You deserve it.' Haunted by the dogs of war, jingoism and conformity, Morel made enemies and lost friends. He later wrote that he had become one of the 'best-abused men in the British Isles'. No dishonour too profound, no motive too base, that it had not been attributed to him.[186]

This pervasive vilification profoundly affected Morel, for despite his fervour he was a sensitive man who felt injustice deeply. His friend, Henry Nevinson, who had known him for many years, was clearly dismayed by his evident distress. 'Once when I was at home on short leave from the Dardanelles,' he wrote, 'I happened to meet him [Morel] in the Strand and he passed me with a cold nod. I ran after him and asked what was the matter between us, and with tears in his eyes (for he never had the average Englishman's way of suppressing the signs of emotion) he replied: 'I did not suppose that anyone would speak to me now.'[187]

Little is known about the effect that this barrage of calumny must have had on Morel's family. Living some distance from London before the radio/TV era, Mary would not have been subject to a fraction of the intrusion that today's media would bring, but it is unlikely that Morel shielded her from copies of papers such as the *Daily Express*, and she cannot have been immune to charges that her husband was a traitor and that he must be in the pay of the Germans. Sadly there is no record of her feelings over these years, but her loyal support for Morel has never been questioned. With four children and one on the way (Oliver, the youngest, was born in 1916), she must undoubtedly have been very busy; fortunately she appeared to enjoy excellent health, but however diverted and robust she may have been, it must have been a deeply stressful period for the whole family. Stella and Roger, the two eldest children, were now in their mid to late teens and both at boarding schools, and the fact that their father was being denounced as a traitor cannot have made life among their contemporaries a comfortable experience.

It is unclear whether Morel travelled daily from Kings Langley to the London office of the UDC. Cherry Croft was quite a large house with plenty of space for a reasonable office, and it is likely that at least a part of his secretarial work was undertaken from home. If so, this must have afforded him some small respite from the growing vituperation that he faced throughout the country. The journalist Douglas Goldring, who got to know Morel following the war, wrote that 'His house and garden, his wife and family, his roses and the man himself all combined to create an atmosphere of peace, love and loyalty which must have impressed everyone who visited them.'[188] But however loving and supportive life was in the family, there can be little doubt that the combination of an enormous workload and an atmosphere of extreme public hostility bore down on him, and in association with an undiagnosed heart complaint caused his fainting fits.

It is tempting to agree with Bertrand Russell that Morel, Norman Angell, Arthur Ponsonby and others, were naively ambitious. Although he was sympathetic to the UDC, Russell remarked that this group seemed, 'like eight fleas talking of building a pyramid'[189] when they plotted means to end the war. This profound feeling of pessimism was well expressed by a UDC supporter, Malcolm Quin. In a letter in the November 1916 edition of the *U.D.C.* he urged members to face the plain truth that the great majority of people cared little for the cause of peace, and that the war policy of imperialism was popular and unchallenged by any of the parties, Conservative, Liberal, Nationalist or Labour. Under the circumstances he felt that the most effective role for the UDC could only lie in the post-war future, since any hope of influencing the terms of peace was also illusory. 'The men who have made the war will make the peace – unless they are deprived of their power as the result of some unforeseen catastrophe.'[190]

Morel, on the contrary, felt that the governing class and its supportive press had no idea that there was universal war weariness in Britain, and considered that it would be possible for millions of British citizens to change their outlook. This was a conflict waged in horrific conditions that was taking the lives of millions of men in Europe, and submitting to a council of despair in the name of some assumed aggressive national sentiment was simply not an option for him. His passionate sense of outrage, and the almost unbearable distress he felt in the face of the suffering caused by the war, are both moving and persuasive, but at the same time he undoubtedly misjudged the mood of the country. Just as he had chosen to ignore the strategic rationale for Grey's care not to offend Belgium when he was campaigning for reform in the Congo, so he now appeared to have made himself oblivious to the true nature of public opinion in Britain.

Yet in many ways Morel was far from a blinkered or a rigid thinker. His political views had developed and changed very considerably as he grew older, and had become much more radical by the time war broke out. His correspondence with Edward Driffill during this period shows particularly clearly how far he had moved to the left. Driffill contacted Morel in August 1916 to say that he had read *Ten Years of Secret Diplomacy* and *Truth and the War*. Obviously a great admirer of Morel (he reported in a footnote that he had sold sixty copies of *Truth and the War* in ten days), he wrote saying that he believed Morel's deduction was correct but that it didn't go far enough. He thought that the occurrence of 'secret diplomacy' was more an effect than a cause. In his view, it was one of the methods used by international financiers to attain their purpose, which was the investment of wealth in undeveloped countries when no suitable alternative could be found at home. 'The ring of financiers of every country are on the hunt for "cent per cent",' he wrote, 'the diplomats back them up and the armies and navies are there to fall back upon when two or more of these rings happen to tread on each others toes or get angry.'[191]

He went on to ask whether Morel did not think that imperial capitalism was the cause of the war? Were not secret diplomacy, militarism and the fear generated between peoples, the tools of capitalism? If that was the case, surely Morel should be upholding the ideal of the destruction of economic competition and its substitution by national and international cooperation? And if Morel held such progressive opinions surely he should become a socialist?

Morel replied, welcoming Driffill's letter. He said that he recognised that national rivalry was largely, though not wholly, economic and industrial, and there was also a dynastic and professional element. Open diplomacy couldn't remove the causes of war, he wrote, but it could work to mitigate those causes. 'Thousands of enlightened and powerful minds would be brought to bear upon their solution and an informed public would insist upon a solution being found.' On the other hand, he didn't think that the war should be used as a vehicle for a socialist revolution, nor did he want the UDC to be seen as an arm of Labour Party politics. He was certain that little could be achieved on the reform front as long as the war remained a threat to Britain. As for being a socialist, he continued, if what Driffill meant by socialism was working for the betterment and increased happiness of humanity, how could he imagine that he, Morel, was anything but a socialist? The unjust and dangerous use of capitalism must be attacked from a thousand sides. It was a hydra-headed monster and must be undermined and sapped in every possible way.

This declaration points to the overt break he was soon to make with the Liberal Party. In his adoption speech to the Birkenhead Liberal Association in 1914 he had publicly declared a more equitable distribution of wealth to be an essential prerequisite of Liberalism, but in identifying himself as a Socialist in his correspondence with Driffill, it appeared he no longer believed in that corollary, and had moved definitively to the left. Over the years, the widening gulf that had opened up between the UDC and the Liberal Party, together with the creation of the coalition government and the failure of that government to pursue any policies for a negotiated peace, had finally brought about his disenchantment. 'Nothing would induce me to stand in with any members of the gang which have brought the country to our present pass. I would never recognise Asquith or Lloyd George, or Grey, or Churchill as my chiefs to whom I owed allegiance.'[192]

In abandoning the Liberal Party Morel was left with the Independent Labour Party (ILP) as the only political organisation which shared his views, and had stuck with its pre-war resolutions to oppose the country's participation in war. It had become a valuable ally of the UDC, who used its press and networks to advance its policies. The ILP, socialist and working class, was very much on the left wing of the Labour Party, and although it sought to recruit its middle class UDC allies, Morel and his colleagues never committed themselves to it. This was very aptly commented upon by Lenin, who observed that E D Morel was a member of the 'pacifist bourgeoisie' who imagined that his international goals could be realised 'without revolutionary actions on the part of the proletariat.'[193] Yet in a way Morel also appreciated that little could be achieved until the democracies of the West realised the impossibility of having a system of government which left them at the mercy of 'the intrigues and imbecilities of professional diplomatists and the ambition of military castes; and helpless in the face of enormously powerful and internationalised private interest dependent for its profits upon the maintenance of that "armed peace", which is the inevitable prelude to the carnage and futility of war.' [194]

This was all very well, but in the here and now of Britain at war, there was little chance of such insight developing. Nor were the social conditions in the country conducive to their evolution. It may seem unreasonable to suggest that a man as compassionate as Morel, who now openly avowed socialist principles and had so clearly pronounced them to his prospective constituents, overlooked the conditions of the working class at the beginning of the 20th century, but it does seem that he underestimated their effect on the mood of the nation. The material circumstances of much of the British population in 1914 could be compared today to conditions in the informal urban settlements in the less developed world: poor health, insecurity, absolute poverty and hopelessness. 'No view of the horrors of the First World War can be complete without a sense of the horrors of the pre-war peace.'[195]

In spite of the Liberal government's welfare reforms between 1906 and 1914 – covering workers, the elderly and children – the conditions of the poor in society remained lamentable. In a study of working class families in 1913[196] it was observed that the proportion of the infantile death rate of upmarket Hampstead to that of Hoxton was 18 to 140. Of the thirty-nine families taken from within the investigation and of the thirty-one outside it with three or more children, the average child death rate was 28%. Wages were in the region of twenty shillings per week, roughly £2 an hour for a forty-five-hour week in today's terms. The chief item in every budget was rent, which could absorb anything up to a third of this sum, perhaps securing only one good upstairs room, or two damp, dark and badly ventilated basement rooms. Little was left for anything other than the sparsest of diets, fuel, bus fares, burial insurance and other essential items. In effect, such grinding poverty meant that life in the forces was increasingly perceived as preferable to a bleak struggle for existence in a working class community at home. Economic hardship thus boosted recruitment figures, which in turn fostered a rise in sentiments of militarism and nationalism within the population.

Casement

During the final years of the Congo campaign Morel and Casement remained in touch, with Casement the main correspondent. Although communication between them was less frequent than before, each kept abreast of the other's work and progress.

In 1910 Grey again sent Casement to investigate allegations made in public of widespread atrocities, this time those committed against Amerindian communities in north-west Amazon. His report, published in 1911, was a devastating exposé of the appalling rubber scandal among the Putumayo Indians in Peru, and it shocked both public and political commentators. Henry Nevinson wrote in *The Nation* in July 1912 that 'We bear in mind only too clearly the misery of the Congo under Leopold's regime; we know well the atrocious system of slavery in Portuguese Angola...But in the cool atmosphere of an official document...we have never read anything to compare for horror with Sir Roger Casement's detailed and substantiated account of rubber-collecting by agents of a British Company under the rule of the Peruvian government.'[197] As noted earlier, this report also occasioned much admiration in a letter from Morel. At the dissolution of the CRA in June 1913 he again took the opportunity to praise Casement for his great contribution to the cause of reform. 'That Consul, that man of noble and generous mind, whose Report, so affecting in its details, yet so temperate in its presentment, so appalling in its implications, yet clothed in such sobriety of language that it moved even the habitual insensibilities of diplomacy.'[198]

In 1916, however, Casement's life and reputation changed dramatically. Casement had retired from the consular service in 1913 and had spent the next three years helping to form the Irish Volunteers. The Irish Volunteers had split in 1914, with 175,000 Volunteers following Redmond's call to join the British Army's Irish regiments as the National Volunteers. The rump of the Irish Volunteers had, by one account, only 13,500 men left, and just before the outbreak of war Casement had travelled to the US to promote their cause and raise money for their activities. Whilst there he had also arranged a meeting in New York with the German diplomat Count von Bernstorff, and had proposed to him that if Germany would sell guns to the Irish rebels and provide military leaders, the rebels would stage a revolt against the English, thereby diverting troops and attention from the war against Germany. The Germans cannot have been greatly impressed by this proposal, as it was not until April 1916 that the Irish were offered weapons and ammunition. Casement himself did not learn of the Easter Rising[199] in Dublin until after the offer of German support was made, and in the event the German arms were never landed, as the ship transporting them was intercepted by the Royal Navy following intelligence reports received from Washington. Meanwhile, Casement travelled to Ireland in a German submarine, and was put ashore three days before the rising in Tralee Bay in County Kerry where he was almost immediately detained.

The uprising was put down in a matter of weeks, and most of the ringleaders were summarily executed on British military orders. Casement was charged with treason and brought to Dublin, and subsequently taken to England where he was eventually put in military custody in the Tower of London. In the middle of May he was placed under civil authority and sent to Bow Street Magistrates Court where he was committed for trial on the 26th June at the Old Bailey, and then taken to Brixton prison.

It is impossible to believe that these events meant nothing to Morel. In spite of Casement's mild rebuke about his confrontation with the Foreign Office, both men remained on excellent terms, and were still united in their approach to most of the issues that mutually concerned them at the time of Casement's arrest. Indeed it seems from Morel's speech to his prospective constituents in Birkenhead that even their views on Ireland coincided to a considerable extent.

The whole sequence of Casement's downfall, from his activities in Germany and his support for the uprising in Dublin, to his capture at Tralee Bay and his ultimate trial and execution, must have affected Morel most profoundly, but unfortunately there is no record of his reaction to the tragedy, other than a passing remark in a letter to Trevelyan that it was 'a beastly complication'.[200] The loss of Morel's family correspondence is regrettable in every respect, but it is especially sad that nothing remains to indicate his private feelings during this extraordinarily harrowing time. Because of Casement's close association with the CRA in the past, his predicament inevitably threatened to bring down further opprobrium upon the UDC and its secretary, and in the public arena Morel remained silent. Nor did he risk any face-to-face contact. Whilst Casement was in Brixton awaiting his trial, he was visited by friends and relatives – but Morel was not among them.

The closest we can come to an intimate explanation of his reasons for not visiting Casement are given in a lengthy confidential letter to Mrs J R Green (Alice Stopford Green), written towards the end of May 1916. In it, he declared that if he had obeyed his own personal feelings he would have responded at once and applied for permission to visit, but he felt he could not act only on those feelings as 'I am associated with a number of honourable men to whose views I am bound to pay attention.'[201] He also said that as he was connected with a movement which he and his colleagues regarded as of immense political importance to the country, he dared not do anything to jeopardise either the UDC or the people involved with it. He added that he had consulted with Trevelyan and Ponsonby, both of whom felt certain that an application to visit would have the worst construction put upon it, adversely affecting the public attitude towards the UDC. He suggested that neither Casement, nor Miss Bannister, his cousin, who had written asking if he would visit Casement, could appreciate how invidious his position was: 'I would not for the world add to the terrible burden he (Casement) is now bearing, by giving him this further source of trouble... The whole movement with which I am connected is faced with implacable enemies...and has led to the concentration of hatred upon me.'

It was undoubtedly true that all those hostile to Morel's cause would have claimed any visit he made to Casement as further proof of his treasonable intent. Casement had rebelled against the state with the support of Germany whilst Britain was at war, and the fact that such support had not been forthcoming was irrelevant. He had also been a champion of the CRA, and sections of the press had even suggested that the CRA had been nothing but a front for plans to transfer Belgian territory in Africa to Germany. Nonetheless, Morel obviously felt guilty about the course he was adopting, and added that he hoped Mrs Green would not think him 'a moral coward'. He also suggested that if she were in his position she might have acted in a similar manner.

Alice Stopford Green wrote back saying that she quite understood Morel's position and appreciated that the situation was one of extreme difficulty, 'in which every obligation has to be give its due place', and she promised to write to Miss Bannister. After visiting Casement in July she wrote again to Morel, saying that 'he told me he thought you were quite right to have accepted the decision of your colleagues...there was no question about it.' In the letter she speaks of Casement's gentle dignity, serenity, his confidence in his friends and absence of distrust. One can only pity Morel in his intractable dilemma, for in many ways he must have longed to confirm Casement's confidence in his 'dear Bulldog' by casting caution aside and visiting him in prison. Such a course would certainly have been a gesture of defiance to Morel's opponents, but they would unquestionably have exploited any behaviour that could be seen to link Morel with the rising in Ireland to the detriment of the reputation of the UDC. It is, however, greatly to his wife's credit that she felt herself to be under no such constraint. In a letter to William Cadbury, Morel reported that Mary had asked Mrs Green where to apply for permission to visit Casement. Sadly it seems she received no reply, perhaps as Morel suggested, because it was less than a week before Casement's trial and 'he would rather not see anyone just now'.[202]

It is also possible that suspicions regarding Casement's homosexuality may have contributed to Morel's decision. There is a general agreement that Casement's sexual preferences did not become public knowledge until after his arrest, and the private diaries found at his flat in London came to light only after his conviction and the rejection of the appeal that followed. In the light of this discovery any possibility of a reprieve disappeared, but long before that point rumour had abounded. Henry Nevinson, in an article in *War and Peace*, writes of the attempts made outside the court:

> ...to poison the sense of justice in the public mind. For some weeks before the trial, and in the interval between the sentence and the execution we were aware...of dim figures crawling about the background, whispering scandal, spreading suspicions, sowing hints against the prisoner's private character...one found the poison at every turn. Those who adopted this filthy means of securing the death of the man whom they wished to destroy knew very well that scandal delights in chatter about vice far more than charges about rebellion. Secretly and carefully they disseminated their malice, and malignity had its reward in the victim's doom.[203]

At a time when homosexuality was a crime and regarded in society with revulsion, these were terrible allegations, and it is at least arguable that Morel's reasons for not visiting Casement may have been influenced by a suspicion that they were true, even if he was determined to deny this possibility to himself. Nobody reading Casement's letters to Morel could be in any doubt of the warmth of his feelings for him, and Morel may have thought that his long, and certainly quite emotional, relationship with Casement would be misinterpreted. Indeed it is possible that he felt that he had been both compromised and betrayed. In his letter to Alice Stopford Green he writes of himself as being surrounded by 'honourable men'. Could he have meant this to infer that by contrast Casement had been revealed as dishonourable? It is interesting that in Seymour Cocks's book, *E D Morel, the Man and his Work*, published only a few years later, the only single occasion Casement is mentioned is in relation to the report on the Congo.

Whatever his eventual feelings, Casement's conviction and execution must surely have caused Morel extreme grief. Casement had been a beloved friend who had shared his most passionate hopes and aspirations, and as well as holding him in great affection, Morel had admired him deeply and relied on his judgement, enthusiasm and moral support. Not only to lose him, but to see him disgraced and reviled throughout the country must have been a shattering blow to Morel's own self-confidence and stamina at a time when he was himself the object of widespread abuse. No doubt this new distress contributed to his fainting fits and growing sense of persecution, as the press continued its virulent attacks on the UDC and its Secretary. Strain and despair were beginning to do their work, and his health as well as his spirit was starting to suffer.

To add to his other worries, he had recently become concerned that the government might decide in some way to obliterate him, in order to rid itself, as he put it, of 'the pest in its midst'. In his unfinished manuscript copy of the *History of the Congo Reform Association* he included a flyleaf with directions for its completion 'in case of my death or disappearance'.[204] Unfortunately this fear could not be attributed to mere paranoia; the forces of the establishment were indeed closing in upon him, and his liberty, if not his person, was soon to come under attack.

The Road to Prison

In August 1917 Morel wrote a pamphlet entitled *Tsardom's Part in the War*. Yet again the principal aim was a refutation of the belief that 'Germany *caused* the war: planned, plotted it, and let it loose at the psychological moment, for ends carefully calculated and thought out beforehand.'[205] The idea that the war was a struggle between opposing ideals of government, between autocracy and democracy was rejected. Britain had entered the war as an ally of Russia, one of the most reactionary autocracies that existed anywhere in the world, and remained its ally until the moment it was overthrown. Democracy was a meaningless term when used in connection with a system of government under which the land and wealth of the country were concentrated in relatively few hands, and where the mass of people lived in conditions of extreme poverty.

Morel went on to analyse the circumstances under which the belligerent countries had been drawn into the conflict, pinning much of the blame upon Russia. 'When the crisis of summer 1914 reached its height, Germany was working with England to find a peaceful solution; a way that…would have led the nations out of the quagmire but for the midnight general mobilisation order issued by a corrupt Autocracy' which had precipitated war against England, and also against a Germany working to find a peaceful solution. This autocracy had:

> …since fallen beneath the blows of a long martyred people…Tsardom is dead – never to be resurrected…will not the peoples of Britain, France, Germany, Austria and Italy see in the disappearance of this vast and active force for evil their opportunity to unite with the people of Russia in insisting that the process of mutual extermination from which their governing classes appear incapable of extricating them, shall be stopped and a peace, inspired by the consciousness of collective past errors and by a universal determination to build a cleaner, sounder civilization, arranged?

It is impossible not to concur with almost all that Morel wrote during this period, and the epilogue to the pamphlet is a stirring and anguished call to action. 'Three years of colossal slaughter finds Europe no nearer the solution of the problems which Europe must solve,' he wrote. 'Why not try another method? *Why not confer?*' But as we know, these entreaties fell on deaf ears, and ironically, far from persuading the belligerent governments to confer, the pamphlet turned out to be the tool that enabled the authorities to bring down its author.

Lloyd George's coalition government, which had replaced the Liberal Administration in 1916, proved to be much less tolerant of dissenters than its predecessor. *Truth and the War* had been published in the same year, and had been a success and widely distributed, but although much disliked by the authorities, no action had been taken against its author. Officials in the new government, however, were fearful for the book's effect on public opinion abroad, and sought ways to bring a prosecution against Morel. Two years earlier the Director of Public Prosecutions had expressed fears that, 'in Mr Morel a defendant might be discovered to whom, provided he could secure a larger publicity for his mischievous propaganda, a prosecution might not be unwelcome.'[206] This irritating dilemma was now the concern of officials and lawyers attached to the new administration who also had no doubt as to Morel's command of his facts, and knew that they possessed little hope of proving any of his statements false if they wanted to achieve a conviction.

As it happened, an opportunity to prosecute Morel without subjecting him to public examination soon arose. The alleged offence revolved around an accusation that he had 'incited' a Miss Ethel Sidgewick to take *Tsardom's Part in the War* to the French pacifist Romain Rolland, who was then living in Switzerland. Miss Sidgewick was the niece by marriage of the former Prime Minister Arthur Balfour, who was then serving as Foreign Secretary, and she had written to Morel in the middle of August saying that Rolland and his sister had a profound admiration for Morel's books and international work, and that she constantly heard his name in France.

Morel had replied the following day asking to which book Rolland was referring – was it *Ten Years of Secret Diplomacy* or *Truth and the War?*[207] He said he had sent Rolland both publications, and wondered if he had ever received them. Miss Sidgewick responded that it was unlikely that Rolland had received any books or UDC pamphlets, but she would confirm that with his sister. She said she herself had received a copy of *Truth and the War* in Paris and given it to Rolland's sister to take to him at Easter, together with another book by Bertrand Russell, as the only safe thing to do was to transport such things by hand. She promised to bring a copy of *Africa and the Peace of Europe* when she crossed to Switzerland in October, before which she would attempt to send the U.D.C. paper and some pamphlets concealed in other journals. On 21st August Morel replied, saying he would be grateful to make use of her in October, and asking Miss Sidgewick if she could perhaps smuggle some copies of *Tsardom's Part in the War* across the border.

This suggestion proved to be a grave mistake. The Defence of the Realm Act had made it a criminal act to send, or incite to send, certain printed material to a European neutral country without a permit, unless it was dispatched through the post from the United Kingdom. The authorities duly seized their chance, and on 31st August Morel was charged at Bow Street with contravening the regulations of the Act.

It is clear that Morel had been under close surveillance for some time. His correspondence had been opened, photographed and resealed by the postal censors; Morel's house, Cherry Croft, and the UDC offices in London had been searched; Miss Sidgwick had been witnessed opening Morel's letter of 21st August.[208] The prosecution now maintained that there was 'a clear understanding between the two correspondents to evade the restrictions binding on every man and woman in the country.'

No action, however, was taken against Miss Sidgewick, despite the fact that she had offered to transport the offending pamphlet to Switzerland, and although her relationship by marriage to a past Prime Minister was undoubtedly a factor in the decision not to prosecute her, it also indicated how little the government was actually concerned by the offence, and how much it was motivated by vindictiveness and a determination to silence Morel. His powers as a speaker, his remarkable command of facts and figures and his debating skills had been amply demonstrated over the previous fourteen years, and they were both recognised and feared by his opponents. When the grounds for prosecution arose which would avoid a close examination of the government's foreign policy, the authorities simply took the opportunity to act. It was described as a disgraceful prosecution, showing how formidable Morel had become and how anxious the government was to put him out of the way.[209] In writing about the trial, Morel commented on this injustice. 'Was the dignity of the law ever seen so shrunk? Was the hand of the political opponent ever seen so plain?'

Unjust or not, the government had finally succeeded in temporarily silencing one of its most vociferous critics. It is true to say that the offence was trivial. The regulations which prohibited sending, or getting somebody else to send, such material to neutral countries or to the United States did not apply to allied countries, and if Rolland had not been temporarily resident in Switzerland no regulation would have been breached. But the government had got its quarry and had no intention of releasing it, however weak its case. Bail was refused, and Morel spent four days in Brixton prison. In his *Thoughts on the War – and Prison,* published in 1920, Morel recalled his feelings at the time. 'Bail refused!' he wrote. 'I recalled with an inward smile that a day or two before, bail had been granted to a man who had shot dead another man whom he supposed, rightly or wrongly – I forget the case – to have been his wife's lover. My crime was so much more heinous!' [210] Bail was in fact refused twice whilst he was on remand.

At his trial in September Morel's counsel argued that *Tsardom's Part in the War* was a 'closely reasoned document written with great conviction and great sincerity; its views were unpopular, perhaps, but not illegal. Mr Morel's personal reputation had been acknowledged by "distinguished English people"' and in the past he had worked closely with Foreign Office.[211] The prosecution pressed the case that UDC publications in general 'had been since November 1916 under close supervision and prohibited from exportation', and there was evidence that Morel had smuggled other publications out of England. It argued that to condone the offence might be to establish precedent for far more serious, analogous offences, and declared that it was the court's duty to pass a sentence that would deter others from acting in a similar manner.

In the event Morel was sentenced to six months in the second division, a category of prisoners that afforded a few privileges over the majority of inmates.[212] Returning to Pentonville in the 'black Maria' on a glorious summer's day, Morel recalled the Sussex garden where he had received the warrant for his arrest. He writes that the scent of roses and the smell of the sea air over the Downs came back to him as if in a dream, adding rather poignantly that 'I used to hunt for bee orchids and chase the chalk-hill "blue" on those downs as a school boy – umpty years ago.'[213]

He describes the sensation of self-contempt he experienced in the black Maria, saying that he found himself shrinking into its wooden walls as the gaze of the occupants of a carriage and pair drew level with his own eyes, peering out through the open bars above the door. For Morel the gulf that separated the normal from the criminal world was as impassable as that which divided life from death, and now he was on the wrong side. He had effected the transfer, as he said, from within to without the pale.

Pentonville

Morel's imprisonment for six months in Pentonville brought a further deterioration in his health, and may well have contributed to his premature death in 1924 at the early age of fifty-one. He was in prison for most of the winter months, when it must have been exceedingly cold, and solitary confinement in the cells lasted from 4.00pm to 8.00am. During working hours he was given the unedifying task of sewing mailbags or making rope mats, and exercise was limited to one hour a day. 'Round and round, usually at a snail's pace, for the space is inadequate for the numbers, nominally for an hour, rarely for more than forty-five minutes. It is called "exercise".'[214] The indignity and frustration must have been very hard for a man of exceptional vigour and intelligence to bear, especially one who had devoted so much of his life to the pursuit of justice and truth.

By any standards of justice the six-month sentence was a harsh one. The government's determination to silence Morel was so apparent that there was little need for anybody to embellish the facts of the case in order to establish him as a martyr. His trial and sentence evoked enormous indignation amongst his friends, colleagues and admirers, including those who did not share his view of the war.

In a passionate address to the House of Commons in October 1917, Colonel Wedgewood, MP declared that:

> It is a real national disgrace that we have put Mr Morel into prison…
> it was in 1911 that all the dignitaries of the churches and the members
> of every political party…came together…to thank E D Morel for his
> wonderful services to humanity. Where are those friends now? E D
> Morel has become unpopular. But because he is unpopular I think it
> would be a disgrace to our country for all those who supported him
> when he was triumphant to forget…the debt of gratitude which the
> world owes to this man…The imprisonment of E D Morel will go
> down to succeeding generations as one of the most serious blots on
> the history of this country.[215]

Friends and admirers rallied to the Morels' side. Arthur Ponsonby wrote a letter for circulation to his supporters suggesting that they should write to Sir George Cave, the Home Secretary, and beg for his immediate release.[216] Throughout the period of his imprisonment Mary received a great many expressions of sympathy, offering help and support from all parts of the country. Amongst the wealth of correspondence were letters from Ramsay MacDonald, Charles Trevelyan and Ethel Snowden, wife of the prominent socialist, who wrote, 'We know that right must triumph in the end and that the country will not always be under the dominion of the yellow newspaper editors and corrupt politicians.' Lord Courtney of Penwith also got in touch, expressing his concern that that the motive of the trial was not only to suppress opinion, 'but to lock up in silence anyone who could form an opinion they would like to suppress.' The Honorary Secretary of The Women's International League passed on its Executive Committee's warm sympathy to Mary and asked her to convey a message to Morel, 'assuring him that his courage and public spirit had been an inspiration to them.' Similar letters were sent from branches of the UDC and the Independent Labour Party around the country. Romain Rolland, the innocent recipient of *Truth and the War,* wrote as well, saying that from everything he knew of Morel, '...from his activities previous to the war, from his apostolic struggle against the crimes of civilization in Africa, from his articles, I regard him as a man of fine courage and splendid faith.'

A petition to the Home Secretary was organised in the middle of September requesting that Morel be transferred within the prison from the second to the first division, where conditions were significantly more comfortable. Although it carried the names of twenty-eight people prominent in public life, amongst them Harry Johnston, Lord Courtney, Conan Doyle, the Bishop of Lincoln, Sidney and Beatrice Webb and the Bishop of Oxford, the petition was rejected. This rejection appears to have been an act of vindictiveness, as a transfer should have been allowed under a rule made in 1910 by the Secretary of State, Winston Churchill. The rule permitted the Prison Commissioners to 'allow such amelioration' provided the offender of the second division had not been committed for an offence involving dishonesty, cruelty, indecency or serious violence. The decision to turn down the appeal, as well as a gratuitous raid that the authorities had made on Cherry Croft and the offices of the UDC a month earlier, were clear reflections of the government's determination to exercise their powers to the full while they had an opportunity to do so.

Although Morel had the support of the great majority of his past allies, some, such as Conan Doyle, remained unforgiving about his role at the UDC. Conan Doyle signed the petition, but in a letter to its organisers he wrote, 'Casement by his treason and Morel by his wrongheaded anti-national attitude have between them dragged the Congo Cause in the dirt and turned a beautiful thing into an ugly one...I have signed a petition today that Morel be put in the 1st Class as a prisoner, but for his conduct towards his country I have nothing but horror.' The Archbishop was also approached, but managed to dodge the issue in his usual prevaricating manner. 'I do not know enough of the facts about his recent trial or enough about prison distinctions to justify me in signing a memorial which appears to me to assume on the part of those who sign it a qualification to decide better than the High Court can decide what exactly should be the character of the penalty imposed after a breach of the present law.'

On 9th September Morel appealed against his conviction on the grounds that he was not guilty of the offence, that the conviction was bad 'on the face of it', that it was bad in law, unjust and against the weight of evidence, and that the punishment was excessive. The appeal was not granted.

Correspondence with the outside world was severely limited, and for both the Morels this must have been particularly hard to bear. On 6th September Mary had been informed in a letter from the Governor that Morel would be entitled to write and receive a letter and a visit – for a quarter of an hour only – after the completion of every calendar month of his sentence. The Governor's letter did at least condescend to allow Morel's denture – which presumably he had left at home – to be forwarded to the prison. Writing to Mary on 3rd October Morel remarked, 'It is rather good to remember, now I am permitted to write, that the first time in the last twenty years we have not written one another daily when absent, is clearly due to *force majeure*.' Later on in his sentence, in the middle of November, Arthur Ponsonby persuaded the Home Office to grant fortnightly visits.

Unlike most of his family correspondence, Mary's monthly letters to Morel while he was in prison have survived. She said that these were limited to 800 words each, but as she wrote at greater length on most occasions, it seems that the prison authorities were not particularly censorious. Her letters all display the great affection and admiration she had for her husband, and it is clear that a very close and loving bond united them. Otherwise their content is unremarkable. They bring news of domestic matters, the children, the garden, and the flood of good wishes from friends and admirers, and give updates on the progress of the UDC, and on the progress of the war. They also express grave concern about Morel's health. These letters were obviously a lifeline to Morel, and he noted on the packet in which he kept them that he carried them everywhere with him in the prison.

His own monthly letters to Mary – all four of them – are written on the official prison letter form, with all the regulations pertaining to visits and letters on the front cover. They are inscribed in a neat and tidy hand, and in one of her own letters Mary complimented him for their legibility. As with Mary's correspondence, much of the contents deal with family affairs. The children were Morel's principal concern, and he wrote at length about the garden at Cherry Croft, advising Mary on a wide range of horticultural questions. He also recalled with great nostalgia their past times and journeys together, and although he complained little about the conditions in which he found himself, it was plain that solitary confinement in the cells for sixteen hours a day, coupled with the poor diet and inadequate clothing in the winter months, were taking a heavy toll, and he was obviously anxious that petitions to the Home Secretary would be successful. However, although there is only the occasional mention of the Congo or the UDC, his work and reputation clearly weighed on his mind, and in his first letter to Mary, he raised the subject of a putative biography, remarking 'Mrs H. If she is seriously contemplating collecting matter for a biography you would, I take it, put my press-cutting books at her disposal temporarily?' Another particularly harrowing passage reads, 'You walked up and down the terrace the other night with me in dreams and said: "isn't it nice you are getting the Nobel Prize?"'

In November, after Morel had endured two months of imprisonment, Mary wrote to the Archbishop asking for an interview. She described how ill her husband looked and how much he needed 'certain small alleviations to make the ensuing months tolerable'. She asked if she could 'place certain matters' before him and seek the help and advice he had so generously given to Morel in the past. The first reply from Lambeth Palace was cast in the usual mould: 'You will understand how extraordinarily difficult it is for His Grace to arrange for interviews except on matters of the highest public urgency, and this week is heavily laden.' However, on reflection, His Grace did rise to the occasion, and in a letter to Mary on 17th November wrote that he was in communication with Morel's friends, and had written to the Home Secretary and expected him to be able to do something about relaxing existing restrictions. He wrote again a few days later saying that he would meet her at midday on 21st November.

This meeting initially appeared to have been a success. In her letter to Morel she described the Archbishop as being 'very nice – saw me off at the front door, and we talked very hard all the way down the nice broad stair way.' Little seems to have come of it, however, as shortly afterwards Mary received a letter from the Prison Commission saying that the Commissioners could not accede to her request to send additional clothing to Morel, and at the end of November the Home Office wrote saying that the Secretary of State would not permit any extra letters to be sent. This was confirmed in yet another letter towards the end of December.

Morel's health was obviously a matter of considerable and increasing concern to Mary. She wrote to Lord Parmoor, who had considered the decision to go to war a disaster and opposed conscription, saying that she feared Morel might have a mental breakdown and that he had recently been visited by a nerve specialist, and asked him to use his influence with the Home Secretary. Amongst other requests she petitioned for better food, warmer clothing and more visits. Parmoor responded saying that he had done his best, but that Mary should not expect much to come of it.

In the event, the Home Secretary, writing in his own hand in response to another letter – this time from Ponsonby – said that he could not allow Morel any visits in addition to those permitted under the rules. Ponsonby, however, proved indefatigable, writing to the Home Secretary again in the middle of January, just over two weeks before Morel was due to be released, to advocate that Morel's sentence be curtailed by a fortnight in view of his mental state, saying that he could be 'in a shattered condition by the time his sentence has fully expired.' In reply, Sir George wrote that he could not find sufficient grounds to justify him in recommending release before the expiration of the sentence, and having made inquiries he had found no cause for anxiety about Morel's health. He tempered this response by sending a further letter, in which he adopted what he apparently felt to be a highly magnanimous tone, saying that he would like to relieve Mrs Morel's anxiety, and if she would undertake to 'get her husband quietly away to Devonshire I would sanction his release for a few days before his time, say on Wednesday instead of Saturday next.'

A few days after Morel's release Ponsonby wrote to him apologising for not being at the gates of Pentonville to meet him. In that letter he declared that there had been one bright spot throughout the previous six months:

Your wife. I cannot describe how much impressed I and everyone else have been during these months by her attitude and bearing which has been nothing short of sublime – no complaints, no grievances, no recriminations, never a querulous note and never a symptom of despair from the outset. Quiet steady courage, unflagging vigilance, keen activity, delightful sympathy and marvellous patience. With all our shortcomings, our distractions, our thoughtlessness and often our absorption in other things, she has never failed to have a kind word for each of us. She seemed determined not to worry us or give a moment of trouble yet some of us well know what her feelings must have been specially in the earlier days...I do not believe there are many women who could have acted as she did.

This brief tribute gives some idea of Mary's character, and of the fortitude that always enabled her to stand behind Morel and support him throughout his campaigns. The fact that his work frequently claimed almost all his time and attention cannot have made her life easy, and Morel himself appears fully aware of how remiss he had often been. In his last letter to Mary from Pentonville he wrote, 'I have fallen short in these twenty years – too much egotism and absorption in self and public affairs: not nearly accessible enough to our dear children. And you have been so magnanimous and patient – it is I who have to do the climbing and you will give me a helping hand.' Later, his description of leaving prison in *Thoughts on the War: the Peace – and Prison* shows how much he depended on his wife's presence and succour: 'With a clang, the gates spring open and inward. The fog rushes in, in eddying billows. But through it there comes the sound of a beloved voice...'[217]

Morel's friends and supporters remained true to him throughout his period of incarceration, and the enormous quantity of correspondence from all quarters that welcomed him back into the world on his release must have helped towards overcoming the stigma of prison. A letter from William Leach, an official of the Independent Labour Party, was typical: 'Last Sunday I announced your release...at our meeting. There was a long burst of thunderous applause that kept on and on...My dear ally and friend, the movement for international unity and good will which owes more perhaps to you than any living man cannot do without you.' Ramsay MacDonald wrote that he would find an enormous change in public opinion since his 'enforced rest cure', but he would also discover that his influence had not suffered in any way. He was presented with a finely bound volume 'From His Friends and Comrades'.[218] Two beautifully illuminated and crafted title pages expressed 'our deep gratitude for the work you have bravely done in sifting from the confused mass of misrepresentation and ignorance the facts about this war and its origin, and of setting forth with equal courage the only policy that will bring peace.' The book contains the signatures of hundreds of members from branches of the UDC all around the country, including the Irish Women's International League.

Morel emerged from prison in a state of nervous exhaustion, and appears to have suffered a short period of near-collapse. As he wrote in a letter to Cadbury on 8th February, 'I was a mere bundle of disordered nerves when I came out and, physically, just fell to pieces for the first few days.'[219] A photograph taken of Morel at Barnstaple in Devon on the day after his release from Pentonville shows him bearded and thinner of face, though considering the privations he must have endured it should also be said that he looks surprisingly cheerful.[220]

Ramsay MacDonald got in touch once more to say how sorry he was to hear about it and that he hoped he was 'picking up again'. Fortunately, he shortly did so, and was sufficiently recovered by 19th February to attend a UDC meeting in Leicester. Molly Trevelyan, Charles's wife, wrote to Mary the following day, saying that 'your man bore himself gallantly and was received with warmest affection by his audience. He was nervous before he got up and found it difficult to sit still. But the moment he began to speak he pulled himself together, and faced the hall with all his old fire.' This verdict was confirmed by Ponsonby, who wrote that he wished Mary had been at the meeting, as it would have made her understand how tremendously Morel was appreciated.

It is striking that throughout this period of correspondence the war is scarcely mentioned. Not far away, just across the Channel, tens of thousands of men continued to die in battle. The United States had joined the conflict but the outcome still remained in question. Yet, only a postcard sent to Mary by Ethel Sidgewick after Morel's release, in which she mentions that her brother Hugh has just been killed in France and she can think of nothing but home for the moment, reminds one of the continuing struggle.

Morel's trial and imprisonment left him burdened with a profound sense of outrage. Later, he published a pamphlet, *The Persecution of E D Morel*, which was reproduced from *Foreward* of 6th July 1918, and based on the transcript of a speech he had given in June at a meeting in Glasgow. In it he attempted to exculpate himself, as well as implying that other sinister forces had been at work. He begins by listing some of the actions wrongly attributed to him over the past years: amongst others, that he had endeavoured to stir up strikes on the Clyde, in South Wales and elsewhere to paralyse national action and prevent munitions from reaching the troops; that the journey he had taken to Nigeria was at the special request of the Kaiser; and that there had been wireless communication between his house and an enemy submarine based off the Cornish coast.

The responsibility for these lies, he said, lay with 'the implacable animosities excited here and abroad, in the breasts of certain influential personages and among powerful financial and political groups, over the movement for purging the Congo of the last atrocious system of slavery which had been established in the vast territory...Rightly or wrongly those who are interested in these projects look upon me as still possessing sufficient public influence to be an obstacle to their designs.'

All this certainly rings true, but a further assertion made in the pamphlet to the effect that he had not attempted to defy the law by sending literature to Switzerland, and that he had never intended to do so, is at first sight extremely surprising, for it appears not to match the facts. Morel declares that it had not occurred to him that Rolland was residing anywhere but in France, and that he only learnt five days later 'after the book had actually left my hands', that he was in fact living in Switzerland. Given that Mary had attempted to send literature to Rolland in Switzerland the previous year, this seems, on the face of it, to be an unlikely claim.

Such a judgement, however, is entirely informed by hindsight, and with hindsight every detail of what later constituted the charge against Morel suddenly assumes critical importance. At the time the book was sent, however, the whole transaction would have been a relatively insignificant incident among scores of others in a busy and complex campaign, one to which Morel probably gave little serious consideration. The exact circumstances surrounding the arrangements would have been unmemorable, and it is quite possible that he had not registered precisely where Rolland was domiciled, or remembered the particulars of one of Mary's numerous activities a year beforehand, none of which would have seemed to be of any remarkable note. Morel claimed, for instance, that Ethel Sidgewick's statements, announcing her intentions of sending literature to Switzerland concealed in newspapers, were entirely irrelevant as far as he was concerned, and suggested that when 'my lady correspondent' eventually informed him of Rolland's actual residence she erroneously – though quite innocently – assumed that he was already aware of where he was living.

Leaving aside the effects on his health, Morel had been both humiliated and stigmatised by his imprisonment, and given the trivial nature of the offence for which he was arrested, and the severity of the penalty he was made to pay, it is understandable that he should have wanted to explain his actions and present himself as the innocent party in the face of the forces of the state. If the pamphlet helped what might be called his 'rehabilitation' then its publication was more than justified, even if some of its content indicates that his original failure to grasp the possible implications of his activities turned out to be a disastrous mistake.

The text ends with a quote from Lord Courtney's letter to Mary following her husband's conviction, and the words are as pertinent now as they were then. 'The motive of the trial was the suppression of opinion, and it became evident that the prosecution not only wanted to suppress opinion, but to lock up in silence anyone who could form an opinion they would like to suppress.' 'And there,' Morel adds at the end of the pamphlet, 'let us leave the matter.'

Morel later wrote some reflections on his experience of Pentonville which were included in his booklet *Thoughts on the War: Peace – and Prison*. His main concern was to ask a number of questions that are still posed today: what was the system's main objective? To deter? Or to punish? If the latter, what was the sense, let alone the justice, in meting out the same punishment to a man who had stolen three bottles of whiskey, and a man who had raped a child? If imprisonment was intended to deter then it was a failure, for very few men could be bettered by their experience of Pentonville. Indeed Morel suggested that most offenders would emerge from their sentence more villainous rather than less so. 'The point is that there is nothing, absolutely nothing in the system which is calculated to point the way to a cleaner, saner outlook, to revive self-respect and strengthen the defences against the onrush of temptation.' Everything in the system, he wrote, militated against these things. The reforms of the past had doubtless done much to bring about material improvement, but as it stood, the system was soul-destroying. It had 'become a sort of science for dealing with men as though they were machines, not creatures of flesh and blood.'

USA Enters the War

At the beginning of 1917, four months before it entered the war on the side of the allies, the United States commanded a large and modern navy, but its army was comparatively insignificant, with just over 100,000 men, no modern equipment and no experience of large-scale operations.[221] 'They will not even come,' Admiral Capelle, Secretary of State for the German Navy, assured the budgetary committee of his Parliament on 31st July 1917, 'because our submarines will sink them. Thus America from a military point of view means nothing, and again nothing and for a third time nothing.'

His confidence was to some extent understandable. President Woodrow Wilson had not wanted to enter the war. In contrast to Edward Grey, and in keeping with Morel's views, he believed that open diplomacy and straightforward dealing between nations was the most effective way of resolving conflict. In 1916 the President had made a determined effort to get the combatants to negotiate on terms that he felt would provide a just solution. He had sent an identical note to all the belligerents asking them to state the terms on which they considered it possible to make peace, '...merely proposing that soundings be taken in order that we may learn, the neutral countries with the belligerents, how near the haven of peace may be for which all mankind longs with an intense and increasing longing.'[222] The UDC had commented on the note, and in March 1917 the UDC General Council passed two resolutions, on the one hand welcoming the appeal to the belligerents, on the other regretting that the government had interpreted the terms as going far beyond the objects for which Britain had entered the war.[223] As it turned out, neither the Central Powers nor the Entente Powers came to any agreement. The President was greatly disappointed by the failure of his initiative, but even up to the spring of 1917 he still had no intention of entering the war, nor was there support for such a move amongst his fellow countryman.

Two incidents eventually changed this position. The first was the exposure of the coded 'Zimmerman Telegram', despatched by the German

Foreign Secretary, Arthur Zimmermann, to Mexico. This message was intercepted, deciphered by British intelligence and transmitted to the American government – although the US State Department had intercepted it independently. It proposed that Mexico should go to war as Germany's ally, and offered United States territory to Mexico, including the restitution of Mexican territory lost during the Mexican-American War, in return for joining the German cause. When the content of the telegram was published in March 1917, it caused outrage in America. The second influential factor was the decision by Germany to resume the unrestricted U-boat campaign to sink merchant shipping without warning in international waters. Within weeks of the publication of the Zimmerman telegram, German submarines had sunk three American merchant ships.

Wilson could not ignore this direct challenge to the United States as a sovereign power, and war against Germany was formally declared on 6th April 1917. Declarations against Austria-Hungary and Bulgaria followed, and selective military conscription was enacted in May. Although the Commander of the American Expeditionary Force, General Pershing, arrived in France in June 1917, the bulk of the United States Army was ill-prepared to take the field and it was some time before troops arrived in any significant number in Europe. By March of the following year, shortly after Morel had left prison, 318,000 men had reached France, the vanguard of 1.3 million to be deployed by August.

Although the collapse of Russia towards the end of 1917 had allowed the German High Command to redeploy some sixty divisions to the Western Front, President Wilson's decision to declare war on Germany and its allies had dramatically transformed the balance of force in Europe. The Germans, 'were now confronted with an army whose soldiers sprang, in uncountable numbers, as if from soil sown with dragons' teeth…Nowhere among Germany's remaining resources could sufficient force be found to counter the millions America could bring across the Atlantic.'[224]

On 8th January 1918 President Wilson had presented Congress with fourteen points on which a peace honourable to all combatants and guaranteeing world harmony could be made,[225] and it was on the basis of the 'Fourteen Points' that the German leadership subsequently decided to approach the allies. The President's proposals were very similar to the peace terms put forward in 1917 by the UDC, and to those advanced by the Labour Party in its memorandum on War Aims. The UDC viewed the Points as a vindication of its own suggestions, and welcomed above all that the foremost requirement for future security was the abolition of secret diplomacy. The last wartime meeting of the UDC's General Council passed an emergency resolution on 31st October in which it heartily supported the Points and the conditions outlined by the President in subsequent speeches, and called upon 'His Majesty's Government to take steps in conjunction with its allies to abrogate all treaties and agreements and to reject all proposals which conflict with these conditions and cooperate openly with President Wilson in his negotiations with the Central Powers for the purpose of bringing about a permanent and immediate peace.'[226]

Further to the resolution, and following the armistice signed on 11th November 1918, a letter was sent by the UDC to the President on the eve of his departure for Europe. Amongst other signatories were Ramsay MacDonald, Morel, Trevelyan and Ponsonby. The letter was lengthy and meticulously detailed and unmistakably came from the hand of Morel. It adopted a rather patronising tone towards the President, and ended by suggesting that the views that were being put before him by the UDC were now shared by the great mass of people in the country. These views, it concluded, would become more apparent when the passions and emotions engendered by the strain of the previous four years were replaced by more normal conditions.[227]

At a time when it seemed possible that a peace settlement might be achieved along the lines of Wilson's proposals, it was not wholly surprising that Morel should have marked the fourth anniversary of the UDC by stridently proclaiming that it had not laboured in vain: 'For the Union's Policy has become the World's Peace-programme – under the sponsorship of Woodrow Wilson. We have not always agreed with the *methods* by which President Wilson hopes to achieve his policy. In the endeavour to reconcile conflicting aims and to parry assaults upon his position he may be led into grave blunders. But his *policy* is ours.'[228] These words may seem rather arrogant, but nonetheless it is true that the UDC's constructive policies had made a significant contribution to a wide-reaching shift in the political climate. While Wilson's proposals certainly reflected this new perspective, in Britain Lloyd George had also aligned himself with the 'New Diplomacy', and his change of outlook was in no small part due to Morel's indefatigable crusade.

For Morel, however, this modification in the Liberal Party's approach was simply too little and too late, and in the period between his release from prison and the end of the war, he moved decisively to the left of British politics. His correspondence with Edward Driffill and his months in prison appear to have concentrated his mind on where his allegiance should lie, and in April 1918 he joined the Independent Labour Party, where he soon became a leading figure. He wrote to Cadbury[229] with the news that he had joined the ILP and added that he would be prepared to stand for Parliament if Snowden and others felt inclined to put him up. 'I have long been gravitating towards the socialist position, of course there is socialism and socialism, and mine is of the reasonable and moderate kind...I can't help feeling that the conglomeration of circumstances which have produced this frightful catastrophe...show that the whole fabric of society is on (the) wrong lines – cut-throat competition instead of cooperation for the common weal. Liberalism – the ideal which secured my adhesion – is dead.' This opinion was to make a considerable impact on the political landscape in Britain, where socialism soon replaced liberalism as the main party on the left of British politics, and remained in this position for many years to come.

At about the same time as Morel declared himself for Labour, he was unexpectedly called up under the Manpower Bill which had extended the age-limit for military service. This was the second time he had been asked to serve his country since the war began. The first request had arrived in April 1916, in the shape of a postcard from the French Consulate in London asking him to attend the Consulate with his military papers within the next few days.[230] On that occasion he had immediately sought the advice of an acquaintance, and had remarked in a letter to his lawyer, Brabner, that this friend had taken 'rather a grave view of the purport which might lie behind this communication', presumably imagining that the authorities had thought up a cunning scheme to get Morel out of the way. Brabner, however, had not been particularly perturbed, and had responded that Morel should not alarm himself unduly. 'I do not for a moment imagine that even if you happen to go over to France that they would shoot you like a rat within twelve hours, not withstanding your view of their being able to pass every day from illegality to illegality'. He had added that as Morel was a naturalised British citizen he was confident that the French could not possibly prove that he had left France to avoid military service – 'it was surely too late for them to attempt to get you over there.' He had also dismissed any idea of a conspiracy between the British and French governments to remove Morel from circulation. In fact had there been a conspiracy, the authorities would presumably have been more persistent, but the demand had been quietly dropped without the French getting Morel into uniform.

The second call up – the British government's attempt to enlist Morel – was rather more disturbing, and this time he had no alternative but to go through the process of appealing against compulsory military service. As he pointed out in a letter to Cadbury, the whole matter struck him as somewhat farcical. In fact Morel, a fine figure six feet tall, with a handsome face and luxuriant moustache, would have cut quite a dash in uniform, but naturally he did not view himself in this light. 'I take it there is this medical examination first,' he wrote, 'and unless vindictiveness operates in my case, I suppose I shall be in class 2 or 3. A ruptured man of forty-five and frequently subject to lumbago and sciatica can't be of much use in the military sense I should imagine.'[231] Nonetheless, he took the issue very seriously and obtained advice from both the National Council for Civil Liberties and a firm of London solicitors on how he should complete the 'Application as to Exemption from Military Service' form, and how to apply to the Appeal Tribunal in his district for an exemption on medical grounds.

He also composed a written appeal against being forced to take part in the war, based on his conscientious objection to 'undertaking combatant service'. As an alternative, he offered to undertake any work that was for the good of the country, 'notably in the increase of its food production, as to which I have a fair amount of knowledge. Or I could work in any unlisted civilian organisation which is concerned with the succour or treatment of the wounded.' He concluded by saying that he had already suffered imprisonment, but would go to prison again, in spite of being in very poor health, 'rather than act against the convictions which I have spent the greater part of my life in upholding'. Fortunately, the powers-that-be never pursued the case for enlistment (their reasons are not recorded) and he was neither imprisoned nor forced into any kind of national service in order to avoid compromising his principles.

But ill health continued to plague him for the rest of his life. When he received a diagnosis some years later it was revealed that he was suffering from Angina Pectoris,[232] a heart disease for which there was little remedy at the time apart from a regime of complete rest, a recommendation that he was not temperamentally equipped to accept. In any case, long before this verdict he had returned to the fray with his usual vigour. He continued to edit and write for the *U.D.C.*, now focusing his attention on the end of the war and the peace settlement that would arise from it. In early 1917 he had warned that there was a great need for civilians to keep their heads during the war because its scale would immeasurably exceed any conflict in history, and the loss of life and suffering would be proportionate.[233] In the August 1918 edition of the *U.D.C*, which coincided with the fourth anniversary of the war, he reminded readers of the scale of the casualties: the dead at that time (and there would be many more to come) were estimated to be 10 million 'of the most physically fit men in Europe'.

> Europe totters to ruin amid the bones of her dead, to the imbecile patter of her statesmen, proclaiming the purity of their motives while the people perish. And for what? What conceivable military success on either side can compensate for the havoc which has been wrought and lies ahead if this thing is allowed to go on? What is the value of ideals if preached in a graveyard?[234]

The Post-War Years and the Treaty of Versailles

It has been said that from 1918 to his death in 1924, Morel directed all his organisational, journalistic and political activities towards a single goal – the destruction of the Treaty of Versailles[235] – and it is true that he devoted much time and energy towards that end. But although he focussed primarily on the Treaty, he embraced a great number of other causes during his last years, and also successfully contested three parliamentary elections.

The first two decades of his public life had been devoted to working on two major and fairly clear-cut campaigns, but now, as Europe came to terms with the devastation of over four years of total war, Morel found himself confronted by a wider range of issues, many of which stemmed from the extraordinary political and national changes that had taken place by the time the conflict drew to a close. In Russia the revolution of 1917 had replaced tsarism. By 1918 Austria-Hungary had disappeared, leaving an empty space in the middle of Europe. The influence of the Ottoman Empire and its enormous holdings in the Middle East was effectively at an end, and Imperial Germany had become a republic.

The conditions of the armistice with Germany had been agreed in early November 1918 between the new government in Berlin, the Allied Supreme War Council in Paris and President Wilson in Washington. At that time, most Germans believed that their country had surrendered on the understanding that Woodrow Wilson's Fourteen Points would be the basis for a peace treaty, and for the first months of the armistice they clung onto this assumption 'like a life raft', with very little sense that their victors might not see things the same way.[236] The UDC, which had warmly endorsed Wilson's initiative, also presumed this to be the case.

In reality, the outcome was to prove very different. Wilson and the American delegation arrived in Europe to attend the Peace Conference, landing at the French port of Brest on 13th December 1918, and from there Wilson went on to a triumphant reception in Paris. In due course he met the Prime Ministers of Britain, France and Italy: David Lloyd George, George Clemenceau and Vittorio Orlando, and there followed five months of heated dispute regarding terms of the Treaty. Although a small German delegation was present in Paris during this time, Germany was not permitted to take part in the negotiations, and there was much disagreement between the victorious powers and their allies concerning the details to be included in the document. However, on 7th May 1919 the text of the Treaty was finally agreed, and was delivered to the Germans, who were given two weeks to consider it.

The terms and conditions it contained were highly punitive to Germany, and bore very little relation to Wilson's Fourteen Points, and for some time it seemed possible that Germany might reject them out of hand. But since the price of doing so was invasion by the allied powers, it effectively had no choice but to submit to its conquerors' decisions, and the agreement was signed by all parties on June 28th 1919 in the palace of Versailles.

Crucial to the terms of the Treaty was Clause 231, the so-called 'War Guilt Clause', under which Germany accepted sole responsibility for starting the war, and for all the damage and losses caused to the allied government and peoples in its pursuance. This clause was used to justify the crippling reparations that the defeated country was asked to pay, a sum eventually estimated at £6.6 billion, roughly equivalent to £284 billion in 2013, well beyond Germany's capacity to render at the time. German colonies were also ceded to Britain and France, and much of its territory dispersed among the allies and other European countries: Alsace-Lorraine was given to France; Eupen and Malmedy to Belgium; Northern Schleswig to Denmark; West Prussia, Posen and Upper Silesia to Poland, and Hultschin to Czechoslovakia. The German army was limited to 100,000 men, and the country was forbidden from having either submarines or an air force. It was also expressly prohibited from uniting with Austria, or joining the League of Nations. [237]

By the time the Treaty was under negotiation, Morel had returned to pick up the reins at the UDC, and had once again become its dominant figure. Unsurprisingly, and in keeping with the UDC's proclaimed manifesto, he was appalled by its contents, not least by the assumption of sole responsibility of 'war guilt' on which its conditions were predicated, an accusation which he had striven so long and hard to deny. He published an article, 'The Fruits of Victory',[238] in the June issue of the U.D.C. journal, in which he set out his views, and expressed his anger and dismay. He declared that the Treaty 'which has at length emerged from the secret conclave at Versailles is at once a great personal tragedy, and a great international tragedy.' It was a personal tragedy because it revealed President Wilson, on whom so many hopes had been pinned, as 'an empty rhetorician', and an international tragedy because it doomed the world to more strife and left mankind with little hope or confidence for the future.

He condemned the attempt to crush the Socialist Republic in Hungary and criticised the conditions being forced upon Austria, writing of them as 'almost grotesque, so amazingly do they ignore the economic and human needs of the Austro-Germans'. He complained of the 'virtual interdict' laid upon German Austria, fusing politically with Germany, and of the proposals to put 2 million Tyrolese Austrians and as many Dalmatian Slavs under Italian domination. He condemned the 'sanguinary and vicious folly which makes of ephemeral Polish adventurers the agents of Allied – notably French – capitalistic finance in Eastern Galicia.' He deplored the vindictive persecution of Soviet Russia and the callous cynicism with which whole nations were being bartered and sold throughout Asiatic Turkey, and reiterated the lines he wrote in an 'Epilogue to the Belligerent Governments' in *Truth and the War* in 1916:

> The 'Victory' you seek is a victory which shall perpetuate your empire over mankind; keep humanity bound in fetters to your cruel and senseless systems; maintain your castes and your monopolies; strengthen your embargo upon the people's liberties; leave your heel firmly planted on the peoples' necks…Thus your notion of 'Victory' means for the people increased poverty and a renewal of fears and hatreds upon which you have thriven, by which you retain them in subjection to your will and through which they perish. For the peoples, your 'Victory' means 'Death'.

Overall, he had not a single good word for the Treaty, which he claimed had been 'imposed upon Germany at the point of a bayonet.' It was, he wrote, 'a document of unspeakable sadness for its revelation of human futility, of human unteachableness (sic); of the depth, and power, and blindness of hatred in human affairs…the deliberate purpose of the Treaty, a purpose disclosed in every section of it, is that of encompassing the utter ruin of a great people.' For five months the Big Four, as he described them, had been squabbling behind closed doors; three of them bent upon loot and revenge; the fourth (Wilson) 'a weak man, as it turns out, really wishful of creating a better world, but inebriated by flattery, infirm of purpose, enveloped from the beginning in that secrecy which he had in advance foresworn, giving way a little here, a little there, until nought remains of his great charter of emancipation.'

He went on to analyse in very considerable detail the chief measures of the Treaty in order that 'we may fully understand the outrage, not upon the German people alone, but upon mankind, which is intended.' (This analysis followed on the heels of an earlier article in the March edition of the U.D.C., 'The Treatment of Germany'.) In his opinion, the Treaty simply violated every essential principle which was alleged to have inspired the war-aims of the allies, and to have justified them in prolonging the war long after it could have been brought to a logical conclusion.

However one judges Morel's profoundly critical views on all the territorial provisions of the Treaty, his extraordinary command of complex national and international issues remains remarkable. He strongly condemned the forced cession of German territory to Poland, which he described as 'rape' and an 'outstanding act of robbery.' He complained of the Sudeten Germans as being subjected by the Czechs to injustices 'in aggravated degree', and denounced the return of Alsace-Lorraine to France: 'Misery and suffering are once again inflicted upon tens of thousands people in the provinces and the seeds of hatred sown with lavish hands.' He deplored the confiscation of German colonies and the demand for reparations by France and Britain, which exceeded any sum that Wilson had envisaged. 'They have got their Knock-Out blow', he wrote, 'and they have made the Peace which they told us was to bring security to mankind. And this is the world they bequeath to the coming generations: A democratic Germany disarmed and reduced to vassalage in a ring of armed foes.'[239]

At the foot of *The Fruits of Victory*, there is a box announcing the forthcoming publication of another pamphlet, *The Betrayal of the Peoples*, and informing the reader that it will contain a further comprehensive analysis of the Peace Treaty and will be indispensable to a real understanding of 'that iniquitous document.'

Morel's views may have been extreme, but they were consistent with, and informed by, all that he had written in the pre-war era and during the war. Nor was he alone in holding them; many others, and not necessarily members of the UDC, adopted a similar outlook. From the moment the Germans signed the Treaty, it was regarded in numerous quarters as unduly harsh, with the potential for creating the conditions for further hostilities in the future. Even Lloyd George had, for a short spell, considered revising its most punishing terms, recognising that it was not in Britain's best interest to 'have a weak and possibly revolutionary Germany at the heart of Europe.'[240] Indeed, Morel's supporters came from all ranks of life – even his old ally the Archbishop declared himself 'very uncomfortable with the Treaty',[241] and the view that it was unjust persisted across a broad spectrum of political opinion for many years to come. Clement Attlee (at the time Major Attlee, and later deputy leader of the coalition government during the Second World War, and Labour Prime Minister following the war) declared himself proud to stand on a UDC platform with those who always protested against the war. The soldiers 'believed, and we believed, that they were fighting for the good of the whole world. That is where the great betrayal comes in.' In 1920, the historian R H Tawney wrote, 'For every man a year ago who knew and said the Peace Treaty was immoral in conception and would be disastrous, there are thousands who say it now...'[242]

In a number of respects this hostile reaction was a strange phenomenon. Generally speaking there had been widespread support in Britain for the war against Germany, and the casualty rates were appalling. It is estimated that between 9 and 15 million people had died during the conflict, including a million from Britain and its dependencies. France lost a higher proportion of its population than any of the other participants. A quarter of Frenchmen between eighteen and thirty (1.3 million young men) had been killed in the conflict, out of a total of 1.7 million dead, and the war memorials in every city, town and village in France still bear witness to the country's loss. In addition, 6,000 square miles of France – which before the war had produced 20% of its crops, 90% of its iron ore and 65% of its steel – were completely destroyed.[243] Besides the enormous physical destruction which had been unleashed upon France and Belgium by the Germans, empires had collapsed and whole societies had been dramatically affected. This widespread devastation and the changing pattern of the power structure in Europe made the task of the Peace Conference extraordinarily difficult, and put a great strain on the leading participants. Indeed, statesmen at the time had the sense of having lived through an exceptional struggle, a unique and total war experience that had shattered the world they knew.[244]

Moreover, as Steiner writes, the central issue of debate in Paris was what to do about Germany. The Treaty was not quite a 'Carthaginian Peace', as John Maynard Keynes would memorably describe it. Rather it was a peace imposed on a defeated nation still intact and vigorous, but unable to defend itself in the wake of a prolonged and brutal war. Germany had surrendered before the conflict reached its frontiers, thereby escaping the physical effects of the fighting and leaving its industrial heartland intact, and although the return of Alsace-Lorraine to France certainly meant that Germany lost much of its steel and coal capacity, it nonetheless made a rapid and impressive comeback.[245] It was hardly the case that it was a nation 'reduced to vassalage'. Even German territorial losses were predominantly of areas in which the population did not think of themselves as 'German', and the fact that Germany was expected to pay reparations was a not unreasonable demand from nations that had suffered huge material damage which Germany itself had largely escaped.[246]

Literature on the Treaty abounds, and it is impossible to analyse and evaluate its terms and conditions in a book of this nature. It is easy to sympathise with the sweeping condemnation accorded to it by Morel and his contemporaries, and to accept the commonly held later assumption that all that went wrong in the 1920s and 1930s could be blamed on the 1919 Paris settlements, but in recent years much scholarship has been aimed at moderating these views. Such revisionism emphasises the extreme complexity of the situation in Europe up to the Anschluss of Germany with Austria in 1938 and Germany's annexation of the Sudetenland in the same year, and points out that the disastrous outcome cannot entirely be laid at the Treaty's door. History has shown Morel to have been particularly percipient in his early conviction that the first war would lead to a second, but in the wake of the Russian Revolution, and with much of Europe and Asia in a state of chaos following the greatest war in history, the chances of bringing lasting stability and prosperity to a devastated Western Europe and the collapsed remains of the Ottoman Empire were inevitably remote, and by 1919 it is difficult to conceive that any settlement could have averted catastrophe. As Margaret MacMillan puts it, 'If they (the Peacemakers) could have done better, they certainly could have done much worse. They tried…to build a better order. They could not foresee the future and they certainly could not control it. That was up to their successors. When war came in 1939, it was the result of twenty years of decisions taken or not taken, not of arrangements made in 1919.'[247]

Some historians join in the debate with an even more unequivocal voice. William Keylor, for example, writes:

> If what has emerged from recent multi-archival research is 'a much more nuanced portrait of statesmen and diplomats striving, with a remarkable degree of flexibility, pragmatism and imagination, to promote their nation's vital interests as they interpreted them', why do even our more learned statesmen continue to repeat the shibboleths of the past?[248]

Morel and his supporters, however, were not present at the table of the Supreme Council, and had not witnessed the tribulations of those seated around it. They had not had to grapple at first hand with the competing interests of the victorious powers, much less with the aspirations of the new nations that emerged from the ashes. Nor had they been compelled to make decisions on commitments that would reverberate into the future, and it apparently did not occur to them that the allies' representatives in Paris might have endured a gargantuan struggle in attempting to meet conflicting demands in a way that would bring peace to the Continent. As Margaret MacMillan suggests, President Wilson might have understood Clemenceau's demands better if he had gone early to see the damage for himself,[249] and perhaps Morel too could have benefited from such a visit. From close quarters, he might better have understood the predicament of the peacemakers, realising that once they began to confer their inflated expectations could not possibly be met, and that quite apart from the personalities of the leaders concerned, their national interests could never hope to be reconciled with the goals of the 'liberal internationalists'.

As it was, he harboured absolutely no sympathy for the protagonists, and when the Versailles Treaty was finally ratified at the beginning of 1920, all he could say was that it was a 'foul deed', an outrage upon all the peoples, revealing 'them to themselves as helpless playthings of a secret diplomacy which perpetrated this thing behind closed doors, in a maze of intrigue and counter intrigue.'[250] This passionate criticism is in tune with his previous campaign against the secret treaties and lies leading up to the war, and as we have seen, much of his hostility towards the Treaty was grounded in his unshakable belief that Germany could not be deemed to carry sole responsibility for the conflict. As a result, his vigorous opposition to the notorious Clause 231, which had been included to establish the German liability for 'reparations', now became the focus of much of his attention:

> What justification is advanced for this levy upon the labour and resources of a great people? There is no dispute as to that. It is not advanced on the ground they were beaten in the war. They have already paid for that in the old-fashioned way – only more so: loss of fleet, ships, colonies, territory, liquid assets, etc...It is advanced on the ground, and only on the ground, that their late rulers were solely responsible for the war itself.[251]

His campaign to obtain a reduction in reparations engendered both considerable support and strong opposition. Norman Angell, a prominent member of the UDC, for instance, was far from sympathetic. He wrote to Morel that he would 'regard it as impolitic for Britain to abandon her

Reparations claims on Germany…The actual payment of large Reparation sums by Germany will not cripple her as a competitor at all.'[252] His old Congo ally, Edward Talbot, the Bishop of Winchester, whose youngest son had been killed in action at Ypres in 1915 aged twenty-three, also took issue with Morel, in particular regarding his views about the critical question of war guilt. Their correspondence is interesting in that it shows Morel defending his stance personally to a friend who had given considerable thought to the matter and whose views were probably shared by a great many people in Britain.[253]

It is not clear from their letters exactly how the matter arose, but the Bishop wrote to Morel in August 1921 thanking him for a copy of 'that bitterly *disappointing* paper the *Daily Herald*', which apparently contained a letter of Morel's. He went on to write that he hated the 'Khaki' election (Lloyd George's election of 1918) with its 'vindictiveness and swagger', and furthermore disliked the Treaty of Versailles for its pervasive triumphalist tone. The Bishop also thought that Germany was not the *only* power responsible for the war – 'no doubt the War emerged out of an international condition unworthy of a Christian civilisation' – but he considered that to imply that the other powers were equally guilty of aggressive intent was 'a half truth, in so far as if there had been no Germany there would have been no war'. He went on to say that it would be 'a great crime to strangle Germany', and that although he thought the allies justified in imposing punitive measures in the first months after the armistice, they should not have committed themselves to pursuing them over such a long period.

He concluded that although history might qualify the judgement that Germany was responsible for the war, it would be very unlikely to entirely abandon that conviction. What concerned him most was that it seemed 'a gross disservice to the morale of a Great Nation to make it believe that Capital, or some other malign cause hoodwinked it into the greatest effort of its history, and that all its beloved dead bled and fell for a big diplomatic mistake.' The Bishop added that he was no admirer of Lloyd George, but had to own up to feeling that the Prime Minister had done his best in dealing with France, which had suffered so much in the conflict. He ended by saying he hoped that none of his words were dogmatic or scornful in tone, and assured Morel that he would not have written at all if he had not held him in great respect.

Morel replied a few days later, hastening to reassure the Bishop that nothing he could write would cause him any umbrage: 'we fought too long and too closely in days gone by for that to be possible', but declaring in very forthright tones 'that those facts to which your mind remains closed are vital.' His ability to write lengthy and detailed letters to ecclesiastics was undiminished, and this letter was typically verbose. He described the Versailles Treaty in somewhat hyperbolic language as a 'punishment of a comprehensiveness, a duration, a vindictive minuteness for which you may seek vainly for any historical parallel since the Birth of Christ.' He maintained that he had met nobody – not even people who disagreed violently with him on the origins of the War, from military men to relief workers – who was not ashamed of it, and who did not condemn it as impossible and monstrous. The Treaty was a crime, and would be the inevitable precursor of further war. Every man who was convinced of this should do his utmost to get it totally recast and revised.

Morel reiterated his usual opinion that Germany should bear some responsibility for the war, but that the Treaty was outrageous in assuming that it was *solely* responsible. He refuted what he described as the Bishop's 'muddled perspective', which he felt had caused him to conclude that Germany alone planned and desired war, and asked the Bishop to specify the facts upon which his allegation was based. He pointed out that this opinion involved rejecting the evidence of reputable historians, dismissing the contents of Russian, Austrian, German and Foreign Office archives (all of which were now available to the public), and repudiating the written works of many prominent statesmen. 'By what process can you dismiss as irrelevant Lloyd George's statement that the more post-war disclosures were studied the clearer it became that *no power* wanted war at that time, but that they all "stumbled and staggered" into it?' Had Lloyd George's statement escaped him, Morel asked, and if not, how could it be that he had not been appalled by its implications? If no power wanted war, what moral foundation could there be for the Versailles Treaty?

He continued in much the same vein, pointing out that in the ten years preceding the war, the level of expenditure on arms by Germany was vastly less than that of the Franco-Russian alliance, a matter which he had raised with the Bishop on two previous occasions. Furthermore the official figures had now revealed that Germany and Austria had faced significant numerical odds from the beginning, irrespective of the power of Britain. He asked the Bishop to explain by what process he rejected these facts as irrelevant, 'which you must do to justify your categorical affirmation to yourself?'

By now the Bishop must have been reeling under the impact of the correspondence, but Morel was far from finished. 'May I not suggest to you with all courtesy and respect,' he continued, 'that *your* perspective may be wrong? You appear to visualise Germany and Britain only…You can't leave France and Russia out of the picture.' He added that he felt certain that Britain had not desired war, but that was not to say it had not been preparing for it from 1906 onwards. His quarrel with the government went back to the secret lies and treaties which had led to the outbreak of hostilities in 1914. Writing with his usual sense of conviction, he ended by saying that he did not believe the Bishop could resist his conclusion 'that the causation of the Great War which has been thrust into our brain by years of intensive propaganda is a legend; a legend whose destruction we owe to our dead, to ourselves, to humanity – and if I may say so, to God'.

The Bishop was generous in his response to what was, by any standards, an extremely uncompromising letter. He expressed himself almost overwhelmed by it, but thanked Morel for the pains which 'you have been at to instruct and convince one who is so little worthy of your steel.' He wrote that he felt he had 'encountered an antagonist who not only wielded the arms of Goliath, but also the skills of David and not a little of his faith'.

He stressed that he and Morel were in agreement over a number of matters, particularly the contrast between the acceptance of Wilson's Fourteen Points at the time of the armistice, and the way they were subsequently dropped in the text of the Versailles Treaty. However, he said that he could not accept Morel's assessment that a significant portion of blame for the war lay with Britain and her allies. 'Were we altogether deceived about the way in which the Professors and teachers in schools taught the children about the supremacy of Germany and the glorification of power?' Nor could he find any fault with secrecy when 'publicity would have meant an offensive challenge to Germany which she could hardly help taking up.'

He was particularly upset by Seymour Cocks's book. He did not consider that 'your favourable biographer was confident of convincing others, and perhaps does not altogether convince himself, by his gallant plea for your methods.' Rather, he felt that Morel had put great strain upon those who believed in him, particularly on account of the company he kept. For reasons that are not entirely plain the Bishop had taken most strongly against the two Trevelyans, Charles and Sir George, Ramsay MacDonald and Ponsonby. Of the latter he wrote he had never read anything so 'grossly unfair' as some of his speeches in the House of Commons during the War.

Morel responded just over a week later, promising not to inflict a further long epistle upon the Bishop. After defending his friends and rebutting much of what the Bishop had written, he launched into another strong attack on the Versailles Treaty, and asked on what basis of humanity or ethics it could be justified. The Treaty was 'an active continuous and devastating wrong' whether or not the Kaiser willed the war. As to responsibility for the conflict, there was nothing in the Bishop's letter to make Morel alter his position. 'A punishment unparalleled in the history of war had been imposed upon the chief defeated nation, on the grounds that the war was solely engineered by that nation.' Only a greater disaster, he wrote, could come from suppressing the truth. Morel concluded the letter with his usual self-confidence, writing that although his method of stating his case might be faulty, his case was itself impregnable. He remained confident that his criticism was legitimate and his facts completely sound.

After that, the correspondence appears to have ceased. History does not relate whether the Bishop was finally convinced by Morel's arguments, but it is nonetheless clear that he continued to hold him in high esteem. Following Morel's death he was one of the many who paid tribute to him in *Foreign Affairs*. He particularly recalled their mutual endeavours in the Congo Campaign, and at the end of the piece he wrote that 'later private correspondence with him about the war expressed marked difference between us. But by his grave I stand by that first noble experience'. [254]

However, although Morel no longer possessed the almost universal support he had enjoyed during the Congo Campaign, many others were in accord with him about the failings of the Versailles Treaty, and agreed that the level of reparations was so high that it would inevitably lead to much humiliation and resentment in Germany, thereby contributing towards the risk of another war.

The dread of further conflict had haunted Morel for almost a decade, and although this fear was now widely shared, it pervaded his post-war outlook almost to the point of obsession. In October 1921 he spoke on 'The Reduction of Armaments' at the London Conference on Economic Recovery and World Peace, and declared that the greater part of London could be destroyed within a few days as a result of an aerial bombardment 'sustained by aeroplanes directed by wireless, dropping huge explosive shells of a size and potency unknown'. This, he assured his audience, was 'a scientifically feasible proposition' which was well advanced and being perfected in 'a hundred laboratories and workshops in three continents.' He imagined that if these facts were generally known, they would provide the driving force for the abolition of war. He called upon mankind to attempt to control the monster it had created, for if it failed to do so it would devour him and his children.[255]

This preoccupation occasionally gave rise to startlingly alarmist journalism. On 3rd July 1924, for example, the *Daily Herald* published a leading article on its front page, not dissimilar in tone to more recent flights of fancy regarding Iraq's Weapons of Mass Destruction. It was entitled 'Explosives Piled up Everywhere', with further sub-headings: 'E D Morel's Exposure of Wholesale Preparations for War' and 'The People Must Cease to Live in a World of Illusion.' The article goes on to say that Europe might at any moment find itself in the grip of another great war and that frantic preparations were being made to that end. 'Mr E D Morel fearlessly makes amazing disclosures of wholesale production of arms and ammunition chiefly in Tcheckoslovakia (sic) and the Austrian state factories…Today,' he warns, 'the peoples of Europe are moving amongst piled-up explosives to which some clumsy or sinister fool, some vile combination of sordid interests, or some section of the European community, exasperated by the hypocrisy of its alien judges and rendered frantic by injustice, might at any moment apply the match.'[256] Rather paradoxically, however, Morel's most forthright criticism on this occasion is directed at the violation of the Treaty and the failure to enforce its conditions. 'Under the Treaty she (Austria) cannot manufacture a single gun, rifle or cartridge. Her armament industry is under the strict control of an Allied military mission.'

He combined his focus on the future with a re-examination of the mistakes of the past, a reprise which may well have been motivated by some desire for self-justification, as well as by a desperate desire to persuade the British government how important it was to exercise effective democratic control of foreign policy. His pamphlet, *The Secret History of a Great Betrayal*, is a lengthy and detailed account of the lead up to the war, reiterating once more the failures of statesmen and politicians. Raymond Beazley writes in the preface, 'Mr Morel is surely entitled to look back with a sorrowful sense of justification upon the efforts he has made, and the warnings he has uttered in International Policy.'[257] A further pamphlet published at much the same time, *The Poison that Destroys, The Case for a National Inquiry into the Causes of the War and the Disaster of the Peace*, also goes back over the circumstances leading to war, and addresses 'The idea that the war was the outcome of a German conspiracy carefully nurtured by every artifice open to the Government'.[258] This subject is approached again in another pamphlet, *Justice Between Peoples*, where Morel writes, 'The truth here is that persistent injustice inflicted upon one of the greatest branches of the human family (Germany) has set up conditions amongst all the peoples of the world which has detrimentally affected mankind as a whole.'[259]

A flood of pamphlets continued to be published, often consisting in transcripts of speeches given in halls around the country to various organisations, or reproduced from articles in *Foreign Affairs*. Their titles clearly reveal their subject matter: *Secret Diplomacy: a Menace to the Security of the State; Peace Overtures and their Rejection; Pre-War Diplomacy Fresh Revelations*, and so on. Morel remained dogged as ever, and his extraordinary capacity for work appeared to be undiminished. Even as he castigated the Treaty and called for its total revision, 'so must we work henceforth to reverse the policy consummated in the Treaty of Versailles',[260] he was writing another book on Africa, *The Black Man's Burden*, which sought 'to convey the fundamental principles of a humane and practical policy in the government of Africa by white men', and was published in 1920.[261] Here he returned to the subject that had so exercised him during the Congo Reform years and up to the outbreak of war – that good governance in Africa was critically dependent on acknowledging the right of Africans to the ownership of their land.

Beginning with the foundation of the slave trade in the middle of the 15th century, he traced the history of the 'civilisation' of Africa down to his own day, dealing successively with Southern Rhodesia, German South West Africa, Morocco, Tripoli, the Congo Free State, and Angola. The whole narrative, as he saw it, was defined by fraudulence and robbery, with all-too-successful attempts to deprive Africans of their land rights, providing a sure route to their exploitation at the hands of 'white capitalists'. He declared that where African communities were divorced from the land, their people would inevitably be reduced to the level of wage slaves, and warned that industrial capitalism and the political interests of the governing class would find common ground in profiting from the opportunities afforded by this debasement. The consequences for local populations were bound to be disastrous. 'Consider the picture of a tropical African dependency – take British East Africa as typical – where policy is directed to ensuring that a dozen or so European concessionaires shall earn large dividends. The first call upon the labour of the country is for work on the plantations and estates of these concessionaires. As a result native villages decay. The population is unable to feed itself.'[262]

Subsequent resource extraction and the impoverishment of the peoples of the countries colonised by the British, Portuguese, French and Italians bears witness to the accuracy of Morel's prediction, but there were very few who called for the rights of Africans when fresh opportunities for settlement and exploitation opened up again after the war. It would take nearly half a century and another even more devastating conflict before any of the African countries achieved a degree of independence, and even then they were typically denied the control of their own resources.

Horror on the Rhine

The Black Man's Burden reflected all Morel's customary concern for the wellbeing of Africans, and advanced his usual trenchant critique of the motives and methods of the colonising powers. It is therefore particularly surprising to find that in the year of its publication he also became involved in an unsavoury campaign designed to rally public opposition to France's implementation of the Versailles Treaty. This campaign was based on deeply racist assumptions, and unfortunately Morel's contribution did nothing but reinforce them. In April of 1920 he gave an address entitled 'Black Troops in Germany'[263] to the Women's International League at the Central Hall, Westminster, and two months later produced a pamphlet called Horror on the Rhine.[264] Both the talk and the pamphlet proved exceedingly controversial, and attracted much public attention.

The only explanation for these extremely uncharacteristic interventions was that Morel was driven by his unwavering determination to resist the enforcement of the Versailles Treaty, and in particular by his disgust at the French use of African soldiers as pawns in the propaganda game. To some extent, this view may have been justified; the French had indeed assigned colonial troops to the occupation of the Palatinate in the Rhineland, partly in order to demonstrate to their erstwhile enemy the extent of its defeat, and Germany's protests against the use of black troops were primarily aimed at turning allied public opinion against France's resolute implementation of the conditions of the Treaty. But regrettably the German protests were couched in overtly racist terms, reasserting prejudices that had already been expressed. Shortly before the end of the war the German Colonial Office had complained that 'the French use of native armies was endangering European civilization,[265] and such had been the concern that in April 1919 the instructions given to the German delegation to Versailles specified that 'coloured troops should not be made a part of the army of occupation.' The French, however, had been undeterred, and by the time the Treaty came into force in January 1920 there were around 85,000 African troops in the Rhineland. As a result, a wave of media and public protest was inaugurated by Berlin, and *The Horror on the Rhine* made a significant contribution to the air of hysteria that permeated the whole situation.

The pamphlet graphically described the atmosphere of fear and danger in the occupied region, and was accompanied by lurid accounts of assaults upon women and young girls by black troops. This sensationalism caught the public's attention, and the pamphlet was translated into German, French, Italian and Dutch, and went into eight editions. Its readership was further titillated by an account of how the local brothels should be managed, and by eighty detailed reports, of which the following two were typical:

> Reported from Erbenheim: Three girls, aged respectively sixteen, fourteen and fifteen attacked by two 'Moroccans', one of the girls seized, dragged into a cornfield and raped, the others escape and get help from the village, assailant seized by the villagers and overpowered after a furious resistance, in the course of which he tries to draw his sword bayonet…as a result of this and similar incidents in the neighbourhood women and girls refuse to work in the fields.

> Reported from Julich: A woman of thirty-four attacked by three 'coloured' soldiers, several people attracted by her cries for help; soldiers make off without accomplishing their design, clothes ripped and torn from the girl's body.

Morel also wrote a lengthy account which he called 'A Prolonged Scandal', concerning the murders of several young girls at Saabrücken. He reported that these atrocities had continued over a period of a year, and described them in a manner that was little short of prurient, alleging that the details had been hushed up by the French military authorities who simply denied the 'bestial deeds perpetrated on German girls by their Black soldiers'. He was obviously not alone in publicising these so-called exposés, indeed, the German propaganda machine ensured that the message of the 'Black Horror' was carried as far afield as Peru and Argentina in similar publications – but nonetheless he played a notable part in the campaign orchestrated by the German government to discredit the French and their use of African troops, and he was strongly criticised for the racist tone evident in both his address and in his pamphlets. Even today his reputation in the Toxteth area of Liverpool is deeply marred by the memory of the prejudices he expressed at this time, and which stood in such extraordinary contradiction to all his previous sentiments.[266]

It has been suggested that Morel became involved in this campaign as a result of falling victim to a clever propaganda campaign organised by a Dr Gärtner, who at the time served as a director of a Rhineland Women's Group financed by Krupp, the armaments manufacturer. Whether or not this was the case, it seems curious that Morel appears to have made no attempt to verify his information. In fact, despite extensive investigations carried out by a number of different groups, the accusations cited in the pamphlet remained largely unproven.[267] It also seems that the wider campaigns, including 'The American Campaign against *The Horror on the Rhine*', failed to produce significant verifiable evidence for the similar claims they made. Morel was warned about this lack of corroboration by his two friends, Ponsonby and Trevelyan, and the latter advised him not to exaggerate, as the only piece of first-hand evidence he had been able to obtain suggested that black soldiers behaved exceptionally well and that native French troops were far more to be feared.

Notwithstanding its doubtful authenticity, however, the campaign resulted in a wave of eye-catching, racially prejudiced newspaper articles. For example, the *Daily Herald* declared that the crime of the French militarists' secret decision to invade Germany was nothing compared to the method of that invasion. Wherever there were black troops, 'long distant from their women-folk' there followed a ghastly outbreak of prostitution, rape and syphilis. Furthermore it claimed that 'The Mayors of German towns are compelled by the French authorities to provide brothels for the primitive sexual passions of these men.'[268] *The Nation* went even further in pronouncing that the bulk of the African soldiers were primitives, and the resulting atrocities were 'attributable to those who had trained barbarism for scientific slaughter, and had thrust barbarians with tremendous sexual instinct into the heart of Europe'.[269] The *Commonweal* gave 'All honour to Mr Morel...for exposing the foul abomination perpetrated by the French Government in sending a horde of Senegal savages to the occupied territory...One would feign believe that no white race exists that would compel a foe to hand over its women to the lust of a black soldiery.'[270]

Fortunately not everyone took all this at face value. For example, Norman Leys, who practised as a doctor in Kenya and was an outspoken critic of the impact of white settlers on the African people,[271] wrote to the editor of the *Daily Herald* that he had lived in tropical Africa for seventeen years and could bear evidence that the so-called physiological facts hinted at by Morel in his pamphlet, and expounded on in the *Daily Herald*, were simply untrue. 'That is to say it is untrue that sexual passion is stronger in Africans than in Europeans. And it is untrue that sexual connection between an African male and a European female is injurious to a European female.'

The first belief, he wrote, was one of the great sources of racial hatred, and should never be repeated by any honest man or honest newspaper.

It has to be said that this letter seems to have brought about a revision of the *Daily Herald*'s views. In an article written a couple of days later the paper stated that the charges it had made about the use of black troops by the French were not designed as an instigation to colour prejudice, nor were the physiological difference to which they had referred the fault of any race or colour. Just to confirm its liberal outlook it declared that, 'We have known many negroes of a far higher degree of kindliness and culture than is to be found ordinarily among the white people.' However, this didn't prevent the writer of the article from continuing to refer to the black troops used by the French as 'men of a primitive and savage state of development.'[272]

The issue continued to be prominently debated in the press for many months, although by the following year the focus had changed. *Labour Leader*[273] published an article in February, also entitled *Horror on the Rhine,* in which it deplored the awful results 'of the white races' use of conscript black troops. The root of the wrong is in the tearing of these black soldiers away from their homes, utterly against their will, for the sordid ends of their Imperialist rulers.' In a letter to the *Daily News and Leader*[274] in February entitled 'Black Soldiers, Enlisted for White Men's Quarrels', Morel too complained bitterly of France's conscription policies and the maintenance of a permanent standing army of 200,000 African troops in Europe. There is no mention in either article of the supposed sexual proclivities of these African troops.

At around the same time as the publication of these articles, the New York paper *Outlook* carried a piece, 'Propaganda about the Black Troops', suggesting that Morel was engaged in a German propaganda exercise against the French. The article claimed that the charges made against the French 'have been denied and disproved.' The French Consul-General in New York called the accusations 'grotesque and malicious',[275] and Morel responded with a letter, 'Coloured Troops in the Rhineland'. He listed the number of troops, mainly Moroccans, Algerians and Senegalese, posted in the area, adding that 'I have consistently urged that this question should be publicly treated in such a way as not to give the impression that those who were instrumental in bringing the facts before the world, are in the slightest degree inspired by racial prejudice.'[276] He refrained from citing any atrocities, merely adding in a postscript that if African troops, who in their 'natural conditions' were polygamous, were quartered without their womenkind (sic) in the European countryside, the results would be inevitable. 'It is the policy itself against which the full force of criticism should be directed.'

There is a distinct change of emphasis over this period, with an obvious move away from the salacious headlines of rape and lust by black troops. There appears to be little evidence to confirm whether or not Morel was aware of being the victim of a carefully contrived propaganda trap laid by Frau Gärtner's Women's Group, or even whether such a plot existed, but he may have concluded that he had blundered in assuming that all the 'evidence' fed to him was verifiable. If this was the case, it was certainly a surprising oversight on the part of a man who in the past had proved himself to be such a consummate master of facts and figures. Even more astonishing was his willingness to present Africans in a manner which all too easily played on the stereotypical prejudices and racial fears of Europeans. He had always displayed a tolerant and deeply respectful attitude towards indigenous institutions, and was fully appreciative of the polygamous nature of much of African society, yet the *Horror on the Rhine* campaign reflected none of this empathy and understanding.

It is virtually impossible to believe that in taking this stance, he failed to appreciate the damage he was doing both to his own reputation and to the image of the continent he had championed over so many years, and the furtherance of his campaign against the Versailles Treaty seems a poor justification for taking such a course. But take it he did, and the dismal outcome is that he is most clearly remembered, in a part of the city that gave birth to his career, for his pamphlet *The Horror on the Rhine*. How much better, and how much more characteristic, had he defended the African soldiers and condemned their exploitation by the Western powers. As Keith Nelson would write some fifty years later:

> And what of the African soldiers who forfeited their time and often their health and even lives in Northern Europe? Hopefully, there was some small benefit for the survivors and their cultures in an increased familiarity with the rationalised and mechanized ways of modern society. Perhaps it was to their advantage that, after the experience of war and occupation, they must have found it more difficult to idealize the white man.[277]

Reparations

The storm over *Horror on the Rhine* appeared to do little to divert Morel's attention from the matter of reparations, an issue that Thomas Lamont, an American delegate to Versailles, would later described as causing 'more trouble, contention, hard feeling and delay at the Paris Peace Conference than any other point of the Treaty.'[278] Almost two years after the signing of the Treaty, the German Chancellor, Prince Max von Baden, was still addressing the issue of Clause 231 in an article in *Foreign Affairs*, and writing that 'no nation has the right to deliver judgement upon another, but all the great peoples of Europe must meet each other as companions in guilt.'[279] But this was not a universal sentiment, and for well over a decade the question of reparations continued to do enormous damage both to the relationship between Germany and the allies, and to such rapport as existed amongst the allies themselves.

Morel obviously remained an implacable opponent of the clause, calling it 'a cunningly devised and intricate system of economic and financial strangulation whose barely concealed purpose was to enslave, starve and break the spirit of a great people in order to make their recovery completely impossible,'[280] and never missing an opportunity to campaign against it. When the Secretary of the Dundee Labour Party wrote to invite him to stand as a candidate for election, he made a point of bringing the matter up again in his reply, stressing that the prosperity of the greater part of Europe depended upon German industry: 'If Germany finally goes to pieces, the economic reconstruction of Europe becomes utterly impossible.'[281] Indeed one of Morel's earliest contributions to debate in the Commons, following his election as an MP in 1922, would be on this very subject. On this occasion he clashed with Lloyd George, asserting that the ex-premier's speeches during the General Election of 1918 had encouraged the idea in Britain and France that Germany would pay the whole costs of the war. The charge was denied by Lloyd George, who responded that his view had always been that Germany should pay 'to the limit of her capacities'. A lively altercation followed, 'Mr Morel asserting and Mr Lloyd George denying, and the House ringing with cheers and counter cheers.'[282]

The issue at stake was fairly straightforward: namely who was to pay for the cost of over four years of war and the massive damage that had ensued, particularly to France? Germany had invaded France and Belgium, and had ultimately been defeated – if it did not pay the price, who would? Lloyd George, perhaps not unreasonably, felt that the British taxpayer should not be called upon to contribute to settling the account. But as we know, Morel did not believe that Germany could be held wholly responsible for the conflict, and consequently held that the demand for reparations was deeply unjust. The only possible moral sanction for imposing reparations on Germany at all, he wrote, would consist in irrefutable proof established before an International Court of Justice that Germany had 'deliberately launched the war upon a guileless, innocent and peaceful Europe.'[283] As it was, he thought the scale of the sums demanded would make the future of international peace impossible.

In a special supplement to *Foreign Affairs* at the end of 1921, Morel wrote a lengthy 'Open Letter to the Friends and Supporters of the UDC', calling for an 'All-Embracing International Conference', independent of the existing League of Nations. Such a conference would not meet for the purpose of imposing punishment upon an exclusively guilty nation – 'this dogma of a guilty nation must be given up'. Rather it would seek an equitable solution to the difficulties created by both the war and the peace.[284]

Despite his considerable following, however, Morel's views on Germany were not shared by the majority of the population. A letter to *The Patriot*[285] from Reginald Wilson, General Secretary of the British Empire Union, is typical of the acrimonious response evoked by his campaign. Wilson wrote of the 'mischievous propaganda' of Morel and the UDC, and their 'lamentable success in permeating their pernicious views on foreign policy'. Since the peace, he went on, 'they have successfully attributed all the evils caused by the aftermath of war to the errors of the Treaty of Versailles, to the wickedness of France and to the cruelty of the allies to "poor dear Germany", who was no more guilty of causing the war than any other country.' The Labour Research Department, he continued, had issued a cheap edition of Keynes's *The Economic Consequences of the Peace* to be sold amongst workers' organisations. Since Keynes was a well known advocate of the cancellation of the German indemnity, this publication was an illustration of how the pro-German minority had taken possession of Labour's foreign policy.

Churchill and Dundee

In April 1920 Morel was invited to stand as a prospective Labour Party candidate for one of the seats in the constituency of Dundee, a seat that had been held for the Liberals by Winston Churchill since 1908. In responding to the invitation, Morel pointed out that his health was not good and that he was under doctor's 'imperative' orders to take two months' complete rest.[286] He went on to say that he must clarify two matters. Firstly, although his whole time would be given to the constituency during the election if he was eventually adopted, he could not pay frequent visits to Dundee in the interval. Secondly, it must be accepted that notwithstanding the fact that he stood 'on the Independent Labour Party's existing platform in every respect, a struggle between Churchill and myself would inevitably resolve itself into a square fight on the issue of militarism and foreign policy...I retreat not one inch from the position I took up on the war when it broke out...you would have to be prepared for an avalanche of mud to be thrown at your man.' He pointed out that there were a number of influential persons in governing circles who would move heaven and earth to keep him out of Parliament.

Despite these caveats, the organiser for the Dundee Branch of the ILP responded very positively, assuring him of a hearty welcome in Dundee and concluding that 'we are not frightened of mud and of the two I think most of the mud would stick to Churchill.'[287]

At the time of Morel's invitation to stand as MP for Dundee, Lloyd George was still Prime Minister and head of the coalition government. Aware of his significant reputation as a victorious wartime leader, he had called an election just before the armistice in 1918, and was swept back into power, but his position was based on extremely uncomfortable foundations. He himself was of course a Liberal, but the elected members of Parliament and key Cabinet members were overwhelmingly Conservative,[288] and many of them clearly resented his radical past. The new House of Commons was described by Stanley Baldwin as 'a lot of hard-faced men who look as if they had done very well out of the War.' Their political instincts were decidedly traditional and they were determined to limit the change war had brought into being.[289]

The country's swing to the right in the 1918 election was to set a pattern for the future. In many ways it was a surprising outcome; the right to vote had been extended to all men over the age of twenty-one, and the 1918 Representation of the People Act had at last extended the franchise to women (albeit limiting it to women over thirty, provided they were householders or the wives of householders). It might have been expected that these changes would have increased the radical vote, particularly as inequality remained rampant, with 90% of the wealth of the country remaining in the hands of the big landowners and industrialists who comprised 10% of the population. However, the traditional structure of British society appeared not only to have survived the war years, but to have become even more entrenched as a result of the conflict. Post-war, the Conservatives dominated British politics, with an ambitious but weak Labour opposition and an eviscerated Liberal Party trailing behind in the polls. It would be many years before Labour would become as formidable an opponent for the Tories as the Liberals had been before the war.

Nonetheless these post-war years were to prove very different from the two decades that preceded them. Although it was not immediately apparent, the war had brought about changes which would significantly alter the old class order. It is true that from the turn of the century up to the outbreak of war in 1914 real wages had failed to rise, and in some cases had actually declined, but on the whole industrial unrest had been rare. However, from the end of the war until the middle of the 1920s the economy entered a period of uncontrolled inflation, followed by a severe slump in 1921-22 with unemployment rising to levels not seen for a hundred years, and workers were much better informed and organised. By 1920, almost 15 million of the working population were manual labourers, and trade union membership had doubled from 4 million in 1913 to around 8 million. As a result, workers were no longer prepared to accept the conditions of the past and were much more ready to challenge their employers.

In the short term, the country faced another election in October 1922, brought about by Lloyd George's forced resignation over the Chanak Crisis[290] and the withdrawal of Conservative support for the coalition. At the time the election was called, Churchill was recovering in London from an appendicitis operation. This prevented him from campaigning, and it was not until four days before the election that he put in an appearance at Dundee. He had sent many manifestos and political pamphlets to his constituents but, in the words of Churchill's biographer, Roy Jenkins, 'they were enmeshed in the assumptions of the inner circle of metropolitan politics, and were far from being skilfully targeted upon Tayside.'[291] Churchill's wife, Clementine, took an active campaigning role in place of her husband, but although Dundee had been solidly Liberal for nearly a century, it was a poor city, and Churchill suddenly found himself facing unexpectedly strong opposition from what Jenkins rather grudgingly describes as a spirit of 'sullen proletarianism'. Nonetheless, Churchill had been returned to Parliament with a huge majority of 15,000 at the previous election in 1918, and although Trevelyan wrote to his wife describing Morel as being in great form and confident of getting in at Dundee, it seems unlikely that he can have viewed his prospects with complete equanimity.

Churchill's National Liberal running mate was an elderly local employer, and three candidates opposed him, all standing to his political left. The most significant of these was Scrymgeour, pioneer of the Scottish Temperance Movement and nominally an independent Prohibitionist, who declared that he was prepared to support Morel, the only Labour candidate in the race, and entered into an unofficial alliance with him for the two available seats. Rather surprisingly, considering he was such an experienced politician, Churchill mistakenly thought that Morel was in partnership, not with Scrymgeour, but with William Gallacher who was running as a communist, although Morel had made it quite clear in a statement in the *Dundee Advertiser* at the end of October that he was the only candidate standing for the Dundee Labour Party, and was 'unalterably opposed to communism'. During the campaign, Churchill attacked both Morel and Gallacher in extreme terms – 'a predatory and confiscatory programme...championed in Dundee by two candidates both of whom were shut up during the late war in order to prevent them further hampering the national defence' – and these slurs went down badly with the Dundonians.

On account of Churchill's poor health, his campaign team had to rely on outside help, and the ex-Lord Chancellor, Birkenhead, was the principal figure imported to boost the campaign. He spent most of his speech attacking the paternity of Morel and mocking his erstwhile French name, Georges Edmond (sic) Pierre Achille Morel-de-Ville. After he had repeated this five times, in an exaggerated French accent, the audience fell into an embarrassed silence. Clementine Churchill was scathing about his performance. 'He was no use at all,' she said, 'he was drunk'.[292] But she too stooped to criticising Morel's origins at a women's meeting, enquiring acidly 'Is it true that he became an Englishman to avoid military service in the land of his birth?'

Morel's response to this remark was mild but effectively crushing:

> My father was a Frenchman, my Mother an Englishwoman, and I was born in Paris. We do not select our parents or our place of birth. I am no more responsible for the fact that my father was French than Mr Churchill is responsible for the fact that his mother was an American...My Father died when I was an infant. My Mother sent me to school when I was eight...Very clever of me to come over here when I was eight in order to escape military service.[293]

There seems no doubt that Churchill completely misjudged the aspirations and feelings of the people he had represented for fourteen years, and his approach was both aggressive and tactless. For example, he attacked D C Thompson, the famous and popular local newspaper proprietor whose tentacles spread all over Scotland, and attended an Armistice Day ceremony wearing his eleven campaign medals, a gesture that was singularly inappropriate in an impoverished and resentful Dundee. In the event, he lost disastrously. His running mate was 8,000 votes behind Morel, and he himself was a further 1,800 behind that. Scrymgeour topped the ballot with 32,000 votes and Morel polled 30,000.

Trevelyan wrote almost immediately to Morel, 'So the wheel has come full circle! From that grim dingy day at Bow Street to Dundee yesterday, the greatest popular triumph of a new movement finding its strength.'[294] Even the *Morning Post*, that pillar of orthodox conservatism as Morel described it, declared that 'Mr Churchill has been defeated by Mr Morel, as a result of which we have only to say that of the two Mr Morel is less dangerous to the interests of the country.'[295] Churchill returned to London, and remarked later that he was left 'without an office, without a seat, without a party and without an appendix.'

Morel and his Constituency

The fact that Morel repeated his triumph in the constituency in the two elections that followed in 1923 and 1924 testifies to the considerable respect and affection with which the voters of Dundee regarded their MP. The UDC's historian, Helena Swanwick, noted that both Morel and his wife had obviously made themselves much beloved there, and remarked that she had never seen political loyalty translate itself into such ardent affection as Morel's constituents displayed. This was especially marked following his second victory at the polls, when he was given a great send-off at Dundee station as he departed for the South. The police estimated that the crowd of well-wishers on this occasion was 20,000 strong.[296] There can be few MPs who have enjoyed the privilege of such a following.

Despite his popularity and verbal skills, however, there was the odd occasion when matters did not proceed as might have been expected. In April 1924, the *Aberdeen Evening Express* reported that there had been 'wild scenes' at a meeting held under the auspices of the Scottish Trade Union Congress in the Caird Hall in Dundee[297] to address the problems in the jute trade.

This issue was of great importance in Dundee, since for many years the city had been principally associated with the production of jute. At its peak in the 1860s and 1870s the jute-processing industry had employed over half the workforce, amounting to some 50,000 people working in over sixty factories. By 1914, the major employers had begun to invest money in setting up jute mills on the Indian subcontinent where they could manufacture jute products more economically by utilising cheap labour, but although this outsourcing had caused the home industry in Dundee to decline, it still afforded employment to a great many of Morel's constituents. He had therefore used the case of the jute export sector to illustrate the economic contradictions inherent in the Treaty of the Versailles and in the subsequent allied proposals in the Dawes Report,[298] pointing out that the Treaty had rendered Germany financially unable to import from Britain, whereas before the war she had been the largest importer of British goods, including jute, in Europe. He declared that if Britain continued to claim reparations from Germany on the scale that was demanded by the Treaty, Germany would be forced to sell off its manufacturing base (which utilised its jute imports) in order to raise the necessary money. This expedient would result in economic loss for all parties concerned, not least the citizens of Dundee. 'In ceasing to trade with Germany,' Morel wrote, 'we are cutting off our nose to spite our face'.

The volatile meeting referred to by the *Aberdeen Evening Express*, however, was not directly related to the level of exports, but had been called to resolve a dispute that had arisen between the Dundee Jute and Flaxworkers Union and the largest of the jute manufacturers, Camperdown Jute Works. The core issue was not a matter of wages but concerned the maximum number of spindles an operator was expected to oversee, and the controversy had led to the stoppage of the whole of the local jute industry.

Morel's sympathies lay with the strikers, whom he felt were being unfairly exploited. He declared that three generations of workers in the city had been ground down by men who had made fabulous fortunes, and he considered that demands placed on local workers were rising unacceptably as a result of employers capitalizing on the use of 'slave labour' in India. Although he was an ardent supporter of free trade as it was then conceived, he felt that such outsourcing was a step too far, and besides being highly exploitative, was grossly damaging to the welfare of his constituents. However, supporters of Mr Scrymgeour, the Prohibitionist MP, created an uproar when Morel strongly defended his support for the strike and the lockout in the trade. In response, Morel said he had been ignorantly criticised, and refuted a charge that he was indifferent to the problems arising from the stoppage as a 'stupid and outrageous' accusation.

Mayhem followed an invitation to the audience to ask questions, and the disorder increased when Morel was asked about a telegram to Mr Scrymgeour but refused to discuss the matter on the grounds that he did not wish to talk about personalities. This reply was met with cries from the gallery of 'You are a liar' and 'You are afraid to answer'. Mr Murdoch Hamilton, the Chair of the meeting, then put a ban on further questions, a decision which met with great disapproval, especially when he called on Mr Smillie to speak. Unfortunately, Mr Smillie was unable to address the crowd owing to the noise created by the Prohibitionist supporters who became so boisterous that the stewards had to use physical force to keep them in order. Refusing to be suppressed, one of the objectors broke the ring and rushed to the platform amid scenes of frantic disarray. Ultimately the Prohibitionists left the meeting, allowing it to continue in peace, but to say the least, it had clearly been an electrifying evening.

On another occasion, when speaking at a meeting in a hall at Broughty Ferry on the outskirts of Dundee, Morel rejected an extraordinary piece of Tory propaganda that depicted the Labour government as responsible for an increase in the infant mortality rate in Scotland. He totally denied the claim, saying it 'went beyond the limit of permissible and forgivable political controversy'.[299] A member of the audience then proceeded to bring an even more outlandish charge, asserting that there was a difference between the people of Russia who were Christians and members of the Soviet government – the latter, he claimed, were Jewish atheists with adopted Russian names. He went on to ask Morel if he approved of Anglo-Russian teacher exchanges, and declared that the teachers were Bolsheviks who regarded all religious instruction with contempt and that they permitted and even encouraged gross sexual immorality amongst the children, as a consequence of which venereal disease was rampant, and the practice of abortion more frequent. Morel was apparently so enraged by these bizarre accusations that, unusually for him, he lost his temper, crumpled up the piece of paper containing the speaker's question, and threw it in his face. As a result the meeting could not be continued and ended in complete confusion.[300] This incident must have worried Morel, for a week or so later he made a half-hearted apology for his outburst, acknowledging that it was always a mistake to lose self-control, but defensively adding that he considered there to be times when anger was justified.[301]

Nine months after his election he wrote a lengthy letter to Ogilvie, the Independent Labour Party's Secretary, setting out 'some account of my actions since they extended to me their confidence with such a full measure of generosity.'[302] He said that he wished he could do more and do it better, particularly with respect to housing schemes, making further provision for unemployment, pressing for a national minimum wage and redressing social inequalities. He also described how he had endeavoured to direct the attention of the Prime Minister and other leading figures in the Cabinet to the important issue of the country's external relations, especially the fact that the reparations policy had caused dangerous discord between France and Germany. He expressed himself as 'deeply troubled' by the grave situation into which the country had been drifting through 'the frivolous incompetence of Mr Lloyd George followed by the well-inspired but futile apathy of Mr Bonar Law.'

He went on to point out that although he had been elected to both the Labour Party's Executive Committee and the International Advisory Committee, he had not neglected the interests of his constituents, and had been engaged in lengthy correspondence with the Secretary of State for Scotland over maternity benefit and child welfare. He concluded by saying that it was exceedingly difficult to convey the range of duties an MP was expected to perform in twenty-four hours. In his case, a working day of fourteen to fifteen hours was not unusual.

At much the same time as this letter was written, *The Outlook* published an article on parliamentary personalities, 'appraising the worth of the newcomers of the Labour Party.' The article bracketed Morel and Emanuel (Manny) Shinwell, later Lord Shinwell, together. Both had made a strong impression, and although they displayed entirely different qualities of character, even those who were antagonistic to their views considered them 'to be possessed by the cardinal virtue of sincerity.' Morel was praised as being the more impressive speaker with the 'soldier gifts of intellect and knowledge.' The paper thought both men were marked out for higher office should Labour be returned to power.[303]

Before *The Outlook* passed this judgement, Morel wrote of his own first impressions of Westminster and the Party. During the election he had been surprised by the sarcasm directed towards 'the so-called Labour Party' because it included men who 'had not delved in the bowels of the earth, or worked in mills.' It was more curious still, he thought, to observe the puzzlement amongst the Conservatives in the House, who now appeared to find the strength of the Labour Party's appeal almost incomprehensible. Morel had contributed significantly to bringing about a realignment in British politics, and he felt that the 'Old Parties' had yet to grasp that the Labour Party had become something greater than a party, that it was 'a social movement embracing men of all types, professions and characteristics, united in common convictions and working for a common end.' He wrote that he was conscious of a sense of exultation and new-found strength in the Labour ranks, combined with a conviction that the party would be well able to hold its own in debate. Morel recognised that unity within the party was absolutely indispensable and that the country was watching and waiting to see how successful it would be.

Morel's doctor would not have approved of his work agenda, and many others, including Ogilvie, were frequently concerned that he was overworking. From his earliest days as an MP he travelled to and from Dundee, even in the depth of winter. In the first of many similar trips to the constituency, he and Mary went up to Dundee in the January following his election, staying from Monday the 15th until the following Saturday, before going on to Glasgow to speak at a study circle the next morning. Morel went on to address a mass meeting at the Town Hall in Falkirk in the evening, followed by an attendance at a big UDC demonstration on the Monday.[304] Engagements of this nature, and there were many of them, were augmented by others elsewhere in the country, where he spoke at UDC meetings or lectured on foreign affairs, and the punishing schedule took an increasing toll on his health. It appears he was unwell again towards the end of 1923 and the beginning of 1924, at which point Mary wrote that he had had a 'beastly time' and that it would be a while before he could take up the reins again.

Swanwick too had been troubled by Morel's obvious exhaustion. She was in Dundee in October 1924 shortly before the election, when the Morels were working in the constituency. Morel was due to address a meeting, and as she accompanied the couple to the conference hall, he had been stuck by a sharp pain in his chest. He had recovered and was able to continue, apparently showing no further sign of distress, but the incident had been alarming. Describing his address, Swanwick wrote, 'He was lavish with the whole of his rich personality and no one in the hall, seeing that upright figure, with his head thrown back to welcome the applause of the densely packed crowd and hearing his warm voice ring out triumphantly would have guessed that Death had just touched him with a warning finger.'[305] Sadly, Death's warning was all too prescient.

Even Morel occasionally admitted in his correspondence with Ogilvie that he was tired, or that it would be nice to exchange a bit of time in the Commons for a few hours of healthy digging in his garden, but in fact the incessant work schedule to which he subjected himself can have left small opportunity for leisure activities. This seems especially sad, as Morel was devoted to his family and had many interests. We know, for instance, that he greatly enjoyed gardening, and was renowned for his 'green fingers'. A photograph of Cherry Croft taken around this time shows him with Mary and Oliver on the patio of the house, which is a bower of flowers and shrubs. The back of the photograph is rather touchingly inscribed, 'He grew things wonderfully'.[306] He also played tennis and continued his interest in moths and butterflies, but there are no records to confirm whether he kept up these hobbies. Nor is there any account of his social life, so we cannot even tell whether he enjoyed wining and dining with friends in Kings Langley and the surrounding neighbourhood.

We do know, however, that life at home was not without its own worries. During Morel's years as an MP, Stella, 'his tall and handsome daughter', had taken on the role of secretary and his study was apparently filled with row upon row of documents all neatly bound up in brown paper, 'a model of orderliness'. She had become his constant companion, comrade and fellow worker – in the words of Swanwick, 'the perfect assistant for one endowed with such an enormous power of work and concentration as Morel possessed'. But Stella became very ill in December 1923, and had to undergo a 'grave' operation. Mary recorded that it had been a terrible ten days, but that Stella had improved and seemed much better by the New Year, when she went off to Switzerland for a few weeks' recuperation. The boys were the cause of intermittent anxiety too, although by comparison their troubles were relatively trivial: Roger did not have a job, and at some stage John had been at home with a badly septic hand, while at another, Oliver had been confined to bed with tonsillitis and gland trouble, which was described as his particular weakness. Mary herself was also unwell during this time, and although there is no record of the exact nature of her illness, it is certainly arguable that exhaustion and worry may have contributed to her poor health.

During the post-war years, both before and after he became an MP, Morel's life was remarkable for the relentless intensity with which he pursued one cause after another, and photographs taken at this period show prematurely grey hair and a steely gaze that speaks of grim resolution. He was clearly driven by a new determination to win the recognition that he felt he justly deserved, and it is hard to resist the conclusion that he was aware of how little time he had left to do so.

In the past he had always focussed on a limited number of major issues, notably the Congo, the run up to the war, and the post-war settlement and the Treaty of Versailles, but although he was now ranging widely over a whole variety of subjects his impressive command of the relevant facts remained undiminished. In some cases he pointed out that the matters he was addressing had direct bearing on his constituents' future, and in others that this impact was mediated by their effect on the future of Europe, but the importance of maintaining peace was always his basic principle. Indeed, all the disparate concerns he espoused in the last few years of his life were informed by his unwavering belief that another war was imminent, and that every possible effort must be made to avert it.

There were many who warned of impending conflict, but there were few who voiced their fears so clearly and so early on. Morel described the threat in unequivocal, apocalyptic terms in 1922 in an article in the *Daily Herald*:

> There was a Great War. We were on the side that won – now nearly four years ago. Today 2 million of our workers are wholly or partially unemployed. In hundreds of thousands of families acute distress has replaced habitual discomfort, wages have dropped unprecedentedly… Europe is on the immediate eve of an economic cataclysm which will deepen the shadows in the homes of our workers – for we are part of Europe. And that cataclysm is the forerunner of something even worse.
>
> Another and a far more terrible war than the one into which our people plunged in 1914 is in the making. It may come in five years; perhaps much sooner. Why these present and prospective calamities? Because when the war ended the winning side closed the war, not by a Peace but by a sentence of enslavement upon the beaten foe – composed of living men and women with hearts to suffer and break like our own. That Sentence is working out its doom – the doom of all of us – being conceived in hate and folly, buttressed by falsehood, imposed by fraud, enforced by starvation. That Sentence, if it be not revoked, will pursue the framers and victims of it alike with implacable, undeviating relentlessness until both fall into the abyss.[307]

Morel's timescale regarding the outbreak of another conflict was amiss by just over a decade, but it is doubtful if even he could have imagined how wholly devastating the 'far more terrible' war he had forecast would turn out to be.

The Decline of the UDC

It cannot be said that the UDC had succeeded in exerting any real influence upon the policies of the coalition government either during, or in the immediate aftermath, of the war. However, the change in political alignment following the armistice, to which the UDC had contributed significantly, was a profound shift and justified a degree of optimism regarding a more promising future. In his book on the UDC, published in 1919, Charles Trevelyan reflected this mood when he wrote:

> Now we face our more hopeful future in the world. There are now only two parties in the world. On one side are the reactionaries, and the militarists who have made the war and the false peace – against them are the repudiators of force, and the believers in internationalism, gathered chiefly in the Socialist and Labour Parties of all lands. The middle people, the President Wilsons and the Liberals, the doctrinaires of the peace-out-of-war policy have pitifully failed. Today the militarists have tried again and won. Tomorrow we shall try again, and win. But our victory can only come by a whole-hearted adoption of international ideas, and by a direct challenge of the central principles of the system that has ended in disaster.[308]

By the end of the war the UDC and its affiliated organisations, most of them local or regional trade unions, had a combined membership of more than 650,000 and although the ending of hostilities somewhat undermined its sense of direction, its members were still committed enough to hold an international conference in Geneva in the summer of 1920.

Arthur Ponsonby described the meeting's cosmopolitan character in an article in *International Affairs*. 'An observant stranger walking in the streets of Geneva in the early days of July might have stared with some astonishment at seeing an unmistakable German walking with an equally unmistakable Frenchman, Englishman, and Italian along the street, engaged in intimate and friendly conversation'. Each was wearing a little silver badge upon which the initials UDC were engraved. 'What' he asked ironically, 'was that useless, traitorous and mischievous organisation up to now?' [309] The twenty-four delegates, of whom over a third were women, are pictured on the steps of the Societé des Arts, with Morel in the front row standing almost head and shoulders over his companions. Ponsonby claimed somewhat grandiosely that where governments had failed to assemble the nations in Paris except 'in their invidious positions of victors and vanquished, and where the League of Nations had failed to assemble more than the dictating representatives of the Allied Powers,' the UDC had succeeded in bringing together the belligerent nations, together with representatives from Poland, Czechoslovakia, Switzerland, Egypt and India.

The conference, which was organised by Morel, lasted for three days and was described as an unqualified success, although also amazingly strenuous. Given 'his unconquerable habit of trying to sit up until 3.00am and then getting up at 4.00am', Morel must have been an exhausting companion, and in a letter to Mary Morel, Ponsonby wrote that they went to bed with their throats sore with talking.[310] Nonetheless, when reading an account of the proceedings over those three days it is impossible not to feel that the delegates inhabited a parallel universe to that existing outside the walls of the Societé des Arts, and it is not altogether surprising to find that the conference seems to have been the last significant international act of the UDC.

Morel's election to Parliament in 1922 was described by Helena Swanwick as 'the country's gain and the UDC's loss', and it certainly meant that the time he could spare for the UDC became extremely limited. An additional problem soon arose, since by law ministers could not be involved with non-party political associations which might at some time be critical of government policy. There were thirty members of the UDC in the 1922 Parliament, and when the first Labour government was formed in 1924 it included five members of the UDC Executive and eight members of its General Council.[311] This meant that the UDC lost a great many of its most able and articulate members, and although Morel continued to edit and write for *Foreign Affairs,* he felt that the time had come to close down the Union and instead form a membership subscription base for the paper.

He talked over the subject with Helena Swanwick and they agreed that unless men of considerable public reputation could speak and work for the UDC, as they had done over the past ten years, the organisation should be wound up and the money saved should be used to fund the paper.[312] In fact, the ending of the war had largely removed the raison d'être of the organisation, and the executive meetings which had taken place on a weekly basis had already been reduced to monthly occasions, while other large meetings had become rare, and mass demonstrations even more so.

On the other hand, *Foreign Affairs* flourished and became the most successful of the various propaganda organs edited by Morel throughout his career. Since it was the only periodical on the left of British politics concerned exclusively with foreign policy, it effectively acquired a quasi-official authority in the mind of many Labour members. It was noted by Trevelyan that international issues were being studied by the 'political working man' and that *Foreign Affairs*, as the one international monthly paper in Britain, had a circulation of 20,000, chiefly among the leaders of the working class.

Ireland

In spite of giving so much of his attention to the Versailles Treaty and the post-war landscape of Europe, Morel was still able to allot time to examining the recurring question of Ireland and its struggle for independence. Following the 1918 election, the Sinn Féin candidates, who had won 73 out of 105 Irish seats, had refused to participate in the Westminster Parliament. Instead they met in Dublin where they instituted the Dáil Éireann, or Irish Assembly, and passed a motion of independence establishing an Irish Republic. This was very much more than the 'Home Rule' envisaged by the British government before the war, which would have created a constitutional arrangement designed to leave Ireland in a position comparable to that of the Welsh or Scottish Assemblies today. The Dáil established ministries, raised a public loan, and called on people to boycott the Royal Irish Constabulary (RIC) as 'agents of a foreign power'.[313] It was not long before volunteers started to join the Irish Republican Army and wage a guerrilla war against both the RIC and the British army. After some months of indecision the government reacted with considerable brutality in an effort to put down the insurrection.

The cause of Ireland was taken up by the UDC in November 1920 when it passed a resolution that it:

> ...protests against the reign of terror which the Government has introduced into Ireland; calls for an impartial inquiry to determine the responsibility for deeds that are disgracing the British nation all over the world, and declares that the solution of the Irish problem

can be sought only through an observance of the pledges of self-determination for small nationalities, proclaimed by the Government in regard to oppressed Continental peoples. [314]

Morel devoted most of a special supplement in *Foreign Affairs* to a debate on the issue, as violence against both the RIC and the British troops stationed in Ireland intensified.[315] His views remained much as they had been before the war when he addressed his prospective constituents at Birkenhead. 'It is primarily then from the international point of view that the UDC regards the tragedy of Ireland; the tragedy of imperialist oppression, of political crime, of military and police reprisals, of burned homesteads and factories, of ever growing embitterment, and worst of all of the apathy and ignorance of the British public in the face of a situation so dangerous and so degrading.' He declared that the Irish people had lost all belief in the British government, in British justice and even in British common sense. 'Things seemed to be working up to a much bloodier crisis than the rebellion of 1916.'

Morel considered that the question of Ireland was essentially one of international politics, and that the country should be permitted to become a member of the society of nations if it chose to do so. He held that Britain's Irish policies had constituted a classic case of British hypocrisy during the war, and as such had been the chief factor preventing the neutral world from accepting 'the professions of the British Government that it was fighting for small nationalities.' Whereas in the past he had forthrightly opposed the idea that half the population of the province of Ulster should veto the aspirations of the Irish people, on this occasion he recognised the need for the government to secure the rights of the minority in Ireland, but he also felt that it would be in the interests of the majority to act towards them in a conciliatory way. (Perhaps he took into account the exhortations of F E Smith's penny whistle[316] and Sir Edward Carson's primitive war-horn, alluded to on page 93!)

Morel's rather optimistic views on arriving at a solution were not shared by A E Russell, the Irish Nationalist, who wrote in a letter to *Foreign Affairs* that he doubted whether any exposition of the Irish question would have the slightest effect in bringing about an Irish settlement. 'Most Irishmen,' he declared, 'do not see that there is anything to be gained by explaining to any generation of Englishman the wrong being done in Ireland.' With hindsight, it is plain that this observation was depressingly accurate. Indeed it would take almost another three generations to reach a satisfactory settlement of the Irish question.

Tour of Europe

Morel rarely travelled abroad, and although we know that he was on holiday in France just before the outbreak of war and made a brief trip to Poland at the invitation of the Polish Socialist Party in 1923, his visit to the United States in the early years of the century and his journey to Nigeria following the end of the Congo campaign, appear to have been his only major forays outside the country. A month-long tour of Europe in the autumn of 1923 was therefore an unusual experience for him. In the course of four weeks he visited Italy, Germany, Switzerland and Holland, and met with a number of prominent figures, including Stresemann, the German Chancellor, and the Presidents of Bavaria and Württemberg, as well as the leaders of most of Germany's political parties.

The *Dundee Advertiser* reported that Morel returned from his travels more than ever convinced that Britain's balance of payment problems and high unemployment rate were vitally linked to the situation on the Continent. He had already claimed that the attitude of the British government had weakened British prestige and interests all over Europe and described all classes in Germany to be desperate and 'well-nigh hopeless',[317] and he now pointed out that the fluctuation of the mark had created social conditions of such extreme hardship and inconvenience that nobody in Britain could possibly appreciate the situation. He wrote that the attempts to create a stabilised currency based on the gold mark to stave off internal chaos must eventually fail, unless the enduring problem of reparations was settled and the Versailles Treaty drastically revised.

Before his trip to the Continent, Morel had been advised by Ramsay MacDonald that the Prime Minister, Stanley Baldwin, was broadly sympathetic to the Labour Party's view on Germany: 'On all essentials his views coincide pretty closely with ours, and the only question is how far he can bring them out and how far he knows the details of the controversy to make the most of them.'[318] It must have been the case that Baldwin was like-minded, as shortly after his return to England Morel was invited to meet the Prime Minister at Chequers for a private interview.

Morel wrote a lengthy account of this meeting, which was focussed solely on Germany, and described it as extremely friendly and perfectly natural. He wrote that for most of the time Baldwin simply sat 'smoking a big curved pipe and listening to me reading notes of my conversations with Stresemann and other German notabilities.' After giving this account, Morel drew the Prime Minister's attention to conditions in Germany as he conceived them, and expressed the need for 'active diplomacy'. Baldwin responded, pointing out that the ultimate sanction behind diplomacy was force, and adding that he believed Poincaré, the French Prime Minister, had pledged himself to negotiate with Germany over the recent occupation of the Ruhr.[319] Morel insisted that 'to an Englishman it is incomprehensible that the French do not see what we are doing, how they are going against their own interests. When Germany unites again, the French will be wiped out. It may take ten or twenty or even fifty years but the end is inevitable.'

Baldwin complained that Morel had no idea of the difficulties entailed in the job of Prime Minister, and of how impossible it was to get anything done in the face of the Rothermere Press and the 'Die Hards'. Morel stressed again the danger of a French hegemony in Europe and said that the only course was a strong diplomatic stand. When Baldwin asked him what he would do if he were dictator of England, Morel answered that it was incumbent upon the government to enter into direct negotiations with Germany. Perhaps this advice had some long-term effect on the Prime Minister, who during his last period of office from 1935-37 was accused of appeasement towards Germany and of failing to rearm the country.

In a much later account of Morel's meeting with Baldwin it was said that both men were aghast when, towards the end of the interview, Morel described the appalling conditions he had seen in Europe over the last years – 'rags in Poland, hunger in Austria, revolt in Hungary.' These depressing thoughts seemed to be almost too much for Baldwin, who apparently lifted a bowl of blood-red roses, enquiring, 'Do you like roses, Morel?' When Morel replied that he did, Baldwin responded with evident desperation, 'Then bury your face in this loveliness and thank God.'[320]

The Anglo-Russian Treaty

From the end of the war until his death, the international issue that preoccupied Morel more than any other was the question of Russia. Given that Morel had embraced socialism, it was not surprising that his article in *Foreign Affairs* roundly condemned the attempt by the allied powers to overthrow the new regime.[321] He described it as a capitalist war, a war between Russian Socialism and French and British Capitalism. In terms that prefigure President Eisenhower's complaint of being 'powerless in the face of the industrial/military complex', and foreshadowing today's sense that our governments are simply pawns in the global economy, he wrote that we must not let ourselves 'make the mistake of imagining that we are governed by Mr Lloyd George. We are governed by the Foreign Office, the India Office, the War Office, the Committee of Imperial Defence, the military and naval clubs and Lord Northcliffe (the newspaper proprietor); by the great vested imperial interests which move behind the scenes, whose power is gigantic and, as yet, barely sensed by Labour.' His view of Russia as a Socialist State, free of external foes and surrounded by other states with which she shared kinship and political alliances was highly idealistic, but the fact that he compared its structure to that of British imperialism nonetheless indicated that he realised that it would become a powerful force in the future.

The year after the tsarist regime collapsed in 1917, Russia had signed the Treaty of Brest-Litovsk with Germany, and the Labour movement had pressed for the opening of full diplomatic and trade relations with the Bolsheviks. It continued to call for this Anglo-Russian Treaty when the Soviet Union was formed in 1922. However, it was not until Labour came to office in January 1924 that full recognition was given to the Soviet Union in response to the considerable pressure from within the party. Much of that pressure had been orchestrated by the Anglo-Russian Parliamentary Committee chaired by the chairman of the TUC, A A Purcell. Morel was a leading member of the Committee and wrote a short leaflet recording the chief reasons for the ratification of the Anglo-Russian Treaty.[322]

Morel had always been well aware of the importance of international trade to the British economy, and he considered that the Treaty was essential if the country was to re-establish and increase its foreign trade. He wrote that one in three of the working population was engaged in the export market, and that a decrease in purchasing power on account of unemployment amongst export workers adversely affected home markets as well. He supported this contention with detailed figures of imports and exports across a range of goods, and pointed out that the country was now afflicted by phenomenal unemployment because her European markets were 'at present deranged'. The greatest achievement of the Treaty would therefore be to normalise relations between the two countries and permit peaceful cooperation in trade and industry in the future.

In the event, the first attempt to ratify the Treaty failed, as negotiations with the Russian delegation broke down. Undeterred, however, a number of backbenchers led by Morel met with Ponsonby, who was now Undersecretary of State for Foreign Affairs, and suggested they should act as intermediaries with the Russian delegation in order to reopen negotiations and find a solution to the problem – 'the amount and method of payment of the compensation to be paid by the Government of the (Soviet) Union in respect of claims preferred by British nationals' – which threatened to derail the talks.[323] After many hours of exhaustive discussion a form of words was found which satisfied both parties, and in due course a formula acceptable to both sides was agreed and the Treaty was concluded. Although he is not specifically mentioned in Ponsonby's account of the talks, the person described as 'one of the most resourceful members of the British Delegation (who) found a form of words on different lines', is almost certainly Morel, and Ponsonby further notes that this exercise in diplomacy turned out to be extremely helpful. Ponsonby himself meditatively described the difficulty of his task, which he found particularly daunting as he had no previous experience of treaty making. 'A Socialist Minister acting on behalf of a Capitalist nation had to make an agreement with a Communist Government – not an easy task to perform.'

A photograph was taken at the Russian offices in New Bond Street, following the acceptance by the Russian Delegation of the formula affecting British owners whose property had been nationalised by the Soviet government. Morel, who obviously considered that he had been the key player in this part of the negotiations, is sitting in the centre of the group of MPs and Russian delegates, with Rakovsky, the Soviet Union's representative in Britain, on his left.[324]

The signing of the Treaty gave the Conservative press a welcome opportunity to attack the Labour government. 'How the Cabinet surrendered', declared the *Evening News*, 'Back bench socialists our real Rulers'; *The Times* wrote of 'Secret diplomacy on the one hand, and the Bolshevist delegates on the other'; *The Morning Post* complained of the 'bullying tactics of men like Mr Morel and Mr Lansbury to which the Prime Minister succumbed without so much as a fight'.[325]

Rather surprisingly Morel seems to have been unaware of the damaging effects that the Treaty would have on the party, just as he appeared unmoved by charges that the conditions of the Treaty had been arrived at without being put to Parliament, a process he would have vehemently condemned in the pre-war years. He claimed in the House of Commons that the government was prepared to go down on the issue and, 'would return with double our numbers.'[326] In fact, at the ensuing election in November 1924, Labour's brief tenure of ten months was overturned by the Conservatives who returned to Parliament with 413 members, against 151 Labour members and 40 Liberals.

The fall of the party was partly attributed to the notorious Zinoviev Letter.[327] Morel, as might have been expected, was the first to suggest that the letter was a forgery and that its release was part of a conspiracy by the Foreign Office to defeat the Labour party at the election. In making such a claim Morel returned to the theme that had dominated his life:

the secrecy and obfuscation of professional diplomacy and the need for more democratic control of foreign policy. In what turned out to be his last speech, he spoke for over an hour to a huge crowd of 4,000 at the Caird Hall in Dundee, and 'warned that the work of pacification undertaken by the Labour Party was being sabotaged by the intrigue of permanent officials'.[328] He described the release of the 'Red Letter', as it came to be known, as 'an act of treachery…unparalleled in the history of this country…a gross, a crude and a palpable forgery.' Denying the Prime Minister's expression of confidence in the Foreign Office, he spoke of him as 'a generous man. He tries to cover a Foreign Office official with the mantle of his own responsibility. He says he "does not complain". Yes, but we complain…the Labour Party are determined that the Foreign Secretary shall be master in his own household.'[329]

As it turned out Morel was not substantially mistaken. The letter *was* certainly forged, though probably by the intelligence services rather than the Foreign Office, and both its forgery and its wide dissemination constituted a deliberate attempt to inflict the maximum damage possible on the Labour government. Although this deception was not exposed for some time, Morel's constituents appeared to relish his charges, and shortly after his attack on the Foreign Office he was returned to the House of Commons with a larger majority than he had gained in either of his other two parliamentary elections.

The Treaty, however, was rescinded by the incoming Conservative government. It was not until Labour returned to power in 1929 that a Protocol was finally signed between Ramsey MacDonald and Christian Rakovsky to re-establish the agreements made in 1924.

Morel Hopes for Cabinet Post

The election of a Labour government in 1924 understandably raised Morel's hopes that he would be offered a senior post in the administration, since his knowledge, organisational skills and powers of oratory were beyond dispute. He aspired to a Cabinet post, in particular that of Foreign Secretary, a position for which he seemed particularly suited. In the words of Helena Swanwick, 'there was one man in the Labour Party unmistakeably marked out for the Foreign Office by knowledge, ability and devotion to all the causes for which Labour stood in its international relations: E D Morel.'[330] Despite this assessment, however, Swanwick knew Morel too well to expect that he would be appointed, writing later that she 'never for one moment believed that the Premier would invite Morel to be Foreign Secretary.'[331] Rather, she perceived that he and MacDonald had 'drifted far apart' and recognised that Morel was not a man to subordinate his opinions to those of a superior whose views were less well founded. Such intransigence would have led to frequent clashes in Cabinet for he was, as she put it, 'more familiar with diplomatic documents than any man I have ever known.' Moreover, an uncompromising disposition might not have been a helpful attribute in a post where a tactful, some might say devious, approach to international negotiations was frequently needed. As a result, Swanwick was convinced that he and MacDonald could never work as a team. She also appreciated that the Prime Minister would not welcome being 'inundated with memoranda', a fate which many of Morel's acquaintances had habitually endured.

On the other hand, Morel had been responsible for many of the Labour Party's pledges on foreign policy and was astonishingly well informed about the international issues of his day. Indeed, as a result of his expertise, he had become the Labour Party's foremost spokesman on foreign affairs. This record placed him at a considerable advantage over others who might have been considered eligible for the post. Nor was it unreasonable to imagine that his close and longstanding relationship with Ramsay MacDonald would count in his favour when matters of preferment arose. But as it turned out, these hopes came to nothing. Instead, the Prime Minister wrote to him expressing his deep regret that 'I have tried hard to get you into something as an under Secy (sic) but have completely failed.' He went on to say that he was not in complete control 'but have to consult heads' and remarked on how sorry he was but would do his best later on if any practicable opportunity presented itself.[332]

Morel had not been alone in thinking that he should have preferment. Arthur Ponsonby wrote to Morel to say that he had 'simply gasped' when 'RM' told him that Jimmy Thomas had got the post of Foreign Secretary. '...to give the job to Jimmy Thomas!!!!, JT knows next to nothing about Foreign Affairs. If we are going to give posts for meritorious Trade Union Service and not for knowledge and capacity, we shall be discredited from the start.'[333] Others wrote to Morel in similar terms: 'someone has blundered, an inexcusable indignity upon one supremely esteemed.', 'I have been much troubled at not seeing the name of E D Morel as the new Foreign Secretary.'[334]

However, although the expectations and disappointment of Morel and his supporters were understandable, objectively viewed there were several specific reasons why MacDonald could not have given serious consideration to appointing Morel to the post. Most critically, France was Britain's closest ally on the international scene, and in view of Morel's past record it would have been inimical to good Anglo-French relations to have appointed him Foreign Secretary. Furthermore, the professional staff at the Foreign Office would not have looked gladly upon a superior who for many years had been deeply critical of almost everything they had done.

Nor can Swanwick's opinion that the Prime Minister suffered from a sense of intellectual inferiority be ruled out. MacDonald may well have felt disinclined to include a minister in his Cabinet who was endowed with a sharper intelligence and a broader vision than he himself possessed. Bertrand Russell referred to this unattractive trait many years later in a letter to Wuliger:

> ...as is now well known MacDonald hated to have around him anyone with superior ability who directed his life according to recognised moral principles; and there was no doubt whatever about the honesty and integrity of Morel. He was a man who would have stood up against the most powerful permanent official and who, I believe, was impervious to corruption. A very dangerous man from the point of view of MacDonald.[335]

There can be no doubt that his exclusion from the Labour government must have been a bitter blow to Morel, and in many ways it undoubtedly amounted to something of a betrayal. Morel had been the life force of the UDC for years – as Swanwick had put it, 'he *was* the UDC' – and without him the Labour Party might never have developed as it had done. Now those who had been inspired by him and had looked up to him for a decade were elevated above him, and although all of them were worthy and able men (they were all men), it must be admitted that they too might have found his presence at the Cabinet table disconcerting, for none of them had the charisma and qualities he commanded.

Morel was greatly dispirited. In a lengthy letter to Lord Parmoor in February 1924, he wrote bitterly of his rejection:

> There is nothing in my attitude on the war and the peace which differs from MacDonald's or Ponsonby's or Trevelyan's, all of whom are THE Government while I am stigmatised as a political pariah which my erstwhile colleagues must avoid, in their interest and in accordance with the national demand, as the very plague itself. Here is even the Morning Post complacently chronicling that Ponsonby and Trevelyan represent the Union of Democratic Control in Government – while I who did more than anyone of them (they would generously admit it) to make it a force, am, forsooth, pilloried and unclean. It is perfectly grotesque. Here in every paper the UDC is revived – MacDonald is even openly described as its founder (he was one of them), Ponsonby's and Trevelyan's connection with it is widely referred to without a suggestion of reproach all over the country – but I am taboo…I am impossible: I am to be wiped out and forgotten. I might have done something disgraceful – instead of being for ten years the close associate and colleague of the men who are running the Government of the country.[336]

Unfortunately, when perhaps he should have let the matter rest, Morel made several more futile efforts to find a place in government. He wrote directly to MacDonald:

> It is already being said and will increasingly be said, that, in view of all the circumstances – my long association with you in less happy times and so on – my exclusion from your government, when so many men from the UDC are in it, can only be attributable to the fact that there MUST be some substance in the various charges and

innuendoes brought against me…I do not know myself how the thing can now be met. But I felt impelled to mention it, because, I confess, it troubles me very greatly, less, if the truth be known, for myself than for my family.'[337]

As the Prime Minister did not deign to reply, Morel again wrote to Lord Parmoor, Lord President of the Council, suggesting that he should be appointed Parliamentary Undersecretary to the League of Nations.[338] This met with a sympathetic response but nothing came of it. It was left to Ponsonby to continue trying to find a post for him, but again the effort proved to be in vain.

Swanwick writes that relations between Morel and MacDonald now assumed an air of virtual hostility, and it was her belief that had Morel survived, he would have become the leader 'of a very energetic opposition to the Prime Minister.'[339] Indeed, it does seem quite possible that MacDonald was frightened of Morel, who once boasted that he had the power to bring down the government. This was probably an empty threat, for it was most improbable that he still commanded sufficient support within the party to bring about a putsch. By this time he had neither the backing of the trade unions (who had taken his part in the debate over the Russian Treaty but were largely indifferent to other foreign policy matters) nor of the professional class of MPs who been involved in the formulation of the Labour government's foreign policy.

The election of a Labour government may not have produced the desired outcome for Morel, but it did result in a unique event taking place in the House of Commons. On 9th of January, very shortly after the election, seventeen members of Parliament who had been imprisoned for religious or political reasons were entertained to dinner at the House. Also present were several non-conformist ministers who were imprisoned as 'passive resisters', a group of ladies who had been sent to prison as suffragettes, a number of 'anti-vaccinationists' (sic) and some conscientious objectors. The invitation described the event as a:

> Dinner in honour of Ex-Prisoner Members of Parliament at the House of Commons', and carries the names of the seventeen erstwhile prisoners, amongst them prominent members of the UDC. The list included George Lansbury, Frederick Pethick-Lawrence and Morel, and also bore the name of Emanuel Shinwell. The *Daily Graphic* published a picture of the party of forty-eight guests round the table the following day. The caption below described it as 'the social side of Parliament being ushered in by one of the strangest political parties on record.[340]

Morel Returns to the Issue of Parliamentary Control of Foreign Policy

Now that he had been denied the opportunity of holding office in the government, Morel returned to the issue of parliamentary control of foreign policy, a matter which had obsessed him since he joined the UDC. Possibly he thought he could now best make his mark in a field in which he had great experience, and where a successful outcome would have been a significant achievement.

The government had already passed a resolution proposed by Arthur Ponsonby 'to lay on the table of the Houses of Parliament every treaty, when signed, for a period of twenty-one days after which the treaty will be ratified.' This followed an earlier resolution put forward the previous year by the Labour Party when in opposition, containing the key proposal that 'no act of war shall be committed directly or indirectly without the consent of Parliament and that no international treaty whatever shall be ratified until it has been submitted to and approved by Parliament.'[341]

Morel sent a letter to Ponsonby congratulating him 'for striking the first blow for UDC policy of Democratic Control in the House'[342] but also expressed his unease. 'While I am sure that the Nation is perfectly safe whilst you and the PM are at the helm,' he wrote, 'the fact remains that the moment you leave office, the Nation is just as insecure as ever.' He pointed out that a mere resolution could not possibly guarantee the necessary binding conditions, and that a Parliamentary Bill would be the only satisfactory solution. He suggested that, since he had spoken to hundreds of thousands of his fellow countrymen over the last ten years on this particular matter, he might be charged with the duty of introducing the matter to the House.[343] Ponsonby responded that Morel didn't understand the difficulties that had to be overcome and that 'a Bill would be the very devil…it would take a whole session and be riddled by constitutional lawyers and at the end be a poor affair.'[344]

It must have been profoundly frustrating for someone who was so accustomed to public acclaim to be prevented from playing any key role in Parliament, particularly in respect to a matter with which he was so familiar. Indeed in view of his extraordinary record of campaigning it was positively humiliating for Morel to be confined to the role of backbencher. It is to his credit that having failed in his pitch for office, there is no record of him having voiced any further resentment.

Instead, he returned to the familiar territory of the written word. He published a lengthy article in *Foreign Affairs*,[345] 'First Steps Towards Democratic Control of Foreign Policy', revisiting the case he had made for democratic control ten years earlier in the run-up to the war. In this piece he reiterated his proposal that the way forward should be a resolution to Parliament followed up by a bill, and at his instigation the Foreign Office was inundated with petitions from UDC and ILP branches and trade unions. But these fell on stony ground. MacDonald, well versed in Morel's tactics, shrugged them aside and no further action was taken on the matter. Morel, always on the lookout for those who stood in his way, blamed this neglect on the Foreign Office 'together with the forces of Society, the Professional classes and military and other circles, armament firms and so forth.' But it has been suggested that the sad fact of the matter may have been that the proposal no longer aroused much interest,[346] an assessment that Morel would have found particularly difficult to accept.

During this frustrating period, Morel's health became increasingly precarious. The letter written by Mary in which she described him as having had a 'beastly time' conveys little of the alarm she must have felt. His spell of illness in the autumn of 1923 had obviously weakened him, and his doctor, White Robinson, wrote to John Ogilvie in March 1924 saying that he had called in to Cherry Croft to tell Morel that it was absurd for him to think of going to Dundee. He was 'pretty well exhausted after having an unbroken and ghastly attack of hiccups lasting nine days and nights.'[347] However, he recognised that if Morel did not visit his constituency he would worry himself to death, and added that if great care was taken of him by those around him, and every possible constraint put upon him to avoid fatigue, the satisfaction of fulfilling his engagement would probably do him more good than harm. Robinson knew all too well that his patient was not easily persuaded to take it easy, and appealed to the whole family for support in restraining him, since another hiccupping attack could easily be fatal.

Matters were not much better a month later. On this occasion Morel had apparently not been fit enough to attend a meeting of the Dundee Trades and Labour Party. The *Dundee Advertiser* recorded that a 'lengthy communication' from him was read to the meeting. This message had included a reference to his recent illness, stating that his ill health had 'converted him into a medical phenomenon, and apart from becoming a repository for most of the drugs in the British Pharmacopoeia, it had left him extremely prostrated, and his recovery was proving to be a slow process.'[348] As he was due to open a sale of work during this visit to Dundee, Morel wrote a further letter of apology to the event's organisers, saying that it was a great disappointment to him not to be able to attend. He added that he could find little consolation in apparently establishing a medical record 'in resisting an assault unprecedented in duration of time, by the particular microbe from whose sinister activities I am now slowly recovering – except such consolation as may be derived from the knowledge that I seem to take a great deal of killing!'[349]

Morel revealed almost no bitterness about his ill health in his correspondence at this time, yet on top of his recent rebuffs it must have been particularly galling to have been struck down in this way. However, he had become a popular and respected MP, and it was perhaps some consolation that he was elected to the Labour Party Executive Committee in 1924. He spoke regularly in the House, where he was able to exercise his speaking skills and display his command of his chosen subjects. He had travelled a long and arduous road from clerk at Elder Dempster in Liverpool to prominent national figure at Westminster, and Parliament provided a comfortable forum in which to exert the influence he now commanded. Unfortunately, the time left for him to do so turned out to be lamentably short.

The Dawes Report [350]

One of MacDonald's first duties on coming to power was to determine the Labour Party's attitude to the Dawes Report. In the past MacDonald had criticised the Treaty of Versailles just as vigorously as Morel and the majority of his colleagues and, in common with the UDC and International Labour, he had also expressed a desire for complete reconciliation with Germany. However, this rapprochement had not taken place, and a crisis arose in January 1923 when France refused to agree to a German request for a two-year moratorium on cash payments to alleviate the country's severe economic distress. Britain had been prepared to agree to this but the French had demanded more in the way of 'productive guarantees', and together with the Belgians, they occupied the Ruhr on 11th January in order to extract the payments due to them. This move caused outrage in Germany, and MacDonald condemned it in forthright terms. For his part, Morel had instantly predicted that the occupation of the Ruhr would be disastrous, and indeed it soon crippled the German economy while bringing few benefits to France.

Responding to the crisis with an attempt to restore Germany's financial position, the Reparations Commission appointed two sub-committees to consider the possible options. In April 1924 one of the sub-committees, chaired by the American financier and future Vice President, Charles Dawes, produced a proposal which was accepted by the Commission. It recommended a loan of 800 million gold marks to help Germany re-establish control over its currency, a reduction in the annual reparations payments, and assurances that the Ruhr area would be evacuated by the French and Belgian occupation forces. Arguably it was not wholly fortuitous that these suggestions were in tune with American self-interest, for although American politicians no longer played any significant role in Europe, Germany was an important market for American businessmen and bankers, and they had no desire to see such a valuable source of revenue permanently curtailed.

Implementation of the Dawes Plan obviously necessitated a substantial revision of the Treaty of Versailles, an emendation that could not be achieved unless it was first agreed by the major powers. Consequently a conference was convened in London in July, made up of representatives from Belgium, Britain, France, Germany, Italy and the United States, and chaired by MacDonald. The Dawes Report was more or less in line with MacDonald's professed views, but he was reluctant to go further at the conference and insist on a substantial reduction in Germany's overall indebtedness. By the time the conference had ended in mid-August agreement had been reached on the withdrawal of the occupation forces and the reduction of reparations to benefit Germany in the short term, with payments beginning at a million marks for the first year and rising over a period of four years to 2.5 billion marks per year.

Meanwhile, the UDC had debated the Dawes Report at a session in May 1924 and had issued a manifesto[351] which expressed the hope that the French and German governments would accept the report's proposals, since they offered 'a possible means of escape from a situation which was rapidly leading to disaster.' It had also confirmed the UDC's view that the imposition of further large sums 'by way of tribute for an unspecified number of years' would be economically disastrous, and had urged the government to renounce any further share in reparations, provided that the sum renounced decreased by an equal amount to the total sum to be paid.

In view of the fact that MacDonald was no longer prepared to demand any major reduction in reparation payments, this manifesto had given rise to considerable alarm in the Foreign Office. Ponsonby wrote to Morel[352] saying that he feared it would 'cause trouble' and that the *Daily Telegraph* was going 'to make the most of it' the following day. He suspected that German nationalists would make capital out of it and the suspicions of the French would be aroused. A statement had had to be issued, he wrote, to the effect that the UDC was an entirely private body and in no way connected to the government. Consequently all members of the government associated in any way with the UDC, amongst them Clement Attlee who had consented to be a Vice President, had been forced to resign. Ponsonby ended by saying, 'But of course our former connections with the UDC make it exceedingly awkward'.

Unsurprisingly Morel simply ignored Ponsonby's rebuke. This was not unreasonable, as in the past the Labour Party had pledged itself to work for the abolition of reparations, and in 1923 had passed a resolution that the payments should be limited to the cost of restoring the devastated areas of France and Belgium. In a letter to the *New Leader*[353] in July Morel wrote, 'Men whose loyalty and services to the Party cannot be questioned are beginning to feel serious concern at the apparent jettisoning, in matters of foreign policy, of convictions and pledges which have been the inspiration of the Party for the last five years, and which have materially assisted in placing the Party where it is today because the country believed those pledges were seriously meant.' A short article in *Westminster* lamented 'the regrettable and growing tendency to treat the parliamentary party in these affairs as a Tame Cat'. This summary disregard of past promises to the rank and file could well prove extremely damaging; how often is it, Morel asked, that a party loses popular support and the confidence of its own followers when principle gives way to expediency in matters where 'its leaders have nailed their colours to the mast so tightly they can only wrench them free by pulling down the mast itself?'

In the end, Morel's campaign against the reparation proposals in the Dawes Plan was unsuccessful, the backbenchers failed to revolt and 'expediency' prevailed. But at least the 'Tame Cat' had an opportunity to make its voice heard when the matter was debated in the House of Commons, where the government's policy was severely criticised and the UDC's manifesto received considerable support.

Nobel Prize

At this period, which would end with his death in the autumn of 1924, Morel's hopes of being awarded the Nobel Peace Prize were rekindled. A letter to the Nobel Committee recommending his candidature for the prize was published in *The Times* on 31st January 1924. It was signed by the Prime Minister, Ramsay MacDonald, eleven members of the Cabinet and over 125 Members of Parliament. The letter praised Morel's campaign against the Congo atrocities, and his devotion to the study of international relations, and commended his appreciation of the dangers that threatened the peace of the world, especially 'the perils growing out of the exploitation of Africa of the Great Powers'. It recognised Morel's struggle during the war to secure a lasting and early peace and his efforts 'to keep before the public of this and other countries the problems of peace and their solutions'.[354]

This was not the first time in Morel's life that the matter of the Nobel Peace Prize had arisen. The idea of being awarded the prize had clearly been present in his mind when he had written to Mary from Pentonville over four years earlier, saying that he had dreamt of how pleased she would be for him if he won the award. It was clear that he desperately wanted recognition for his efforts, and above all hoped that the honour might finally cast off the shadow of prison, which he felt profoundly sullied his reputation. He had later lobbied to have his name put forward for nomination, and had gained a level of support. Some eighteen months before *The Times* letter was published, Lord Loreburn, who had been Lord Chancellor before the war, told Morel that he had most willingly sent a letter to the Nobel Prize Committee along the lines he had suggested.[355]

Apparently nothing came of Lord Loreburn's letter, although over a year later he was still in correspondence with Aino Malmberg,[356] wife of a Finnish politician and writer, who recorded that she had received a letter from an 'important man' (not identified) commending Morel in glowing terms to the award committee in Norway. The recommendation had been sent on to Dr Moltesen, Chairman of the Danish Inter-Parliamentary Group, who agreed to propose Morel for the honour, but again the approach had been unsuccessful.

The Times letter of 1924 was the third occasion that Morel's name was put forward in public. In a leading article responding to the letter it had published the paper wrote:

> Great stress is laid on his attitude during the War. That at least is remembered. It deeply offended all classes in this country; it evoked, for instance, a strong protest from the National Union of Railwaymen. Otherwise Mr Morel is unknown...his name might have been safely forgotten. Recalled at the moment when the Labour Government is being watched by the world with a critical and curious eye, it may provide distrust, or at best amusement. Mr Morel seems to be one of those pacifists who disturb the peace and act as a perpetual irritant.[357]

The Daily News adopted similar views, and *The Birmingham Post* accused him of being a Bolshevik. *Outlook* described him as a 'strange and sinister figure', and *The Belfast Newsletter* (perhaps unsurprisingly, in view of his long association with Casement and his support for a united Ireland), described him as engaged in all kinds of pro-German propaganda, and remarked that 'happily the Nobel Committee has shown appreciation of the effect such an award would have both in GB (sic) and France.'

Morel was outraged by *The Times* response. In a telephone conversation with Mrs Malmberg[358] he pointed out that the paper, which reported he was 'otherwise unknown', had appointed him as its special correspondent in Nigeria in October 1910. He wrote to Lord Parmoor, Lord President of the Council, complaining that, with the exception of *The Westminster Gazette*, every single liberal paper, including the *Manchester Guardian*, had suppressed his nomination to the Nobel Prize. His sense of persecution and betrayal was profound. 'This is only one indication out of many that the opportunity is being taken by my enemies, the Die-Hards, to smother me with abuse, the hostile liberals with the most efficacious of all weapons to extinguish me by silence. I am "impossible". I am to be wiped out and forgotten as *The Times* puts it.'[359]

In spite of his critics' hostile response, however, there were many who felt Morel justly deserved recognition. Thirty-three representatives of the Church of England from across England and Scotland sent a letter to the Norwegian Committee endorsing the recommendation that the Nobel Prize should be awarded to him.[360] 'We believe,' they wrote, 'that his work from 1900 onwards has rightly entitled him to the very high place he occupies amongst those who have sought for world peace and the establishment of that rule of justice, truth and generosity upon which alone it be founded.' Amongst other signatories were the recently retired Bishop of Oxford, Charles Gore, the Canon of Westminster Abbey and Chaplain to the King, B K Cunningham and the Provost of Inverness Cathedral, A D Mackenzie. Further support for his candidature came from other members of the government, amongst them Josiah Wedgewood, Clement Attlee and Emmanuel Shinwell, as well as many friends and associates including writers and journalists. There was also a strong endorsement from abroad. The Prime Minister of Egypt, Zaghloul Pasha, Brigadier-General Burnham, Secretary of the White Cross in Canada, groups from the United States, Austria, Russia, France, China and Hungary, and even the *Japan Chronicle* all promoted his cause.[361]

In view of his heart condition Morel must have been well aware that his life could be cut short at any moment. It is not unreasonable to suppose that he wanted the award for posterity as much as for the present, but as it turned out no decision had been taken by the Nobel Committee at the time of his death in November. It has to be hoped he imagined in his last few months that his expectations might yet be fulfilled.

The Closing Months

I have never known a life that so completely fulfilled itself. I have never known a catastrophe where, apart from personal sorrow, I felt less inclined to chide at fate. The amount achieved by E D M was prodigious. He had done, actually succeeded in realising, far more in his twenty-five years of political activity than do most important statesmen who live to eighty. It is quite true that his work was not finished. But he had done the rare thing of completing one definite policy of good for mankind, which is a record that falls to few.

Charles Trevelyan to Mary Morel
21st November 1924, family papers

Although the Labour government lost heavily in the election of 1924, Morel himself triumphed for a third time and was returned at the top of the poll at Dundee, 3,000 votes ahead of Scrymgeour. But his punishing work schedule and his continued bouts of ill health were taking a heavy toll, to the extent that he was driven to take periodic rests stretched out on the terrace in the House of Commons. The Anglo-Russian Treaty, and Morel's attack on the permanent staff at the Foreign Office hinting that the Zinoviev letter was a forgery and part of a conspiracy to discredit the Labour Party, were to be the last significant political activities of his life.

Following the election he returned to Cherry Croft, and shortly afterwards travelled down with Mary to Teignmouth in Devonshire to stay for a period of recuperation with his sister-in-law, Winifred Richardson. On 12th November, accompanied by Winifred, he drove out to Aller Farm on Dartmoor, close to North Bovey, and together they walked up through Luckdon Woods towards Easdon Tor. Many years later his eldest son Roger, in a letter to Wuliger,[362] described Morel as being very tired but enjoying the fresh air of the moor. 'He sat down to rest awhile, his back against a tree and just died there, quietly, like that.' He was only fifty-one.

A stone in the woods inscribed 'Edmund Dene Morel died here on November 12th 1924' marks the spot where he died.[363] His body was taken to North Bovey Church and then brought to London where it was cremated at Golders Green cemetery. The tablet on the wall of the crematorium reads, 'Edmund Dene Morel, Vindicator of Freedom for Natives of the Congo, Champion of Peace amid the Passions of War, Fearless Advocate of Truth.'

A memorial service was held at St Martin-in-the-Fields on 25th November. Helena Swanwick wrote that the church was filled with some 2,000 people. Around another 4,000 attended a memorial service in his Dundee constituency where it was said that groups of men strove in vain for self-control; that poor, working women spoke of Morel and his wife with tears running down their faces; and that more tears were shed in Dundee on the day of Morel's death than had been shed for any reason for many a long day.

Somewhat later in February the following year, over a thousand people attended a Memorial Meeting in the Community Church in New York to commemorate his life and work. There was 'a long series of superb addresses' in his honour, including a poem dedicated to him, written and read out by the American poet Edwin Markham.[364]

Morel's death provoked numerous obituaries from countries around the world – Egypt, India, New Zealand, and Australia, amongst others – and a great many tributes from friends and admirers. Bertrand Russell wrote to Stella shortly after her father died, declaring that:

> ...his death is far more than a personal loss. In a very real sense he was the embodiment of causes and principles. He was a public man par excellence; his interests lay in men and the world, he cared for justice, for truth, for high endeavour...His method was that upon which all great fights for truth must proceed. He mastered his facts. On the subjects which he made his own few men were better informed. His moral energy had at its command the most formidable assemblage of rational weapons which could be brought together.[365]

Russell went on to say that 'time', which had already justified him, would go on doing so. Sad to say, this has not proven to be the case.

Ponsonby in his turn wrote to Mary regretting that more people did not know her husband personally. 'He was of a so shy and retiring disposition that for years he could not be persuaded to join a club.' This was largely due to absorption in his work but could also be accounted for by his home life, which 'yielded all he wanted in the way of relaxation. He seemed unaware of his exceptional social gift and charm.'[366] Later Swanwick, who admired Morel greatly and understood him particularly well, gave an affecting description of her feelings for him in her memoirs:

> I felt something volcanic in the man. He has fires smouldering always at his heart. Agonies of sympathy with his beloved black man; agonies of indignation and shame at cruelties or stupidities of which he thinks his own people guilty; almost, one would say, so poignant are they, agonies of delight in beautiful things of nature, flowers and trees and cloudy skies. No half-life for him. I think when he dies, people may say he died of living, and how can anyone do more with his life?

She declared that she had never met a man with whom she could talk more freely of public affairs; who was so deeply versed and informative about them, and was yet so willing to discuss them as an equal, enabling her to say anything she wanted to say. She added that although they nearly always talked about international matters, she occasionally met him at home at Cherry Croft, and on these rare occasions he could be cheerful and congenial. She also reflected that despite his ceaseless activity, he was extremely sensitive and that 'a kinder world might have prolonged his days.'[367]

Swanwick's affection for Morel does not appear to have been in any sense physical, but although women rarely appear in the record of his life, Morel was unquestionably very attractive. The journalist Douglas Goldring described an occasion in 1919 when he first met him at a dinner in London.[368] Amongst those present were Charles Trevelyan and Bertrand Russell, and the principle guest was Madame Madeleine Marx, 'a chic, very attractive Parisienne, in her middle thirties (who) made full use of her sex appeal' and who greatly admired Morel's books. After being introduced she could hardly take her eyes off him and at intervals was to be heard murmuring '*Ah, comme il est beau!*' Morel was still tall and broad-shouldered, but already sported white hair that contrasted strikingly with his dark eyebrows and moustache, and Goldring acknowledges that he was conspicuously good-looking.

But despite the numerous plaudits, not all Morel's obituaries were favourable.[369] As *Labor*, a national weekly newspaper based in Washington DC, proclaimed in a headline, 'The Tory and Liberal Press spits on his grave, which shows how gentlemen can hate'. The article recalled its previous editorial describing the stir caused by Morel's first appearance in the House of Commons in 1922, when as a Labour candidate he had beaten no less a 'warrior' than Winston Churchill, the then Chancellor of the Exchequer. On that day the paper had declared that:

> ...silk-hatted, hard faces who had wondered what could be done about the traitorous, pro-German snake-in-the-grass, French born liar and cad, found themselves confronted by a tall, grey-haired, courteous man speaking as if he had been in Parliament all his days, and dealing in facts as if he were accustomed to having facts carry the day for him. It was a shock. Some gentlemen in England may have wondered if they should revise their opinions about Morel!

A good many gentlemen, however, were not prepared to make this revision. One comment in *Outlook* described Morel as a 'strange and sinister figure in British Politics, the founder of that preposterous organisation the UDC.' The *Catholic Herald* published a lengthy and excoriating article comprehensively condemning Morel's campaign against Leopold in the Congo, and the CRA as a body. The *Birmingham Post* complained of 'his warped judgement that impelled him in strange directions' and suggested that its readers might never know how much mischief he was responsible for during the war years. In slightly less disparaging terms the *Daily Graphic* wrote that 'like so many fanatics and cranks Morel was nonetheless a very likeable man.'

Several opinions about him were similarly guarded, and even a number of his devoted friends were apparently unable to express their affection and esteem without qualification. C P Scott's assessment was typical of many who held Morel in high regard, but could not bring themselves to embrace his radicalism. 'Personally I admired Mr Morel very much for his disinterestedness and devotion, but I found myself in frequent disagreement with his political attitude, not because I disagreed in essentials but because to my mind he often spoiled a good case by the way he stated it.'[370]

Others took a slightly different, though in some ways more dismissive view. Thirty years later in his book *Edwardian Portraits*, W S Adams wrote that 'he [Morel] was not what one would normally call a great man. His abilities were not transcendent though they were considerable; his personality was not luxuriant though it was perceptible even if pitched in a minor key. He represented the decent Englishman determined to seek the truth with the equipment at his disposal, determined also to proclaim and maintain it.'[371] Contrasted with Russell's enthusiastic tribute, this seems a surprisingly lukewarm appraisal. It is difficult to imagine why somebody writing a book on famous Edwardians should have been quite as dismissive of a man whose qualities so many contemporaries clearly admired.

Yet after his death, Morel's memory did indeed fade rapidly from view, leaving only a handful of acquaintances to record their recollections of his life and work. Some of the reasons for this silence have already been explored, but they still seem insufficient to fully explain it, while much of the criticism levelled at his character in such writings that do exist is remarkably unpersuasive. The allegation that he was disdainful of power politics, and with his simplistic moral judgements and appeal to moral principles he thereby attracted the British Left, hardly constitutes a shortcoming. And while it is true that 'his ideological approach gave his views a clarity and an aura of certainty which attracted dedicated disciples and carried conviction to a substantial following',[372] surely that quality cannot be considered a defect? To the contrary, it was the key to the foundation of his commitment and attraction.

It is true, however, that the warmth of his personality was not always readily discernible from his written work. Ponsonby (confirming the *Labor* article) wrote that he too knew of men who, having been suspicious of Morel from what they had heard about him, 'succumbed immediately to the fascination of his unexpectedly agreeable personality', but that this changed perception appeared to require face-to-face contact. Arguably, this observation provides a further clue as to why memories of Morel appear so sparse following his death. In the parlance of the present day he simply wasn't a networker, and definitely not one to 'prop up the bar' in the House of Commons. His oratorical and writing prowess, his mastery of facts and detail, his astonishing work ethic with its accompanying output – all traits recognised and indeed often feared by his opponents appeared to many to be the characteristics of an unapproachable, rather fearsome and radical preacher. Yet at the same time, he was by all reports an immensely popular and charismatic figure to his constituents, with whom he connected so ably using just such skills.[373] In spite of his short tenure in office his name was still held in high regard sixty years later when Cline visited Dundee and spoke to members of the Labour Party.[374]

Morel himself seemed unaware that he may have appeared arrogant and unsociable to those with whom he had no personal contact, particularly if they did not share his views. Rather, he saw the opposition as fundamentally misguided, and always hoped that sheer perseverance would eventually persuade them of the righteousness of his cause. Josiah Wedgewood captured something of his spirit when he wrote, 'he who had more enemies than any man in public life – had an almost pathetic faith in those enemies. If he could only show them the truth they must believe.

His heart was so right, his equipment so perfect, ever more and more convincingly perfect – surely these reasonable men would be persuaded at last. And the "reasonable men" only hated him the more for believing they were reasonable.'[375] One can only conclude that this hate contributed in no mean part to the conspiracy of silence that followed his death.

Extinguished by Silence

As far as African policy was concerned, everything that Morel stood for was epitomised in his report[376] to the WALC just before the outbreak of war, in which he made absolutely clear his commitment to the Kinsgsleyite principle that the African people should have control over their own land. As Bernard Porter writes in his *Critics of Empire*, Morel's solution lay in abolishing Leopold's system and replacing it by its antithesis – indirect instead of direct rule, free trade instead of monopoly, peasant instead of company proprietorship. But Porter's dismissal of Morel's proposals ('a curious mixture of various attitudes and strands of thought; anti-capitalism, anti-militarism, anthropological empiricism, the old fashioned Cobdenism of laisser-faire and free competition') as 'nostalgic reactionary idealism' is largely contradicted by his own assessment that 'the strength of these century-old critical ideologies is that they furnish a critique of empire that takes on board the problems that present-day imperialists – or humanitarian interventionists – say they are grappling with, but with a far more sophisticated understanding than theirs.'[377] Even in his own terms, therefore, defining 'Morelism' as a 'one sentence answer to a two volume question' (an oversimplification Porter claims to account for its campaigning success)[378] seems an unduly harsh verdict on Morel's extremely well-researched and thoughtful approach to the exploitation of Africa.

In fact, the countries present at the Berlin Conference of the Powers, where the European nations planned the carve-up of Africa at the end of the 19th century, had little time for any such scruples. Rather, they were engaged in an unprincipled contest for power and resources, and one of the worst outcomes of this 'scramble' was to be the destruction of the Congo. The war inevitably slowed down the dash for riches, but peace in Europe allowed the victorious powers to resume their previous exploitation, all of which was predicated upon conditions of direct rule and the monopolisation of land. It was most certainly not in the interests of the large international corporations to abide by the principles Morel had championed during the CRA campaign and to which he subscribed on the WALC, and the intervention of a world war of unprecedented scale and ferocity made it all too easy to forget them. The gulf between the pre-war and the post-war years was enormous in both societal and international terms, and after the conflict ended there was little motivation for anyone, other than personal friends and admirers, to revisit a campaign that seemed to come from a different era. As a result, any aspirations for systems of land tenure were to all intents and purposes swept aside, and the memory of Morel with them.

The extent to which Morel's principles were rejected in almost every respect in the post-war years is epitomised by the partnership between Lever and the Huileries du Congo Belge (HCB). In 1922, the Belgian Colonial Minister and Lever discussed the question of awarding the industrialist a further monopoly over the palm-nut trade across the five 'circles' that had been granted to him. These circles totalled 5.5 million hectares, almost twice the surface area of Belgium.[379] Lever's concession was confirmed, and a government decree of the same year, which remained in force with only minor modifications until the end of the colonial period, set out the conditions under which Africans' labour contracts should operate. These conditions encompassed almost every aspect of the hired labourer's life: his wages, his rations, his bedding and accommodation, his medical care and the fines he would incur for absence, or prison sentences that could be given for minor crimes and violation of work discipline. The Governor General, Maurice Lippens, described as an advocate of forced labour in the Congo, deplored the fact that the authorities did not always lend sufficient support to the colonists, traders, agents and directors of the commercial and industrial firms of whatever scale.[380] To meet the needs of labour entire villages in the Congo were encouraged to move to the 'circles' granted to HCB. In a report written in 1923, following a six-day tour of inspection in the Lusanga circle, Dr Lejeune, the medical officer for Congo-Kasai province, described a shocking situation. Rations, accommodation, and clothing were inadequate and the medical services provided for the African worker were deplorable.[381]

There was to be little improvement thereafter, and there is no way now that the people of the Congo can be compensated for the damage inflicted upon them by King Leopold, and later by Belgium. Their land was stolen, they were enslaved or murdered and subjected to institutionalised racial hierarchy, and their resources were, and continue to be expropriated. If Morelism can be dismissed as 'a one sentence answer to a two volume question' what is the alternative? Is it simply to ignore the atrocities and profiteering and believe, as is now the case in some quarters, that the 'good' achieved under imperial and colonial rule outweighs the damage? In the case of the Congo in particular, this is plainly an outrageous claim, while in Africa more generally it would seem indisputable that a philosophy driven by greed and power has left many countries in turmoil and their people greatly impoverished.

In the light of these past and ongoing abuses, today's more radical thinkers may find Morelism unacceptably paternalistic, but in respecting the African people, their trading rights, and the land they lived upon, it was very far in advance of the attitudes of its day. As the emerging powers of China and India join the dwindling hegemony of the EU and the United States in the pursuit of diminishing global resources, the future fate of the African nations will depend to a large extent on the degree of respect and consideration that is accorded to them. It can only be hoped, although unfortunately with little confidence, that the abandoned principles to which Morel adhered will play some part in determining their future.

While his proposals for Africa may to some extent have been eclipsed by the war, the same cannot be said of his work in the anti-war movement, or of his subsequent campaign against the Treaty of Versailles, and here the obliteration of his memory appears to have been much more deliberate and vindictive. The fact that he exposed the 'secret treaties and lies' that preceded hostilities did not endear him to those who had been party to them, while his passivism was an embarrassment both to the statesmen who had led their country into a terrible conflict, and an affront to the patriotic masses who had fought and suffered as a result. Again, his condemnation of the Versailles Treaty, and especially of the war-guilt clause, was highly discomfiting, and although history would prove him right, his prediction that it would lead to another and even more disastrous war was especially unwelcome. If ever there was an activist who proclaimed 'inconvenient truths' it was Morel, and the charge of being 'a traitorous, pro-German snake-in-the-grass', although dismissed by many people, was potent enough to assist the process of erasing his reputation and his name. Moreover, at a time when society was trying to put the memories of a horrific war behind it, and fears for the future stability of Europe were again being voiced, the passing of a prominent Jeremiah in society may have been met with some relief.

As a result, and although there were still those who admired and respected him, there were few who appeared inclined to champion his work after his death. Nobody took up their pen to record his life until Wuliger wrote his thesis a decade after the Second World War, and Catherine Cline her book nearly thirty years later.[382] Indeed Morel was entirely justified in fearing that the memory of his life and work would be obliterated. Even the book published in 2008 to commemorate the history of Liverpool when it was designated European City of Culture, carries only the merest reference to Morel and the Congo Relief (sic) Association.[383] It acknowledges his 'exposure of the barbarous imperial machine of Leopold of Belgium' and the success of the campaign to end the atrocities, but dismisses Morel and his 'coterie' as having failed, due to the lack of solid economic backing or wide popular appeal, 'to establish a Liverpool "sect" or "third party" opposed to both racial condemnation and racial condescension in imperial policy in West Africa'.[384]

The Labour movement retained the UDC's principles until August 1939; in the words of A J P Taylor, 'it [the Labour movement] still held the outlook of Keir Hardie and E D Morel, of Brailsford and J A Hobson. No issue of principle divided Attlee from Cripps so far as foreign policy was concerned. Two simple sentences expressed it all. Imperialist capitalism was the cause of the war. Socialists should oppose both war and capitalism'.[385] But despite these precepts, the party failed to keep his memory alive or accord him the renown his contribution demanded. 'Trouble makers' was what Taylor called the radicals of Morel's time – and trouble makers they were, with Morel prominent amongst them. Clearly some truths are too disruptive, and some polemic too disconcerting to be electorally attractive to a voting public anxious to avoid discomfiture and guilt.

Morel's death at the end of 1924 marked the end of an epoch, and no single figure took his place.[386] Without him, the UDC rapidly lost its influence and was no longer counted as an effective force, and although other groups and organisations arose over the interwar years, none of them replaced it as a convincing campaigning organisation prepared to question the zeitgeist of the age. Then as now, a brave politics was required, and then as now a courageous and inspirational figure was needed to challenge the establishment and call for fundamental change. A rare combination of hard work and intellectual rigour, conviction and vision, passion, sincerity, selflessness and fortitude is a necessary characteristic for a leader of this kind, and in a materialistic and solipsistic global culture, these attributes are hard to find.

Morel, however, possessed them in ample measure, and displayed them to great effect all his life. A tribute which appeared in *Forward* just after his death gives a moving description of how precisely these qualities won over the initially sceptical citizens of Dundee.

> They found him to be a simple, straight, courageous man, with a message of vital moment to our generation, convinced that truth must prevail over falsehood, that the average man and woman in

the end will identify sincerity, and will respect it when they see it, certain that they will respond to a lead given by anyone who serves Truth faithfully, who will rather die than bear witness to falsehood and conscious error. 'I cannot play the hypocrite amongst you,' he wrote when he refused to compromise with his convictions so as to retain the position of Liberal Candidate for Birkenhead. And because he could not play the hypocrite the people of Dundee gave him their trust and confidence, and the gift of deep and abiding affection. But they did not accept his message because they loved the man; they loved the man because he made it possible for them to identify the root causes of social disease and of international strife and disorder, because he gave them a faith to live by and a hope to live for.[387]

It would be difficult to study Morel's work in any detail without being impressed by his integrity, and captivated by his perseverance and dedication. But is also virtually impossible not to be moved by the adversity of his life. Despite his talents and industry, he was humiliated and imprisoned, consistently misrepresented and vilified, and ultimately relegated to obscurity by a resentful establishment. That he died at fifty-one, leaving so many objectives unfulfilled and a loving family desolate, was the final tragedy in a life that was frequently marked by personal anguish.

The Morels were a particularly devoted couple, and Mary, who had always cherished and encouraged her husband with such steadfast enthusiasm, was now left alone to raise a young family riven by grief and loss. As was her wont, she continued to be a source of strength to her children, the youngest of whom, Oliver, was only eight years old. Stella, who was by now twenty-seven and had been very close to her father, was clearly especially devastated by his death. In a touching letter written to her on 1st December and beginning 'My own precious Daughter', Mary attempted to comfort her:

> Thank you for telling me about your feelings last night. It is inevitable – this down in the depths, and we shall both have to go through it. Dear old Roger and Geoff too, in their ways. But it hurts him if you don't just get through the mood and the depression as soon and as quickly as you can – and open yourself to absorb his spirit day by day...how he just adored you – loved you calling him by your pet name.' She went on to say how much her father had valued her help, and had spoken of it 'in the last half hour we were here together.[388]

The boys too attempted to console one another. Geoff, then eighteen, and writing to his elder brother John, also spoke of the solace their mother had provided. 'Then, I was with Mother in Devon after a few days. She talked to me up on Dartmoor in that wonderful calm and peaceful voice. She made me feel that it was a beautiful and happy ending; that his had been a courageous and fine life and that his influence and spirit was still with us as a family.' And again, writing to his mother, Geoff recalled, 'I have a beautiful memory of Dad. His face to me is always clothed in that wonderful smile and understanding. I feel and know that he is with us all, and always will be. We all have our battles, and with the thought that he is helping us, they will be easier to win.'[389]

It would be pleasing to feel that the family's misfortunes, grave though they had been, had come to an end, but in fact much worse was to follow. Geoff died of pneumonia in 1929 aged only twenty-five, and Stella, already the mother of two little girls, died in 1931 of mastoiditis, an acute middle ear infection that was extremely difficult to treat before the advent of antibiotics. John also predeceased his mother, and died following severe mental health problems in 1942. The shocking and untimely deaths of three of her children must have caused Mary almost unbearable heartbreak, but valiant to the last, she went on to bring up Stella's children and lived into her eighties. One can only hope that she continued to be sustained by the 'faith to live by and hope to live for' that her husband had once possessed, and had communicated so widely.

Unfortunately, the conviction and motivation that Morel engendered in his family, and in his followers and readers, are in short supply today. But his trenchant criticisms address many issues that are with us still, and his proposals for reform are far from outdated. His call for social justice, political transparency, and above all global peace, is of critical importance in our current circumstances. Clearly some of his thinking was informed by the established mores of his age, but much of it can be seamlessly transposed into the present, and we badly need to revisit it. We should no longer allow his memory or his message to be 'extinguished by silence'.

Appendix I

Woodrow Wilson's Fourteen Points

Woodrow Wilson's Fourteen Points were first outlined in a speech Wilson gave to the American Congress in January 1918. The Fourteen Points became the basis for a peace programme and it was on the back of the Fourteen Points that Germany and her allies agreed to an armistice in November 1918.

1.   Open covenants openly arrived at (No secret agreements between nations).
2.   Freedom of the seas in peace and war.
3.   Removal of economic barriers between nations as far as possible.
4.   Reduction of armaments to needs for domestic safety.
5.   Adjustment of colonial claims with concerns for the wishes and interests of the inhabitants as well as for the titles of rival claimants.
6.   Evacuation and general restoration of conquered territories in Russia.
7.   Preservation of Belgian sovereignty.
8.   Settlement of the Alsace-Lorraine question.
9.   The redrawing of Italian frontiers according to nationalities.
10. The division of Austria-Hungary in conformance to its nationalities.
11. The redrawing of Balkan boundaries with reference to historically established allegiance and nationalities.
12. Turkish control only of their own peoples and freedom of navigation through the Dardanelles.
13. The establishment of an independent Poland with access to the sea.
14. A provision for a general association of nations under specific covenants (Subsequently the League of Nations).

Columbia University Press, Fifth Edition, 1993

Appendix II: Photographs

Morel, the keen gardener at Cherrycroft, Kings Langley.

Ramsay MacDonald and Morel in Dundee 1923.

Morel's Children. Clockwise from top left Geoffrey, John, Roger, Oliver & Stella.

Dundee Committee Room with ED and Mary Morel and agents.

Stone marking the place of Morel's death on Dartmoor.

Endnotes

The Early Years

1. Handwritten note by Mary Morel, *Snowden's Biography*, Vol 2, p.578, Morel Papers, LSE, F1/1/14.
2. Morel E D, *Truth and the War* (National Labour Press, London, 1916), p.127.
3. Hattersley, Roy, *The Edwardians* (Little, Brown, 2004).
4. Cline, Catherine, *E. D. Morel, The Strategies of Protest* (Blackstaff Press, 1980) p.4.
5. Morel papers LSE, 1/1/9, Bertrand Russell to Mary Morel, 1946.
6. Morel papers LSE, F17/2/4, Douglas Goldring to Mary Morel, 23/2/46.
7. Cocks, Seymour, *E. D. Morel: The Man and his Work* (George Allen and Unwin, London, 1920), p.24.
8. Adams W S, *Edwardian Portraits* (Secker and Warburg, London, 1957), p.177.
9. Morel to Alice Stopford Green March 1909, quoted Cline, Catherine, op. cit, p.4.

The Congo Campaign

10. Pakenham, Thomas, *The Scramble for Africa* (Weidenfeld and Nicholson, London, 1992), p.17.
11. ibid, p.18.
12. *Pall Mall Gazette,* quoted Cline, Catherine, op. cit, p.24.
13. Morel, E D, *Red Rubber* (Haskell House Publishers Ltd, New York, 1970) Intro. Johnston H.H. p.xv.
14. Louis, Roger and Stengers, Jean (eds), *E. D. Morel's History of the Congo Reform Movement* (Oxford, 1968)
15. Morel, E D, *Affairs of West Africa* (London, William Heinemann, 1902) p xiii.
16. Morel, E D, *Great Britain and the Congo* (Howard Fertig, New York, New Edition, 1969), p. 87/88.
17. ibid, p.34.
18. Morel, E D, *Affairs of West Africa,* op. cit, p.331-332.
19. Morel, E D, *Red Rubber,* op. cit, p.100.

20. Morel, E D, *King Leopold's Rule in Africa* (London, 1904), p.111.
21. Louis, Roger and Stengers, Jean (eds*)*, op. cit, p.262.
22. *The Speaker,* The Congo Scandal: The Domaine Prive. 28/7/1900; 1/9/00; 1/12/00.
23. Hochschild, Adam, *King Leopold's Ghost* (Pan MacMillan Ltd, London 2006), p.187.
24. Morel Papers LSE, *West Africa*, Vol. ii. No 11. 2 March 1901.
25. ibid, Vol. iii. No 26. 15 June 1901.
26. E D Morel, *Affairs of West Africa*, op. cit, p.353.
27. Wuliger, R, *The Idea of Economic Imperialism with Special Reference to the Life and Work of E D Morel* (PhD. LSE, 1953), p.31.
28. ibid, p.31.
29. Morel Papers LSE, *West Africa,* Vol. iii, No 67, 29 March 1902 and No 68, 5 April 1902.
30. Cocks, E S, op. cit, p.78.
31. Wuliger, R, op. cit, p.48.
32. ibid, p.1.
33. Pavlakis, Dean, *The Congo Reform Movement in Britain, 1896-1913* (PhD. Diss., SUNY at Buffalo, 2012), p.155.
34. Morel, E D, *Great Britain and the Congo*, op.cit, p.25.
35. Morel, E D, *History of the Congo Reform Movement,* op. cit, p.83.
36. ibid, p.55.
37. Louis, Roger and Stengers, Jean (eds), op. cit, p.107.
38. Morel, E D, *Affairs of West Africa*, op. cit, p.124.
39. Morel Papers LSE, Morel to Conan Doyle, July 1909.
40. Louis, Roger and Stengers, Jean (eds) op. cit, p.128.
41. ibid, p.12.
42. ibid, p.130.

The Congo Reform Association

43. Morel papers LSE, F8/16 Nov 1903.
44. ibid, F8, Casement to Morel, Jan 1904.
45. ibid, March 1905.
46. Inglis, Brian, *Roger Casement* (Penguin Books, London, 1973), p.392.
47. William Cadbury too had concerns of his own. As a Quaker and director of the chocolate firm Cadbury Brothers Ltd he had been concerned for some time about the working conditions of African labourers in the Portuguese Colonies of Angola and the islands of Sâo Tomé and Príncipe. There had been widespread rumours that slave labour was being used for harvesting cocoa. In 1903, at the time the Foreign Office sent Casement to report on

conditions in the Congo, Cadbury was also seeking someone to investigate conditions in Sâo Tomé. Travers Buxton of the Anti-Slavery Society suggested that Joseph Burrt, friend and employee of Cadbury, should go. It seems that Cadbury's assessment of labour conditions and attempts to improve them were widely praised. Higgs, Catherine, *Cocoa Islands* (Ohio University Press, Athens, Ohio, 2012).

48. Morel to Deuss. Quoted, Cline, C, op. cit, p.47.
49. *New York Times*, 18/10/1904.
50. At some time during his trip to the US, Morel also met the author Samuel Clemens, aka Mark Twain. The latter was greatly moved by Morel's reports of atrocities in the Congo, and in the following year produced his swingeing political satire, *King Leopold's Soliloquy*. The pamphlet, somewhat contemptuously dismissed by Catherine Cline as 'a lengthy demonstration that earnest humanitarianism does not produce great literature', was sufficiently effective to prompt a strong rebuttal. In *An Answer to Mark Twain*, Leopold's regime denied all the charges laid against him in the *Soliloquy*.
51. Claparede, Rene, *Deux Journalistes, J. Condurier et E. D. Morel, 1919*, Family papers.
52. Cocks, S, op. cit, p.201.
53. Wulinger, R, op. cit, p. 105.
54. Morel, E D, *Red Rubber*, op. cit, Intro p.vii and viii.
55. Wulinger, R, op. cit, p.107.
56. Morel Papers LSE, F8/92, Johnston to Morel, 23 December 1906.
57. ibid, Doyle to Morel, 10 Jul, 10 Aug, 15 Sep 1907.
58. Hansard, Fourth Series, 160, 260. Quoted Wuliger, R, op. cit, p.183.
59. Morel Papers LSE, F8/12/24.
60. Adams, W S, op. cit, p.196.
61. ibid.
62. For all correspondence see Morel Papers LSE, F8/14.
63. Morel Papers LSE, notes by Mary F1/1/4.
64. ibid, F8/11.
65. ibid, EDM to Harris 26/4/06, et al.
66. ibid, F1/1/4, Recollections Mary Morel.
67. Morel to Casement, Dec 1908, Casement Papers. Quoted Louis, Roger; Stengers, Jean, op. cit, p.203 Fn.

The End of the Congo Campaign

68. Wuliger, R, op. cit, p.199, Morel, E D, Memorandum on talk with Grey, 30/6/08.

69. Morel Papers LSE, F8/145, Morel to Sir George White, 14/4/09.

70. ibid, F10/17, Letter Book, p. 484.

71. Morel, E D, *Great Britain and the Congo*, op. cit, p.xii.

72. ibid. p. xxvi.

73. ibid, p.xxv.

74. Gondola, Didier, op. cit, p.77.

75. Morel Papers LSE, F8/15, Morel to Canterbury, 7/6/10.

76. Morel, E D, *Memorandum to His Majesty's Government from the Congo Reform Association on the Reports of His Majesty's Consular Staff in the Congo as Presented to Parliament Nov 1911.*

77. Autograph ABP, *The Republic of Congo* (London 2010).

78. Quoted in Cocks, Seymour, op. cit, p.145.

79. Morel Papers LSE, *The African Mail*, 8/10/1912.

80. ibid, F14/1/13 and 14, West Africa Lands Report, Morel, E D, Hodgson, F M, Napier, W. It appears that the Draft Report was not presented to the Colonial Office until 1917.

81. Cocks, Seymour, op. cit, p.145.

82. *Official Organ of the Congo Reform Association*, Final Issue, July 1913.

83. Didier, Gondola, op. cit, p.84.

84. Morel, E D, *Africa and the Peace of Europe* (National Labour Press, London 1917).

85. *Official Organ of the Congo Reform Association*, Final Issue, July 1913.

86. Hochschild, Adam, op. cit, p.280.

87. Morel, E D, *Red Rubber*, op. cit, p.56 and 116.

88. Evans, M A, *Brussels and Bruges*, Frommers, (John Wiley and Sons, Chichester, 2011) p.24 and 172.

89. Morel Papers LSE, Letters F8/99 & F8/100.

90. Griffiths, Jay, Slow Motion Genocide, *The Guardian*, 30/12/10.

91. Birkenhead News, 19/4/13. Quoted Wuliger, R, op. cit, p.312.

92. Wuliger, R, op. cit, p.269.

93. Morel Papers LSE, *Liverpool Journal of Commerce*, 18/12/1.

Nigeria: Its Peoples and its Problems

94. Morel, E D, *Nigeria: Its People and its Problems*. See espec. p. 3, 7, 19, 20, 27, 53, 67/68, 82, 136, 215, 247.

European Alliances

95. Cline, Catherine, op. cit, p.69.

96. Ferguson, Niall, op. cit, p.10.

97. Morel, E D, *Thoughts on the War: The Peace and Prison,* EDM.

98. Trevelyan, G M, Grey to Sir A Hardinge, *Grey of Fallodon* (Longmans, Green and Co, London, 1937), p. 200.

99. ibid, p.199.

100. Morel, E D, *Great Britain and the Congo,* op. cit, p.245.

101. Morel Papers LSE, Gilmore to Morel, 5/10/1909.

102. ibid, Casement to Morel, 31/7/1909.

103. Trevelyan, G M, op. cit, p.196.

104. See page 46.

105. Hattersley, Roy, op. cit, p.468 and ff.

106. Lloyd George, Mansion House speech, 17 July 1911. Quoted Ferguson, Niall, op. cit, p.69.

107. Hurd, Douglas, *Choose your Weapons* (Orion Books Ltd, London, 2011), p.226.

108. Cline, Catherine, op. cit, p.74.

109. Morel, E D, *Ten Years of Secret Diplomacy,* Reprint of *Morocco in Diplomacy* (Smith, Elder and Co, London 1912), p. xxviii.

110. Adams, A S, op. cit, p.201.

111. http://www.ons.gov.uk/ons/dcp171776_271539.pdf

112. *Manchester Guardian*, 9 November 1912: 'The Liberal Candidate for Birkenhead'.

113. Taylor, A J P, *The Trouble Makers* (Hamish Hamilton Ltd, London, 1957), p.108.

114. Hattersley, Roy, op. cit, p.475.

115. Ferguson, Niall, op. cit, p.33.

116. Morel, E D, *Ten Years of Secret Diplomacy* (National Labour Press Ltd, Manchester 1920). A reprint of *Morocco in Diplomacy.*

117. ibid, p.178-179.

118. Kettle, Martin, Openness Against Secrecy has a Rich History of Struggle, *The Guardian,* 3/10/2010.

119. Taylor, A J P, op. cit, p.119.

120. ibid, p.121.

121. Morel to Holt, 5/2/12. Quoted Wulinger, op. cit, p.304.

122. Morel – Private memorandum.

Union for Democratic Control

123. Swanwick, Helena M, *Builders of Peace* (Swarthmore Press, London, 1924. New edition. Garland Publishing, Inc., New York and London, 1974) and Swartz, Marvin, *The Union of Democratic Control in British Politics During the First World War* (Clarendon Press, Oxford, 1971).

124. Trevelyan to Morel, 5 Aug 1914.

125. Swanwick, H M, op. cit, p.24.
126. ibid, p.26.
127. Morel Papers LSE, F6/1.
128. Swartz, Marvin, op. cit, p.25.
129. Morel, E D, *The Irish Problem. Its Fundamental Aspects. 'Ulster' and 'Loyalty'.* Delivered at the Drill Hall, Birkenhead, 2/4/1914. (Wilmer Bros and Co., Birkenhead)
130. ibid, p.3.
131. ibid, p.12.
132. Morel Papers LSE, F6/1.
133. Cocks, Seymour, op. cit, p.199.
134. Quoted in Ferguson, Niall, op. cit, p.57.
135. Wilson, K M, *British Foreign Secretaries and Foreign Policy: from Crimea to the First World War* (Croom Helm Ltd, Kent 1987) p.172.
136. Ferguson, Niall, op. cit, p.57.
137. ibid, p.58.
138. ibid, p.58.
139. Wilson, K M, *The Policy of the Entente* (Cambridge University Press, 1985), p.34.
140. ibid, p.17.
141. Ferguson, Niall, op. cit, p.59.
142. Wilson, K M, *British Foreign Secretaries and Foreign Policy,* op. cit, p.178.
143. Pilger, J, Why Have Journalists Colluded with Governments to Hoodwink Us? *The Guardian G2,* 10/12/2010.
144. Taylor, A J P, op. cit, p.138.
145. Hansard 8/11/86. From LSE F/6/7. Morel was made the subject of personal slander in the House of Commons (5 Apr 1916). 'Mr Thorn, M.P. asked the Home Secretary whether it was not a fact that the UDC was founded in August 1914 with the avowed object of inclining public opinion in favour of a dishonourable peace with the central powers: whether Mr Morel was not obviously guilty of receiving German money, and whether the time had not come for the Government to take steps to find out definitely whether he was in communication with the enemy or whether he was to be trusted.' On being asked whether allowing the Parliamentary Question-Paper could be used for personal slander, the Speaker agreed the question was not in order. The Home Secretary explained that although he had heard of Mr Morel's work, no definitive information against Morel had been laid before him.
146. Morel, E D, *Truth and the War,* op. cit, p.xvi.
147. Swanwick, Helen, op. cit, p.75.
148. Wilson, K M, *British Foreign Secretaries and Foreign Policy,* op. cit, p.188.

149. ibid, p.189.
150. Gooch, G P, *Europe before the War,* History, April 1921, Vol. vi, No 21, p. 20–21.
151. Hurd, Douglas, op. cit, p.230.
152. ibid, p.36.
153. Stevenson, David, *1914/1918: The History of the First World War* (Penguin Books, London, 2005), p.9.
154. Ferguson, Niall, op. cit, p.165.
155. Truth and the War, op. cit, p. xvi.
156. Stevenson, David, op. cit, p.9.
157. ibid, p.46.
158. Morel, E D, *Truth and the War,* op. cit, p.122.
159. Stevenson, David, *The First World War and International Politics* (Oxford University Press, 1988), p.8.
160. Morel, E D, *Truth and the War,* op. cit, p.126/127.
161. Stevenson, David, op. cit, p.37.
162. Swartz, Marvin, op. cit, p.51-52.
163. Morel, E D, *Thoughts on the War: The Peace - and Prison,* p.7.
164. Morel Papers LSE, F1/7/1.
165. Swartz, Marvin, op. cit, p.50.
166. ibid, p.52 fn 20.
167. Morel Papers LSE, F3/15.
168. ibid, F8/24, Morel to Casement, 13 October 1913.
169. Keegan, John, op. cit, p.191.

British Society and the War

170. U.D.C., Vol. 1, No. 1, November 1915.
171. Morel, E D, *Truth and the War,* op. cit, p.286.
172. DeGroot, Gerard J, *Blighty: British Society in the era of the Great War,* (Longman, London, 1995) Gregory, Adrian, *The Last Great War: British Society and the First World War,* (CUP 2008).
173. *Manchester Guardian,* 3 August 1914, p.2. Quoted Gregory, Adrian, ibid, p.15.
174. Gregory, Adrian, ibid, p.15.
175. Ferguson, Niall, op. cit, p.163.
176. DeGroot, Gerard, op. cit, p.143.
177. Russell, Bertrand, *The Autobiography of Bertrand Russell,* Vol 2 (Boston, 1968), p. 38-39.
178. Cocks, Seymour, op. cit, p.237.
179. Morel Papers LSE, F8/101, Scott Lidgett to Morel, 18/12/15.
180. Morel, E D, *Ten Years of Secret Diplomacy,* op. cit, p.xvii.

181. Morel Papers LSE, F8/50, Doyle to Morel, 13 Aug 1915.

182. ibid, F6/1, Scott to Morel, Aug/Sept 1914.

183. ibid, F8/9/14, MacDonald to Morel.

184. Swanwick, Helena, op. cit, p.91/92.

185. ibid, p.105/106.

186. Morel, E D, *Truth and the War,* op. cit, p.xi.

187. Nevinson, Henry W, Letter to Editor, *Manchester Guardian*, 14/11/24, Private Papers.

188. Goldring, Douglas, *The Nineteen Twenties* (Nicholson and Watson Love, London and Redhill, 1945), p.164.

189. Hinton, James, *Protests and Visions* (Century Hutchinson, London, 1989), p.44.

190. U.D.C., Vol. 2, No. 2, December, 1916.

191. Morel papers LSE, F/6/4, Driffel to Morel, 9/8/1916.

192. ibid, Morel to Ponsonby, July 1917.

193. Cline, Catherine, op. cit, p.207.

194. Morel, E D, *Democracy, Nationalism and the War System* in *Thoughts on the War: The Peace - and Prison.* Talk given at the Metropole Theatre, Glasgow, 24/10/1918.

195. Gregory, Adrian, op. cit, p.278.

196. Reeves, Maud Pember, *Round About a Pound a Week,* G. Bell and Sons Ltd, 1913.

197. Mitchell, Angus, *Casement* (Haus Publishing Ltd, London, 2003), p.68.

198. Supplement to *The African Mail,* 27/6/1913, p.6.

199. The Easter Rising was a rebellion mounted by Irish Republicans during Easter Week in 1916 with the aim of ending British rule in Ireland and establishing a Republic.

200. Cline, Catherine, op. cit, p.100.

201. Morel papers LSE, F8/25, Morel to Mrs Green, 25/5/1916.

202. ibid, F17/2/23, Morel to Cadbury 16/6/1916.

203. *War and Peace, 1916* (undated).

204. Morel Papers LSE, F4/28, 1916.

The Road to Prison

205. Morel, E D, *Tsardom's Part in the War* (National Labour Press, London, August 1917), p.3 et al.

206. Matthews to U.Sec. of State, 16 Oct 1916, FO, quoted Cline, Catherine, op. cit, p.111.

207. Morel papers LSE, Rex v E D Morel, F13/7 U.D.C.

208. ibid, p.7-8.

209. Swanwick, H M, *Builders of Peace*, op. cit, p.103.
210. Morel, E D, *Thoughts on the War and Prison* (Published by the author, London, 1920), p.50.
211. Rex v Morel, op. cit, p. 12-23.
212. ibid, p.29-30.
213. ibid, p.51.
214. Morel, E D, *Thoughts on the War,* op. cit, p.52.
215. Cocks, Seymour, op. cit, p.263.
216. For all subsequent letters see Morel Papers LSE, F1/4 and F1/5.
217. *Thoughts on the War: The Peace - and Prison,* op. cit, p.70.
218. Morel Papers LSE, F6/18.
219. ibid, F8.
220. ibid, F1/8/5.

USA Enters the War

221. Keegan, John, op. cit, p.401.
222. Ponsonby, Arthur, (ed), *Peace Overtures and their Rejections,* (UDC, London, 1918) p.7.
223. Swanwick, Helena, op. cit, p.80.
224. Keegan, John, op. cit, p.441.
225. See appendix 1.
226. Swartz, Marvin, op. cit, p.139.
227. Swanwick, Helena, op. cit, p.114.
228. Swartz, Marvin, op. cit, p.140.
229. Morel Papers LSE, F1/6, Morel to Cadbury.
230. ibid, LSE, F1/1/8.
231. ibid, et al, LSE, F1/6.
232. ibid, diagnosis from Dr Reginald Fisher, 5/12/21.
233. Morel, E D, *Thoughts on the War: The Peace - and Prison,* op. cit, p.15.
234. *U.D.C. After Four Years*, Vol 3, August 1918 , p. 249, Morel papers LSE, F6/16.

The Post-War Years and the Treaty of Versailles

235. Cline, Catherine, op. cit, p.116.
236. MacMillan, Margaret, *Peacemakers: Six Months that changed the World* (John Murray, London, 2001), p.27.
237. Those wishing to read the full text of the Treaty of Versailles will find it at http://www.firstworldwar.com/source/versailles.htm
238. Morel papers LSE, F6/17. Also published in the form of a pamphlet, *The Fruits of Victory,* Morel papers LSE, F13/7.

239. ibid, p.335.
240. MacMillan, Margaret, op. cit, p.478.
241. ibid, p.478.
242. Swanwick, Helena, op. cit, p.61
243. MacMillan, Margaret, op. cit, p.36.
244. Steiner, Zara, op. cit, p.14.
245. ibid, p.17.
246. Gregory, Adrian, op. cit, p.295.
247. MacMillan, Margaret, op. cit, p.500.
248. Keylor, William, Versailles and International Diplomacy, *The Treaty of Versailles*, p.471. Quoted in Dockrill, M and Fisher, J, (eds), *The Paris Peace Conference* (Palgrave Ltd, 2001) p.13, Steiner, Zara, *The Treaty of Versailles revisited*.
249. MacMillan, Margaret, op. cit, p.36.
250. Morel papers LSE, F6/19, *Foreign Affairs*, No 8 Vol.1, February 1920, p.16.
251. Morel, E D, *Reparations and the War Guilt, The Nation and the Athenaeum,* 8/8/1924, p.589.
252. Morel Papers LSE, F7/3, Norman Angel to Morel, 3/7/1924.
253. ibid, F8/149, Bishop of Winchester to Morel, 23/8/1921 et al.
254. *Foreign Affairs,* Vol 6, No 6, December 1924, p.126.
255. Morel Papers LSE, F/15/4/3, press cutting 'Stoking up the Hell of War', 14/10/21.
256. ibid, *Daily Herald,* 3/7/1924.
257. Morel, E D, *The Secret History of a Great Betrayal* (Foreign Affairs, London).
258. Morel, E D, *The Poison that Destroys* (The Independent Labour Party, London, 1922), p.4.
259. Morel, E D, *Justice Between Peoples* (The Free Religious Movement, 1924), p.8.
260. Morel, E D, *The Fruits of Victory* (The U.D.C., London, 1919), p.19.
261. Morel, E D, *The Black Man's Burden* (National Labour Press, Ltd., London, 1920).
262. ibid, p.238.

The Horror on the Rhine

263. Morel, E D, *Black Troops in Germany.* Address given to Women's International League, Central Hall Westminster, 27/4/1920, *Foreign Affairs*, Vol.1, No 12, p.v.
264. Morel papers LSE, F13/5/2; Morel, E D, *Horror on the Rhine* (UDC, London, 1920).
265. Nelson, K L, 'The Black Horror on the Rhine: Race as a factor in Post-World

War 1 Diplomacy', *The Journal of Modern History*, Vol.42, No 4, Dec 1970, p.608 et al.

266. The author in conversation with Martin Pinder, Community Development Officer, Newham New Deal Partnership Ltd.

267. Cline, Catherine, op. cit, p.127.

268. Morel Papers LSE, F15/3/4, *The Daily Herald*, 12 April 1920 , p.23.

269. ibid, *The Nation*, 27 March 1920, p.22.

270. ibid, *Commonweal*, 17 April 1920, p.25.

271. http://en.wikipedia.org/wiki/Norman_Leys

272. Morel Papers, op. cit, *Daily Herald*, 14 April 1920, p.23.

273. ibid, *Labour Leader*, 24 February 1921, p.91.

274. ibid, *Daily News and Leader*, 16 February 1921, p.91.

275. ibid, *Outlook*, 1 March 1921, p.94.

276. ibid, *The Freeman*, 27 April 1921, p. 94.

277. Nelson K L, op. cit, p.627.

278. Macmillan, Margaret, op. cit, p.191.

279. *Foreign Affairs*, March 1921, p.135.

280. ibid, December 1919, p.2.

281. Morel Papers LSE, F2/1/7, Morel to Ogilvie, 30/9/20.

282. ibid, F15/4/4, *Daily News*, 15/12/22.

283. ibid, p.137.

284. ibid, December 1921, Special Supplement, p.8.

285. Morel Papers LSE, F15/4/3, *The Patriot*, July 1922.

Churchill and Dundee

286. Morel Papers LSE, F2/1/7, Morel to D Watt. Morel's ill health, diagnosed as angina towards the end of 1921, as noted earlier, appears to have affected him badly during the 1920/21 period, to the extent that in December 1921 his doctor wrote that it was absolutely necessary that he should deal with no business matters whatsoever and should not even read books or papers of a political character.

287. ibid, E Carr to Morel.

288. In the 1918 election the Liberals won 28 seats, Labour 63 and Conservatives 348.

289. DeGroot, Gerard, op. cit, p.312.

290. The Chanak crisis arose when Turkish troops threatened to attack British and French troops stationed near Chanak guarding the Dardanelles.

291. Jenkins, R, *Churchill* (Pan Macmillan Ltd, London, 2002), p.370 and foll.

292. Jenkins notes that a problem with Dundee in that transport era was that it was very difficult to arrive from the south for an evening meeting other than in the

morning. Birkenhead had consequently fallen back on the hospitality of the Conservative Eastern Club to occupy most of his day.

293. *Dundee Advertiser*, 'Morel replies to Mrs Churchill', 10/11/1922, Morel family papers.

294. Morel Papers LSE, F2/1/8, Trevelyan to Morel, 17/11/22.

295. ibid, Morel to Ogilvie, 27/11/1922.

296. Geoffrey Morel to his brother John. Undated letter. Private papers.

297. Morel Papers LSE, F15/4/4, *Aberdeen Evening Express*, 20/4/23.

298. The Dawes Report is more fully discussed on page 195.

299. Morel Papers LSE, F15/4/4, Dundee Courier, 16/10/24.

300. ibid, 21/10/24.

301. Morel Papers LSE, F15/4/3, *Dundee Advertiser*, 24/10/24.

302. ibid, Morel to Ogilvie, 16/7/1923.

303. Morel papers LSE, F15/4/4, *The Outlook*, 25/8/23.

304. ibid, Morel to Ogilvie, 4/1/1923.

305. Swanwick, H M, *I Have Been Young* (Victor Gollancz, London, 1935), p.421.

306. Morel Papers LSE, F1/8/6.

307. ibid, F15/4/3, *The Daily Herald*, 26/8/22.

Decline of the UDC

308. Trevelyan, Charles, *The Union of Democratic Control: Its history and its Policy,* (Simpson and Co Ltd, London, 1919), p.9.

309. Morel Papers LSE, F6/20, Ponsonby, Arthur, *Foreign Affairs,* No.2 Vol.11, August 1920 et al.

310. Ponsonby to Mary Morel, 9/7/1920, Family papers.

311. Swanwick, H M, *Builders of Peace*, op. cit, p.152, 167.

312. Swanwick, H M, *I Have Been Young,* op. cit, p.377. Swanwick was appointed editor of *Foreign Affairs* following Morel's death. Morel's daughter, Stella, became secretary.

313. Branson, Noreen, *Britain in the Nineteen Twenties,* (Weidenfeld and Nicolson, London, 1975), p.57.

314. Swanwick, Helena, *Builders of Peace,* op. cit, p.138

315. Morel Papers LSE, F6/20, *Foreign Affairs*, Vol. 11. No.5, November 1920.

316. In 1919 F E Smith was ennobled by Lloyd George to become Lord Birkenhead.

317. Morel Papers LSE, F/15/4/3, *Dundee Advertiser*, 17/10/23.

318. ibid, F8/106, Macdonald to Morel, 17/8/23.

319. As a consequence of Germany's default on the payment of reparations France and Belgium had occupied German territory in the Ruhr.

320. A P Lee (British Broadcasting Corporation) to Mary Morel, 17/6/40. Family papers.

321. Morel Papers LSE F6/19. 'The why and wherefore of the War against Russia', *Foreign Affairs,* Vol 1, No 12, June 1920.

322. ibid; Morel, E D, *The Workers and the Anglo-Russian Treaty,* (Centropress, Ltd., London), Sept 1924.

323. Ponsonby, Arthur, *The Anglo-Soviet Treaty of 1924, Recital of Events that Led to their Conclusion,* Journal of the Royal Institute of Foreign Affairs, Vol. 5, No.3, May 1926.

324. Morel Papers LSE F6/24, *Foreign Affairs,* Vol. vi. No.3, Sept 1924, p.53.

325. *Evening News,* 26/8/24; *The Times,* 27/28/24; *Morning Post,* 12/8/24. Quoted Wuliger, op. cit, p.517.

326. *Hansard,* p.175, 3140-42, 7/8/2. ibid, p.518.

327. The Zinoviev letter was one of the greatest political scandals of the last century, although its influence was not as crucial as may have been imagined, as Macdonald's Government had already lost a confidence vote and the Liberal support on which it depended had slipped away. Later research has almost certainly proved the letter was forged by an MI6 agent's source and leaked by MI6 or MI5 officers to the Conservative Party. The letter, purported to be from Grigori Zinoviev, President of the Comintern, the international communist organisation, called on British communists to mobilise 'sympathetic forces in the Labour Party to support the Anglo-Soviet Treaty and to encourage agitation propaganda' in the armed forces. Four days before the election the *Daily Mail* carried headlines across its front page claiming: Civil War Plot by Socialists' Masters; Moscow Orders to our Reds; Great Plot disclosed. Files later showed the forged letter was widely circulated, including to senior army officers to inflict maximum damage to the Labour Government. 'The Zinoviev Letter', Norton-Taylor, Richard, *The Guardian,* 4/2/1999.

328. Morel on Russian Revelations, *Dundee Advertiser,* 27/10/1924, private papers.

329. Cline, Catherine, op. cit, p.144.

Morel Hopes for Cabinet Post

330. Swanwick, H M, *I Have Been Young,* op. cit, p.373.

331. ibid, p.256 and 375.

332. Morel papers LSE, F2/1/12, MacDonald to Morel, undated.

333. ibid, Ponsonby to Morel, undated. Jimmy Thomas was Secretary General of the National Union of Railwaymen. As it turned out MacDonald combined the role of Prime Minister and Secretary of State for Foreign Affairs. Jimmy Thomas was appointed Secretary of State for the colonies.

334. ibid, Aitken to Morel, 4 Feb 1924, Grindle to Morel, undated.

335. Russell, Bertrand, to Wuliger, 20/12/51.

336. Morel papers LSE, F2/1/12, Morel to Lord Parmoor, 2 Feb 1914.

337. Morel to MacDonald, 24 January 1924, quoted Cline, Catherine, op. cit, p.137.

338. Morel papers LSE F2/1/12, Morel to Parmoor, 2/2/1924.

339. Swanwick, H M, *I Have Been Young,* op. cit, p. 375.

340. Morel Papers LSE, F15/4/5.

341. *Foreign Affairs,* Vol.5 No. 2, August 1923, p.23.

342. Morel papers LSE F2/3/1, Morel to Ponsonby, 4/4/1924.

343. An article in the *Brighton Herald* in August 1922 reported on a large meeting in the Union Church in Brighton where Morel gave 'a rousing attack on "secret diplomacy."' His 'fiery eloquence' so impressed his audience that they passed unanimously a resolution that no treaties, agreements or understandings involving the potential use of armed forces of the Crown should be concluded by Government without the express sanction of Parliament.

344. Morel papers LSE F2/3/1, Ponsonby to Morel, undated.

345. *Foreign Affairs,* Vol v. No.11, May 1924, p.215.

346. Cline, Catherine, op. cit, p.139.

347. Morel papers LSE F/6/1, Robertson to Morel, 19/3/24.

348. ibid, LSE F/15/4/5, *Dundee Advertiser,* 10/4/1924.

349. ibid, LSE F/1/6, Morel to his constituents, undated.

350. Kitchin, C J, *Prime Minister and Foreign Secretary: the Dual Role of James Ramsey MacDonald in 1924,* Review of International Studies, Vol.3, No.3, CUP, 2011.

351. Morel papers LSE, F8/123, *Proposed Manifesto by the Executive of the UDC,* undated. No authorship is credited to the Manifesto but it would be safe to assume that Morel was principally responsible for it.

352. ibid, F8/123, Ponsonby to Morel, 23/5/24.

353. ibid, F15/4/5.

354. ibid, LSE, F1/6.

355. ibid, Loreburn to Morel, 7/5/1921.

356. ibid, Malberg to Morel, 4/7 and 16/7/1923.

357. ibid, F1/6.

358. Wuliger, op. cit, p.500.

359. Morel to Parmoor, 2/2/24. Quoted Wuliger, op. cit, p.500.

360. Morel Papers LSE, F17/2/3.

361. *Foreign Affairs,* Vol. vi, No 6, 1924, p.124.

The Closing Months

362. Morel papers LSE, F1/7/1, Roger Morel to Wuliger, 29/5/1953.

363. ibid, F1/8/6, Mrs Dixon to Mary Morel, 25/5/1955.

364. ibid, F1/7/1, Haynes Holmes to Stella Morel, 2/2/1925.

365. ibid, Bertrand Russell to Stella Morel, 22/11/24.

366. ibid, Ponsonby, undated letter.

367. Swanwick, Helena, *I Have Been Young*, op. cit, p.376/7

368. Goldring, Douglas, op. cit, p.162.

369. Morel papers LSE, F1/7/2.

370. ibid, LSE , F1/7/1, C P Scott, 8 Dec 1924.

371. Adams, W S, op. cit, p.202.

372. Cline, Catherine, op. cit, p.148.

373. Morel was criticised by his opponents for neglecting the interests of his constituents, but there appears to be little evidence to support this.

374. Cline, Catherine, op. cit, p.134.

375. Morel Papers LSE, F1/7/1, Wedgewood, Josiah, undated.

376. The West African Lands Report by Morel and his co-authors is a most comprehensive and detailed account on the subject of land tenure in Britain's West African Territories. It describes the traditional rules of title to land of the African peoples in the countries concerned and provides recommendations as to how those titles should be protected by law to prevent 'wholesale mortgaging, the grip of the money-lender, the creation of a landless class, with resultant poverty – now unknown – the inevitable decay of native industries, the conversion of a land-possessing population into labourers, the crumbling of the native social structure with all its long misery and chaos... the native system of tenure allows of private property in land, minus the power of sale, and under the native system an arboricultural tropical industry has grown up unparalleled in the world.' (see p. 65 above)

377. Porter, Bernard, *History Today*, Vol. 157, Issue 10, 2007.

378. Porter, Bernard, *Critics of Empire*, (Macmillan, 1968), p.287.

379. Marchal, Jules, *Lord Leverhulme's Ghost*, (Verso, London, 2008), p.19.

380. ibid, p.19.

381. ibid, p.27-35.

382. The Duke of Bedford also wrote a short pamphlet in 1941 entitled *Diplomacy and War Guilt: A tribute to the Vision and Peace Aims of the late E D Morel,* (The Strickland Press, Glasgow, 1941.). Morel Papers LSE, F1/7/4. The aim of the pamphlet is not clear as the author does not appear to draw parallels with 1914.

383. Belchem, J and MacRaild, D, *Cosmopolitan Liverpool,* in Belchem, J, (ed). *Liverpool 800: Culture, Character and History.* (Liverpool University Press, 2000), p.311-388.

384. Nworah, D W, 'The Liverpool "Sect" and British West African Policy', *African*

Affairs, vol.70, p.349-64, 1971. Nworah is referring here to Mary Kingsley and those who supported her 'kingslyite' principles.

385. Taylor A J P, op. cit, p.199.
386. ibid, op. cit, p.169.
387. *Forward,* Saturday November 22, 1924.
388. Morel family papers, letter from Mary Morel to Stella, December 1, 1924.
389. Letters from Geoff Morel to his brother John (undated) and to Mary Morel, 17 November 1924. Morel family papers.

Bibliography and List of Sources

Morel's Family

Three of Morel's grandchildren have been most helpful and supportive, but due to Morel's premature death and the destruction of many family papers there is very little in the way of first-hand personal recollections.

Morel Papers

Catalogued and listed in the London School of Economics Archive Library, pages 1-342; includes letters, pamphlets, newspaper articles and memorabilia.

Books published by Morel

Red Rubber, Haskell House Publishers, 1970.
Great Britain and the Congo, Howard Fertig, 1969.
Affairs of West Africa, William Heinemann, 1902.
King Leopold's Rule in Africa, London, 1904.
Nigeria: Its Peoples and its Problems, London, 1968.
The Black Man's Burden, National Labour Press, 1920.
Truth and the War, National Labour Press, 1916.
Thoughts on the War: Peace – and Prison, Simon and Co. 1920.
Ten Years of Secret Diplomacy, Reprint of *Morocco in Diplomacy,* Smith, Elder, 1916.
Tsardom's Part in the War, National Labour Press, 1917.

Newspapers edited by Morel and included in the Archive collection

West African Mail, 1901-1903.
West African Mail (renamed *African Mail* in 1907), 1903-1907.
Official Organ of the CRA, 1904-1913.
U.D.C., 1915-1919.
Foreign Affairs, (successor to *U.D.C.*), 1919-1924.

Secondary Sources

Adams, W S, *Edwardian Portraits,* Martin, Secker and Warburg, 1957.

Belchem, J and MacRaild, D, *Cosmopolitan Liverpool,* in Belchem, J (ed), *Liverpool 800: Culture, Character and History,* Liverpool University Press, 2000.

Branson, Noreen, *Britain in the Nineteen Twenties,* Weidenfeld and Nicholson, 1975.

A and G Bulens Bros (eds), *An Answer to Mark Twain,* Brussels, undated.

Cline, Catherine, *E.D. Morel: The Strategies of Protest,* Blackstaff Press, 1980.

Cocks, Seymour, *E D Morel: The Man and his Work,* George Allen and Unwin, 1922.

DeGroot, Gerard, *Blighty: British Society in the Era of the Great War,* Longman 1995.

Dockrill, M and Fisher, J, (eds) *The Paris Peace Conference,* Palgrave, 2001.

Evans, M A, *Brussels and Bruges,* Frommers, (John Wiley), 2011.

Ferguson, Niall, *The Pity of War 1914-1918,* Penguin Books, 1999.

Gregory, Adrian, *The Last Great War: British Society and the First World War,* Cambridge University Press, 2008.

Goldring, Douglas, *The Nineteen Twenties,* Nicholson and Watson Love, 1945.

Gondola, Didier, *The History of the Congo,* Greenwood Press, Westport, 2002.

Goodman, Jordan, *The Devil and Mr Casement: One Man's Struggle for Human Rights in South America's Heart of Darkness,* Verso, 2009.

Gott, Richard, *Britain's Empire, Resistance, Repression and Revolt,* Verso, 2011.

Gregory, Adrian, *The Last Great War, British Society and the First World War,* Cambridge University Press, 2008.

Hinton, James, *Protests and Visions,* Century Hutchinson, 1989.

Hurd, Douglas, *Choose Your Weapons: The British Foreign Secretary,* Phoenix, 2011.

Hattersley, Roy, *The Edwardians,* Abacus, 2006.

Hochschild, Adam, *To End All Wars: How the First World War Divided Britain,* 2011.

Hochschild, Adam, *King Leopold's Ghost,* Pan MacMillan, 2006.

Inglis, Brian, *Roger Casement,* Penguin, 1973.

Jenkins, Roy, *Churchill,* Pan Books, 2002.

Keegan, John, *The First World War,* Hutchinson, 1998.

Louis, Roger and Stengers, Jean (eds), *E. D. Morel's History of the Congo Reform Movement,* Oxford, 1968.

Llosa, Mario Vargas and Grossman, Edith, *The Dream of the Celt,* Farrar, Strauss and Giroux, New York, 2012.

Marchal, Jules, *Lord Leverhulme's Ghost,* Verso, 2008.

Martel, Gordon (ed), *The Origins of the Second World War*, Unwin Hyman, 1986.

MacMillan, Margaret, *Peacemakers: Six Months that Changed the World*, John Murray, 2002.

Mitchell, Angus, *Casement*, Haus Publishing, 2003.

Nworah, D W, *The Liverpool 'Sect' and British West African Policy, African Affairs*, vol.70. 1971.

Packenham, Thomas, *The Scramble for Africa*, Wiedenfeld and Nicholson, 1992.

Pavlakis, Dean, *The Congo Reform Movement in Britain 1896-1913*, PhD., SUNY at Buffalo, 2012.

Porter, Bernard, *Critics of Empire*, MacMillan, 1968.

Reeves, Maud Pember, *Round About a Pound a Week*, G. Bell and Sons, 1913.

Russell, Bertrand, *The Autobiography of Bertrand Russell*, Vol. 2, Boston 1968.

Stevenson, David, *With our Backs to the Wall: Victory and Defeat in 1918*, Allen Lane, 2011.

Stevenson, David, *The History of the First World War*, Penguin Books, 2005.

Stevenson, David, *The First World War and International Politics*, Oxford University Press, 1988.

Swanwick, Helena, *Builders of Peace*, Garland Publishing, 1973.

Swanwick, Helena, *I Have Been Young*, Victor Gollancz, 1935.

Swartz, Marvin, *The Union of Democratic Control in British Politics During the First World War*, Clarendon Press, 1971.

Taylor, *The Trouble Makers*, Hamish Hamilton, 1957.

Trevelyan, Charles, *The Union of Democratic Control: Its History and its Policy*, Simpson and Co, 1919.

Trevelyan , G M, *Grey of Falloden*, Longmans, Green, 1937.

Twain, Mark (Clemens, S L), *King Leopold's Soliloquy*, International Publishers, New York and Seven Seas Books, Berlin, 1970.

Wilson, K M, *British Foreign Secretaries and Foreign Policy: From Crimea to the First World War*, Helm, 1978.

Wilson, K M, *The Policy of the Entente*, Cambridge University Press, 1975.

Wuliger, R, *The Idea of Economic Imperialism with Special Reference to the Life and Work of E. D. Morel*, PhD., London School of Economics, 1953.

Acknowledgements

My particular thanks to Dean Pavlakis, the foremost authority on E D Morel and the Congo period, who was writing his PhD on Morel in the Research Library at The London School of Economics at the same time as I was writing this biography. He shared much of his research with me and commented frequently and most constructively upon the book. Thanks too to the staff at the library who for over three years were always most helpful to me with my requests for material from the Morel Archive.

My thanks also to John Douglas, Rachel Douglas, Richard Ellis, Gerry Kennedy and Paul Schultz for their valuable comments on reading the manuscript, and to Morel's grandchildren, Marya Fforde, Stasia French and Mary Kelly, who encouraged me to write about their grandfather and allowed me to see what family records they had in their possession.

Most of all, many thanks to my wife, Susanna, for all the time and encouragement she has given to me. Her help and advice have made the book what it is.

Index

B/2/P

9 781781 321782